Bird Sounds and Their Meaning

mL

3/97

By arrangement with the
British Broadcasting Corporation

Rosemary Jellis

Bird Sounds and Their Meaning

With a Foreword by
Frank Fraser Darling
and drawings by
Derek Goodwin

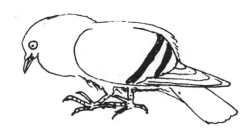

Cornell University Press

ITHACA, NEW YORK

© Rosemary Jellis 1977

Paperback edition first published 1984
by Cornell University Press.

Printed in the United States of America

Library of Congress Cataloging in Publication Data

Jellis, Rosemary.
    Bird sounds and their meaning.

    Bibliography: p.
    Includes index.
    1. Bird-song.   I. Title.
QL698.5.J44   1984   598.2'59   83-73212
ISBN 0-8014-9276-9

*The paper in this book is acid-free and meets the guidelines for permanence
and durability of the Committee on Production Guidelines for Book Longevity
of the Council on Library Resources.*

Contents

Preface

Bird Sounds and Their Meaning was first planned by Terry Gompertz and Rosemary Jellis after listeners had responded enthusiastically to the BBC Radio series of the same title with which they were both associated. Later, Terry Gompertz' series 'Birds in their element' and her documentary programme 'A lifetime of Johnny', about her years of watching and listening to Great Tits, confirmed their impression that many people are interested not only in learning to identify bird sounds but in the recent scientific research which is gradually cracking the code of bird sound-communication.

Most of the studies described in this book are of birds that can easily be heard in the British Isles and Continental Europe and it is intended primarily for people with little knowledge of bird behaviour who watch and listen for pleasure. But it should also be useful to experienced amateur observers, who can make a valuable contribution to our knowledge; to ornithologists with different specialisms, and to others in need of an introduction to this new and exciting branch of the study of animal behaviour.

The visual presentation of bird sounds helps both amateur and professional to 'fix' these brief and rapid utterances and to compare them at leisure. Some of the diagrams in this book are linked with recordings of the same sounds on the disc which has been prepared to accompany it. However, as these diagrams are in a standard form which is not difficult to interpret, the book can be read on its own.

Foreword

There are times when the contemplative naturalist must wonder why some fields of animal behaviour have lain fallow so long or have at best been desultorily worked. The very subject tended almost to be outside science and in the realm of folklore and anecdote.

The truly scientific approach was adumbrated by Darwin in *Expression of the emotions in man and animals*: Romanes followed soon after with *Mental evolution in animals* but unfortunately fell into the trap of anecdotalism. There was a long gap before the delving of Lloyd Morgan and a succession of American experimentalists leading to Washburn's *The animal mind*, a masterly review up to 1930.

Possibly Julian Huxley's paper on Great Crested Grebes, of 1914, was the beginning of an entirely new outlook on animal behaviour, ushering in a phase which continues to this day. Animals in the wild state gained a new dignity as objects of behavioural study. Eliot Howard, an intellectual amateur naturalist, developed the observational, disciplined research into bird behaviour which has profoundly influenced work of the past half century and drawn many people into enquiry in the spirit of science, without any loss of aesthetic or literary delight in animal behaviour and of bird watching in particular.

Yet, when all this is said and grateful acknowledgement made to an earlier generation, there is for me something of shocked surprise in our neglect of the field of auditory communication between animals. Anecdotally, man has had a constant interest. The songs and sounds of birds have filled our literary and musical imagination and have even led us to wrong conclusions which for too long were not questioned.

Then, within the last fifty years and particularly in the last twenty-five, there has been an awakening in which amateur and professional have each contributed their enlightenment. Margaret Nice, in the United States, concentrated on the Song Sparrow and showed us the worth of such imaginative concentration. The pioneering school at Cambridge under Professor Thorpe steadily built up a relevant structure of research and now other universities here, and many in the United States and Canada, are devoting resources to these studies. The Germans, Danes, Swedes and French have made an immense and thorough contribution, developing the use of instruments. Then the growth of broadcasting and the technical development of recording sound made possible so much that was impossible at an earlier time.

Broadcasting since the early 1920s has been the popular force from which the auditory side of natural history has gained a great spin-off, to use the current colloquialism. Indeed, broadcasting in education and entertainment has made its own special contribution for which we are grateful. The song of the Nightingale on 'the wireless' in the 1920s was romantic: the recordings and commentaries of Ludwig Koch reached a very large audience. Interest and technology were there together for enlarging our knowledge of auditory communication among animals. We have now heard Leviathan and his cousin the dolphin talking in the wastes of seas, as inspiring to our lyrical sensibility as when we 'have heard the mavis singing his love song to the morn'. Our imagination is uplifted and I would think art and science are married in this research into animal communication. To me it is deeply moving that the barrier of Babel between us and our lowlier brethren may be to a larger extent breaking down. Many of us have had experiences of momentary, intimate communication with animals, wild or tame; they are indelible in the memory.

It was not fortuitous that Terry Gompertz and Rosemary Jellis should have come into this field: they were educated women of musical ability, intensely aware of the world of nature, who came together in the activities of Broadcasting House. The juncture of art and science was a natural trend in their minds which were intellectually equipped to lead them on to more than they knew. I sat at their feet in those days, somewhat awed in watching their ideas and technical skill grow into a florescence. They had something new to impart which gave, in Berensen's phrase, enhancement of life.

One small but significant fact became plain: here were two women of no great physical strength, living mainly in a suburban environment and earning their living, who were reaching into a new field without the trappings of a laboratory, expensive equipment or fellowship grants, nor undertaking arduous expeditions. They opened their windows and the birds came in, and went out; especially the Great Tits, those positive, intelligent birds – related to the crow tribe, believe it or not. I like to think my two friends and the Great Tits co-operated in this matter of communication, though only the human side could set out their findings and interpretation. Terry Gompertz and Rosemary Jellis travelled in Europe and in the forested regions of this country. They met their fellow workers and it is one of the special values of this book that recordings are included which are auditory documents of analysis from a wide range of sources and of birds we cannot hear easily. Others are familiar but made revealing.

Terry Gompertz died suddenly at the end of June 1973, while listening at Knighton Bushes in the Berkshire Downs. Rosemary Jellis has completed this phase of their work together and by her clarity has added to that appreciable body of English literature inspired by the behaviour of birds. Gilbert White, who two hundred years ago differentiated some species by their voices, would have liked this book and made his bow to the two ladies.

FRANK FRASER DARLING

1 Listening to Birds

Despite the changes in man's attitude, his response to the utterances of birds has retained so much from the past that in appreciating bird song and what has been written about it we become alive to insights and sentiments widely shared. It is an achievement of great music, visual art and literature that they alleviate our loneliness and enable us to realize that, although the centuries have brought great changes, others have stood where we stand and been inspired by universal, enduring things – not least by the songs of birds. *Edward Armstrong*

All of us, including those who are convinced that they will never be able to tell one bird song from another, have aural memories of this natural accompaniment to our lives. We have brought our tame birds, as well as our domesticated mammals, into the towns with us and wild-living birds have followed us of their own free will.

Even in the heart of London, Blue Tits prance about in the trees overhanging the Law Courts. In spring a rhythmic little high-pitched song will suddenly pierce the traffic noise of the Strand, like a piccolo ringing out over the orchestra in a brief solo phrase. The parks and many of the tree and shrub-planted squares are full of the chatter without which few bird species seem able to conduct their daily business; and the surrounding suburbs with their gardens and, very commonly, their feeding tables have become desirable residences for avian as well as human families.

Birds, in general, are mobile, exploratory, opportunist. They have adapted to an environment that mobile, exploratory, opportunist man has been tampering with since he had the tools to alter it on any significant scale. But they have been around for much longer than we have. The evolution of birds from reptiles began about 200 million years ago. About half a million years ago, perhaps, our immediate ancestors in the genus *Homo* won time and safety to begin expanding their experience of the world around them, and extending immeasurably their vocal communication. By this time most of the modern families of birds had already evolved: among them the true songbirds, the youngest of this ancient line. The sounds they made were the first music man heard and they have influenced his music making directly or indirectly ever since.

Music is something that we share with the birds alone among living things. We respond to their sounds and to some extent they react to ours. Species like the Blackbird and the Starling, living closely with man and possessing a capacity for imitation, incorporate human whistled calls into their repertoire (see Chapter 10). But more sophisticated forms of human music may also produce a response.

The hand-reared Great Tits who shared the home that Terry Gompertz and I had made together, where music was part of the normal day, frequently joined in. After roosting time radio and gramophone had to be kept at low volume. The first of these house-living Great Tits, a foundling, human-fixated and a constant companion in all our activities, distinguished herself as a youngster (when birds often experiment freely with sound) by extemporizing a warbled obbligato to a Haydn sonata I was playing on the piano. She adapted to Haydn in pitch and rhythm with increasing accuracy as she went along. Even the sounds of speech – its emotional tone, not the sense – can have meaning. Bird keepers know that where touch may frighten, it is often possible to gentle a distressed bird, as we would a child, with soft crooning words.

This tells us something about the level of communication that our species has in common with the birds: conveying mood, reacting to events in the environment, or to the behaviour of familiar or unknown companions. Many scientists would say that the intention to communicate does not exist in birds: that it is all a response to the input of information through the senses and an indication of the 'mood', or internal state, of the bird. This may well be so. At the same level, some of our own utterances are unintentional responses. Nevertheless these signals are understood by members of the same, and sometimes other, bird species. Over millions of years they have been elaborated into an effective code which is part of the system that regulates social relationships between birds, and also helps to ensure the sharing out of food and living-space.

Because birds, like ourselves, rely so much on the senses of sight and hearing we can enter their world, in most other ways so utterly different from our own, with some degree of comprehension. No doubt when early man began to listen consciously to these companions in his environment, competitors for the nuts and berries that were part of his diet (and also a food source in themselves), he gradually learned how birds behaved. Probably he linked some of the sounds birds made with satisfaction, distress, danger, nesting: helpful signals for human purposes.

Only a generation or two ago countrymen who snared birds for food, or for sale as captive pets, as they still do in many parts of the world, knew a great deal about the behaviour of the species they were interested in, including their songs and calls. But much of this lore remains unwritten, and sounds – so evanescent in the memory, and difficult to transcribe – were the last aspect of a bird's behaviour to be studied scientifically.

That study is comparatively recent and very incomplete. Apart from the pioneering work of a few experienced and aurally talented individu s, it could not begin seriously and on any scale until equipment for high quality, mobile sound-recording had been designed. Recording has done for the study of sound what photography did for the study of movement. In the last twenty-five years, the widespread use of tape-recorders in the field and the sound-spectrograph and other electronic gear in the laboratory has meant that sounds can be repeated again and again, slowed down, seen as visual patterns and analysed aurally, electronically and visually. Recordings can be played back to birds in the wild to check their reactions and so arrive at some understanding of 'meaning'.

Since this technical revolution, the study of bird sounds and their meaning has moved from its pioneering stage to become an important branch of ethology, the science of animal behaviour. At one end of the scale this study is adding to our understanding of the subtle, interlinked behaviour patterns of individual birds. At the other end it is contributing to our comprehension of the process of evolution itself. Some of us think that one day it may be possible to demonstrate that these very distant relatives of ours, whose precursors diverged from man's ancestral stock about 250 million years ago to take a totally different evolutionary pathway, have an aesthetic appreciation of sound. It is rudimentary, but akin perhaps to man's art of music.

This book is a progress report on what we are learning from the results of these last few years of rapid development, and an introduction to the growing scientific literature for those who would like to read more deeply in it. But the book is also intended to help those who just want to understand bird sounds for enjoyment. Many of us, both amateurs and professionals, who have worked in this field have done so not only out of scientific curiosity; not only because it is a promising and interesting area of research, part of a much larger study with possible implications for our understanding of the springs of human behaviour; but, quite simply, because the sounds and their makers are so beautiful.

At the end of a day of lectures and discussions at the four-yearly International Ornithological Congresses, there is nearly always to be found a small group of such people from, say, North America, France, Germany, the Scandinavian countries and Britain continuing the discussions round a tape-recorder. Sooner or later, someone, looking a little shamefaced (because this, after all, is a strictly scientific gathering), will suddenly stop talking ornithological Latin and bio-acoustic technicalities and say 'Would you like to hear this? It's the XYZ bird' (his or her favourite species). 'It's nothing to do with what we are talking about but I brought it over with me because it's such a glorious sound.'

I was reminded of this, and of how comparatively easy it is now for anyone who wants to learn about bird sounds for pleasure, one afternoon in late July 1975 when I was staying in a friend's house in the Dordogne. It was my first visit to southern France, with cave-paintings, châteaux and a superb countryside to be explored. Mercifully it was the wrong time of year to pursue my specialized interest in the songs and calls of the tit species and I was determined not to take bird-watching too seriously – just to enjoy what came my way. However, knowing that there would be some unfamiliar birds and that my ears would refuse to take a holiday, I had listened before leaving England to some of the easily available commercial recordings of their songs and calls and made a few notes.

So there I was on this hot, sunny afternoon, lying under an archway of vines at the foot of the wooded hillside garden, doing precisely nothing, with the ornithological paraphernalia of binoculars, bird books and notebooks unused beside me. Then, almost overhead, I heard a call – clear cut, clarinet-like in quality, repeated several times; not a bird sound I had ever heard in the wild. But somewhere in my notes? It couldn't be a Golden Oriole? I found the right page and there, in my particular system of bird notation, was an outline transcribed from one of the recordings I had listened to in England that matched the sound I had heard. (The section on 'Notating bird sounds' (p. 226) includes an illustration of this call.)

The invisible bird moved up the hillside and I followed it as quickly and quietly as the steep slope, overgrown bushes and brambles permitted, reflecting bitterly that all the books emphasize how difficult it is ever to see a Golden Oriole. Its size and brilliant yellow body feathering, with black wings and black and yellow tail, leave no doubt about sight identi- fication of the male bird even for an observer as inadequate as I am outside the species I know well. But it has lurking habits and rarely emerges from leaf-cover to provide a good view of its astonishing presence.

I scrabbled my way uphill with the caller still invisible, first in an acacia tree, next in a sumac. Then, quite suddenly, the sound was a long way away. I broke through the top thicket, almost upending myself on the shaky, barbed wire fence, into an open field with trees on the far border, further up the hill. The bird must be there, somewhere. And equally suddenly, there it was, breaking out of leaf-cover on the top- most branch of an oak – indubitably a Golden Oriole, and calling.

An hour later, after I had had my fill of watching and listening to two males and at least one female, I stumbled happily down the hillside, my denim jeans memorably stained with squashed sloes from the hedge under which I had taken cover, and returned to the vines to put down my binoculars and pick up the bird books to re-read the familiar descrip- tions, now come alive. I was thinking how easily, from ignorance, I could have missed such an experience and yet, nowadays, how easy it had been to achieve it – stains and scratches apart. I had started my preparations in England with little more knowledge about the birds I might see in southern France than the average mildly interested holiday maker.

The necessary information is easy enough to pick up from the excellent Field Guides now published for so many areas of the world, and especially Europe where generations of hardworking naturalists have built up detailed pictures of the whereabouts and habits of every resident, and regular migrant, species. These are presented in the guides in notes and maps which, though brief and simplified, are sufficient for all but the most specialized birdwatching needs.

The greater problem is the presentation of sound. Most current English bird books offer as a clue to this Golden Oriole call the phonetic transcription *weela-weeo*. In the French translation of one of them this appears as *tuolio* and in the German edition as *düdelio*. It is interesting that French, German and English speakers should give such different renderings of the same call and underlines the difficulty of conveying musical sound in words. None of them would have given me much help in identifying the sound on first hearing though afterwards a phonetic label serves as a reminder and provides a name of sorts for the call. However, this gap in the provision for beginners is now increasingly well filled by recordings on disc or cassette, at least for the songs and typical calls of most species. Of course not every sound a species may make can be heard in this way. The full repertoire of some quite common species has not yet been studied properly.

As with all living things, it will always be difficult – demanding time, concentration, energy and often discomfort – for an observer to learn to know a great deal about even one species of bird. But to know a little, to understand a little, and to come to share in the enjoyment of those others who 'have stood where we stand' is relatively easy now, with the assembled knowledge of so many patient watchers and listeners.

Remembering that afternoon when I sat lazily under the vines in a French garden, still hearing the distant calling of the Golden Orioles from their oak trees in the field, I am grateful.

It is a glorious sound.

2 The Communication System

We can study life and we can study environment but we must not divorce them if we are to study behaviour. *Eliot Howard*

A bird is a complex organism, subtly adjusted in its whole way of life and in the finest details of its behaviour to its environment. This book is mainly concerned with only one aspect of that way of life, that adjustment: the sound signals that are part of the bird's communication system. These signals give us clues, when we are able to interpret them correctly, to many matters – from a bird's daily routine to the probable evolutionary relationship of its species with others. But like any other aspect of a bird's behaviour or its appearance, its physiology and its choice of habitat, they cannot be considered in isolation. Everything interlocks.

First then, it is important to consider in very general terms how sound signals relate to other parts of the communication systems in different bird groups and how the systems are adapted to different environments. That is the subject of this chapter.

Birds fly. This has profound implications for their communication systems. For example, the smaller songbirds in woodland and scrub country are active for a high proportion of the daylight hours. They may not travel great distances but within their daily range they are extremely mobile, mainly foraging for food. The small size of the prey that many of them take or the seeds they eat, the speed of their digestive processes and the high daily intake of food in relation to their body weight are such that they rarely rest for more than a few minutes before flitting off to look for the next meal.

At any moment members of the same species within an area of a few hundred square metres may be on the wing from one tree to another, clambering up a tree trunk, perched somewhere on an outer twig investigating a leaf, hopping along the ground, or preening on a branch. For essential maintenance activities like preening, when the usual alertness for danger must be temporarily relaxed – it is difficult, even for a bird, to keep a watchful eye on the surroundings with head turned backwards and beak probing under a wing – they normally choose to be well concealed.

If they are brightly coloured they may catch a glimpse of

each other from time to time in the course of these spatially varied activities. But for obvious reasons the females and the young, at least, tend to have dull, camouflaging plumage. So while they are bound to be better at it than we are, it is not only the human observer who has cause for complaint about the difficulties of identifying a small brown bird diving into a bush, as one exasperated ornithologist put it.

When you get to know a species and its sound-repertoire well it becomes evident that its members often mislay each other, particularly in the heavy summer foliage. Mates lose track of mates, parents lose offspring and vice versa. Without mid-distance contact calls which indicate the species, the individual identity (it is almost certain that this important piece of information is also carried in these calls) and permit assessment of direction and approximate distance, they would have as much difficulty in finding each other as human beings might at a mainline railway station.

If our folk memory carried us back to the information situation in primitive societies, especially in forest country, we should have a far deeper understanding of the communication predicament facing these small woodland birds. It has been resolved in the course of evolution by the elaboration of a variety of sound signals, characteristic for each species, which save the birds time and energy in looking for each other as well as for their food.

We might expect to find that most bird species which spend a lot of their time in leaf cover make considerable use of sound in their communication systems; and, in general, this appears to be so, whether the cover is the broadleaf woods and copses of the temperate zone in Europe and North America or the dense rain forest of the tropics. Bird species belonging to families which are otherwise quite different in their habitats, but which share the woodland habitat, indicate many of their moods and activities by sounds.

Go through a woodland in spring when the affairs of the bird community are at their busiest and there is a continuous stream of sound traffic: Robins, Willow Warblers, and perhaps a Blackcap singing their various fluting phrases; a Blackbird *chinking*, a Song Thrush excitedly giving his clear trumpet signals and mellow glides; a Jay screaming harshly, a Great Spotted Woodpecker drumming, a Chaffinch *pinking*, a Wren chittering, a Great Tit *churring* imprecations if it misjudges its landing on a twig. If the wood is in Continental Europe an Icterine Warbler may add to the human listener's confusion by imitating other species while delivering his own message. The birds themselves, of course, are attending mainly to the sounds of their own species unless one of them spots danger and utters an alert which is understood and promptly acted upon by the rest of the smaller species in the community.

A wood in spring, then, is neither the place nor the time for the beginner to start learning to recognize bird sounds. It is far better to start in a garden, where the birds are more easily seen, and in the late winter months. Then only the resident species are singing and it is easier to single out each voice in turn. Once the residents can be identified by voice alone they can be ignored and the songs of the summer migrants gradually learned, as the birds of these species arrive in the spring.

In tropical forests the sound picture is even richer. The tree species are more numerous, their growth higher and more dense. They shelter an extraordinary range of bird species (600, for instance, in the forests of the Amazon). Some species, brilliantly coloured, with loud, sometimes raucous voices, live mainly in and over the tree tops where visual contact and display is easier. Others spend most of their time at lower levels in the trees or near the forest floor and are often well camouflaged in plumage, highly dependent on sound-signals for contact between individuals. Harsh or musical calls, whistles, simple and elaborate songs intermingle. In the dense parts of African rain forests where large, thick leaves predominate in the undergrowth, the sounds are comparatively low in pitch and many species have long, pure, whistled notes – a type of sound that has great carrying power in such an environment. In the less dense parts of the forest, the forest edges, and in woodland savannah, the sounds tend to be higher in pitch and more varied in their tone-quality. It is interesting that of the species which, so far, are known to 'duet' – one bird inserting notes with beautiful precision into the songs or calls of its partner – a high proportion live in tropical forests or woodlands, using their elegantly contrived, individually identifying duets to keep contact as they forage in the thick foliage (see Chapter 10).

It is also true that most of the world's finest bird singers, judged by human standards, are woodland species. We are attracted by the more musical and extended songs. Probably these qualities, which must be of use and significance to the birds, have evolved in response to the evolutionary stimulus provided by the great forests of the temperate and tropical zones.

This is one clue to the communication systems that different species of birds have evolved. The systems have to be effective in the particular habitat to which the species has become adapted. Specializations of body and behaviour, such as feeding and nesting habits, have evolved in response to the demands and opportunities of a particular habitat. The communication system, too, has been appropriately adapted.

A further clue is to be found in the basic pattern of a bird's life. There are events and activities in which communication is essential: for example ownership of a living space with the need to proclaim it to others; mating and rearing young; threat from a member of a bird's own species, or danger from another. Then there are occasions when communication occurs incidentally – experiences which induce fear, distress, pain or satisfaction; a change of mood; an intention to engage in some activity. Any of these elements of living may be expressed, often involuntarily, in a movement or utterance which is understood by other birds in the vicinity.

A third clue is in the social organization of a particular species. If it nests in large colonies for instance, like the gulls, the living space for each family may be a small one; not much more than the area immediately round the nest. Proclamation of ownership is over a very short range, though usually fierce and frequent, since at such close quarters it is easy to tread on a neighbour's toes. On the other hand if a pair of birds have several hundred square metres of woodland round their nest site, the situation is quite different. Once the boundaries have been established, neighbours are a long way off and all that is normally needed is a periodic vocal statement from the owning male that he is in residence and ready to deal with trespassers.

The final clue, then, is implicit in the other three. It is a matter of distance. There are situations which can be dealt with at long range and situations of direct confrontation. Most birds have to cope with both, but social organization, specialized behaviour and habitat affect the balance between close and distant situations, and the combination of signals which make up a species' communication system.

For sound signals are only part of the system. When individuals are in sight of one another, information conveyed by plumage and movement can be received and understood. Body shape and plumage patterns indicate the species, movements convey the mood or intention of the individual.

In situations of direct confrontation such visual information is particularly important. Stylized movements may enhance the eye-catching effect of part of the plumage as, for instance, when a Robin engaged in threatening a rival puffs out the red throat and breast to maximum size. But movements may be supplemented by sound. If the rival fails to wilt at the sight of that rich expanse of red feathers the Robin often makes doubly sure, according to the intensity of the threat, or its own mood of the moment, by singing a terse, strangulated phrase quite unlike the normal fluent song.

So the visual signals of plumage and movement may operate alone, or be combined with vocal signals, in the displays which regulate the relationships between one bird and another. Such displays are entirely characteristic for each species but there are often family resemblances in the displays of closely related species. The situations in which displays are used, however, are the common situations of a bird's life, and however different the expression in different species, the messages are the same.

All species, for example, have one or more forms of threat display. It may be a threat directed at a rival of the same species, as with the Robin. In a mixed flock feeding on the ground it may be a threat at any bird, even of another species, which comes too close for avian comfort. For except in the special circumstances of the nest, most birds like to keep an 'individual distance' around them – an invisible, personal living-space. This is presumably because, ever conscious of danger, they feel the need of at least a wing length on either side of them for a quick take-off in emergency. Here, as in so much bird study, we may note a phenomenon and even measure it precisely, as observers have done for individual distance, but rarely, if ever, explain why it occurs or why, in some cases, it does not. The tiny estrildid finches, for example, birds of tropical forest and semi-desert, are among the 'contact' or 'clumping' species. In aviaries they are often seen in a companionable huddle on a perch.

This 'individual distance' requirement in the make-up of most bird species is relevant to all direct confrontations. But it is most obvious in courtship displays, for the male and female have to break down their normal reaction to a close approach during the process of forming a pair and getting to know each other as individuals.

The male, at least, has also to overcome his first, aggressive

Bronze Mannikins

reaction to the approach of an apparent intruder. In many courtship displays, the movements reveal this conflict between attraction, fear and aggression. Though the whole performance is now a highly stylized affair, communicating the intentions of both partners and normally leading to copulation, movements incorporated into it can often be traced back to totally different situations in a bird's life. Ethologists have a special word – ritualization – for the evolution of stylized displays. Such displays may include the transfer of a movement or a sound from its original context to a different one, and its exaggeration to enhance its effectiveness as a signal.[1]

Courtship display movements may also show some special feature of the plumage to advantage. One of the most familiar and dramatic examples of this is the Peacock spreading open its shimmering, vibrating train. On the smooth lawns of an English stately home, the effect, even from a distance, is theatrical. But it has to be seen in close-up to appreciate fully the brilliance of the 'Peacock's eye' near the tips of the tail-coverts which form the great fan, and the lacy effect of the grass-green barbs on these graceful feathers. Among the undergrowth of the Peacock's natural home, in and around the rain forests of India and Ceylon, these feathers blend in with the tall, waving grasses they closely resemble. But the raucous, far-carrying call would attract the females to a closer attendance at the display.

The vocal sounds of courtship displays are delivered in great excitement. Among small birds especially, however, most of them are very quiet. Because it is difficult for an observer to get close, courtship and copulation calls for a number of species whose behaviour is otherwise quite well known have not yet been recorded.

[1] This approach to the interpretation of certain forms of behaviour as a balance between conflicting 'drives' or tendencies was developed by Professors Konrad Lorenz and Niko Tinbergen and has proved a valuable analytic tool, in the study of bird displays in particular. It was in these that it was first and most fully developed. There are, however, still problems at a deeper level. We cannot suppose, for instance, that in all forms of bird behaviour a drive or tendency to do something is rigidly fixed and invariable, or has a single cause. It may arise from hormonal or other physiological changes in the bird. It may be a response to some stimulus from the environment or to the behaviour of a partner or a rival. Whatever the cause, it may wax or wane over a period of time, and according to the strength of the stimulus. Theories are modified as knowledge accumulates and anyone interested in these wider considerations in animal behaviour should read some of the general works listed on p. 239.

Paired birds usually have other mutual displays, frequently both vocal and visual, associated with all their strenuous breeding activities such as choosing nest sites, building nests, greeting each other after a period of separation, incubating and feeding the young and protecting them while they are still dependent.

In all close range situations whether of pairing, or of threat to rivals, the effect of habit and of habitat makes itself felt. Think again of the Robin and that expanse of red. In the woodlands where the display evolved, it was important to be able to beam the red breast at the rival like a searchlight, whether the other bird was on the same level, or on a branch above or below. So there are different postures to make sure that wherever the rival is, the threatening red breast will be in full view.

If it happens to encounter a rival on the ground, the Robin tends to stay on the same spot, as it would on a branch, until one or the other of them gives way. We once watched two males and two females, rival pairs, in such a display. They were posed like the musicians in a string quartet, swaying from side to side, with vocal accompaniment, but otherwise immovable on the disputed boundary between the territories of the two pairs. Occasionally encounters between rival males lead to actual fighting. Robins, in particular, are rather belligerent birds. But with most bird species, in most situations, the threat display, conveying its message 'Keep off – or else . . .', is enough to prevent conflict.

Blackbirds, though also birds of woodland and hedgerow, treat their habitat somewhat differently. They make the best of two worlds – a concealing environment and an open one. Pairs hold a territory which includes at least some woody growth, even if it is only a few garden shrubs or a climbing rose, to provide cover for their nests. They may also spend the night on their territory. But if there is shelter on a larger scale in thickets or copses, they often gather from quite a distance to roost communally. Yet for their threat and their courtship displays they frequently come into the open.

Threat posture

Blackbirds make full use of the space that any open ground provides. They posture and prance forward or retreat, in a sequence of stately movements like a dance. With no patches of colour on their plumage to show off, they have a great range of body postures with wings and tail feathers raised or lowered, spread or sleeked, according to the intensity of their mood and the occasion.

Submissive posture

In spring a garden lawn of any size provides a stage for posturing Blackbirds. Drivers know the hazards of the quiet residential road which, too often, has become a disputed boundary, or (even more dangerous for the Blackbirds' survival) part of the territory owned by a pair. In this case, in early spring, courtship may be in progress and both partners more than normally oblivious of an approaching car. In late spring one of the parents may dive out of the hedge, flying low and swiftly, from a food gathering trip on one side of the road to the nest on the other. Our own favourite male Blackbird, six years a resident in our garden and a notable singer, was killed in just this way in late April.

Blackbirds, like other woodland species, sing in the breeding season but – and this is an interesting point about this species – they may already have acquired a mate and settled the boundaries of a territory before they begin to sing. Possibly it is less necessary for them to sing as early in the season as many other territorial species because of their different behaviour. These matters can often be settled on the ground for which their displays are so well adapted.[1]

Song, however, is the first line of communication for most species that occupy the concealing environments of forest, woodland, thick swamp or reedbed, and whose way of life requires them to stake a claim to a piece of territory within these habitats. It is a long-distance proclamation of ownership to deter rivals and to attract potential mates. Song may be followed up by visual and vocal displays at close range if border disputes become particularly troublesome.

Songs of species in these concealing environments tend to be clearly patterned, lengthy or reiterated, sound signals. These carry far without being absorbed or deflected by obstacles, and can be well differentiated from the signals of other

[1] Dr David Lack's *The life of the Robin* and Dr David Snow's *A study of Blackbirds* are enjoyable accounts of their scientific studies of these two species and should be read for a more detailed discussion of the displays briefly described here. Like many ornithologists I am indebted to both these authors for the interpretation of my own less extensive observations.

species liable to be sounding off at the same time. In what better way could the problem of providing long-distance information be solved in such conditions?

What, then, about the birds that spend most of their time in open environments – in the fields, on the plains or the tundra; in open marshland, on the water or the shore? There is plenty of surface space for visual display and all the air above it as well. The line of sight for effective long-distance signalling is limited only by the size and general visibility of the bird. In exploiting these opportunities, different bird species have evolved extraordinarily varied combinations of sound and visual displays. Here are just six examples.

The Skylark, fairly small and with unobtrusive colouring, is virtually invisible as you casually scan the ploughland or pasture where it is feeding, alone, with its mate or, in winter, in a small flock. But few people have not seen and heard what happens next – and it can happen on almost any day in the year.

Near a downland village in Berkshire which I often visit, a lane winds steeply uphill from a secluded dry valley. There are hawthorn thickets by the road and farm fields on either side. Often, just as I have reached the highest point on the great sweeping hillside to turn the corner and go downhill again to the village, a Skylark rises vertically from the field on my left, with a continuous stream of trilled, gliding or staccato sound as it goes up and up. Then it hovers, singing and beating its wings, sometimes circling over the field. Before it has risen far its rival in the field on the other side of the road is airborne too. They sing against each other for minutes on end, until the pattern of notes and phrases changes as they come down, giving a few final song notes before the last, sudden, and silent, drop to the ground.

In the same fields there are often Lapwings, or Green Plovers as they are also called: larger, more powerful birds than the Skylark and with an impressive presence – black throat and head, surmounted by a delicate crest; white on their cheeks and underparts; their back and wings glinting green and purple, and a chestnut-coloured patch under the tail. Their outline and colour show up in striking contrast with the ground as they parade about the fields, slowly and with dignity, stopping from time to time to feed or preen.

For most of the year Lapwings live in large flocks. They will not allow an intruder to approach too closely and take

to the air immediately, relying on numbers and aerial agility, not on concealment for safety. In autumn they execute great flock manoeuvres in the air, the black and white plumage patterns changing as they wheel and alter direction of flight. Like the Skylarks, they may move over considerable distances, feeding on moorlands and tidal flats as well as cultivated fields.

In spring and early summer the flocks break up into territorial pairs who rear their young in scrapes in the furrows. The Lapwings are not 'songbirds' in the avian systematists' reckoning – they belong to a group commonly known as waders. Nevertheless, in the breeding season they have a short but splendid 'song' or display-call. They can be heard in chorus, especially at dawn and dusk, and sometimes well into the night. By day their spectacular tumbling and turning song-flights over their territories ensure that they are seen and heard by rivals or by intruders of other species.

When Lapwing flocks rise – disturbed – circle and come to rest again, the birds often use the *peewee* call which has given them their most familiar name – the Peewit. There are numerous dialect variations of this name, showing the familiarity of the sound to the people for whom these birds of open country provided a daily spectacle. Unfortunately Lapwings are less numerous than they used to be, probably because of changes in agriculture, but the dialect names are still in use. I remember, not so many years ago, a forester friend in the North Riding of Yorkshire giving me his version – 'Teäfit'.

The various displays of the Lapwing and the Skylark resemble each other in little but their use of aerial space above an open ground habitat. Different habits, and spectacular plumage in one species, unspectacular in the other, are associated with a different balance between vocal and visual signals.

In recent years many people, particularly in the south of England and the Midlands, have had the opportunity to see

the Great Crested Grebe. Once almost exterminated in Britain for the grebe fur (its breast feathers), the species has made a remarkable recovery largely because of fashion changes, protection and especially the increase in the number of reservoirs and flooded gravel pits. These have provided it with a highly suitable habitat which it has rapidly occupied.

I live near a chain of gravel-pit lakes and like to spend a restful hour watching the Grebes drifting across the smooth water surface, sometimes asleep, with their long, elegant necks twisted backwards along their backs and head buried in the wings, so that they present the outline of a raft. This can be seen at any time of year, because even in the breeding season there are usually a number of bachelors keeping silent and somewhat distant company with each other. They seem to spend most of their day doing nothing, interrupting their inactivity only by an occasional long submergence to catch a fish.

In spring, on other parts of the lake, there is tension and excitement – discordant calls, or the graceful ceremonial dances of courtship in which the birds display to advantage the ear tufts and neck frill that are part of the breeding plumage of both sexes. As in a pas-de-deux by a fine choreographer, the birds make full use of their water stage in some of these dances, approaching each other at speed and suddenly rearing half out of the water as they meet breast to breast in a dazzling contrast of white fronts, wet and gleaming, topped and framed by the warm chestnut and deep browny black of their headdress.

Great Crested Grebes are essentially water birds, nesting for preference on a floating platform of their own making, anchored among aquatic plants. On the gravel pit lake, which is still rather short of these building aids, they sometimes use the edges of the little islands that break the surface of the water here and there and are gradually being colonized by herbaceous plants and shrubby willow. They are rarely seen on the wing, except in short flights during courtship. From time to time, and mainly at night, they fly from one stretch of water to another. But it is not a matter of routine and in years of occasional watching I have never seen one in the air.

In contrast with the graceful balletic courtship duets of the Great Crested Grebe, there is the bizarre communal display of the Ruff. This is a bird of marshes, swamps and damp meadows and once bred in numbers in Britain. It has the distinction of different names for the sexes: the Ruff and the Reeve. The species became extinct here as a breeding bird before the middle of the 19th century, partly as the result of drainage of the marshes and fens but even more because it was good to eat. It reappeared sporadically to breed in East Anglia and since 1963 it has re-established itself there in small though increasing numbers.

I have only seen the display on the island of Gotland in the Baltic Sea. It was fairly late in the season when the number of displaying cocks, the Ruffs, was smaller and their ardour less intense than earlier in the spring, but it was still an astonishing sight I witnessed on a circle of ground, scraped bare and dusty by the Ruffs' activities, in some partly drained marshland.

These birds do not pair and take up individual breeding territories. Instead the males assemble in spring on a communal display ground. Here they stake out their rights to a particular stamping patch within the arena and go through a series of formal postures and gyrations, sparring with each other in a state of high tension. They are settling a hierarchy and the most successful males have a better chance of selection as mates by the females. This is display fighting and rarely turns into the real thing. Amidst these competing, dominant males, some subordinate or 'satellite' males seem to be virtually excluded from the ritual trial of strength. They are often permitted to approach other individuals more closely – if they show submissive behaviour – but have much less chance of attracting a female than the dominant members of the displaying group.

The Ruffs, each bird on its small stamping patch on the arena, conduct their fantastic manoeuvres in silence. They are gaily coloured and individually identified by different colour combinations of bill, legs and huge feather ear-tufts as well as the ruffs which have given them their name. The satellite males are usually white ruffed and tufted. So the sparring company, with the fully erected ruffs bowing, twisting, turning, apparently of their own volition, and seeming

Territorial Ruff and satellite male

A Reeve soliciting
a Ruff

to overbalance the birds' small bodies, makes an ever-changing pattern of colour and movement quite extraordinary to the human observer. It is a commonplace matter to any watching Reeve. The Reeve, in her sombre, ruff-less dress, arrives at the arena, chooses the male that she is interested in and solicits him. But it is not a permanent relationship and the ceremony is repeated day after day.

A number of species of the grouse family display in a somewhat similar way. They are often referred to as 'lek' birds from the name for the arena of the Blackcock, one of the most famous. This Swedish word, from Old Norse, has ancient associations well suited to the excited activities on the lek. It still survives in the dialects of northern England with the original meaning of 'play, dance'.

The Blackcock – the male Black Grouse – belongs to a different family from the Ruff and is much larger: about 53 centimetres long compared with the Ruff's 28 centimetres. It is promiscuous but in other ways very different from the Ruff. It is dignified rather than grotesque in display (to our eyes) and very vocal. The severe blue-black plumage, with white shoulder spot, wing-bar and undertail feathers, is relieved only by the scarlet combs on the head. Blackcock favour a larger arena than the Ruffs and each bird occupies a sizeable piece of ground within it. In Britain the average size of the individual stamping patch is given as 30 square metres if the birds are in clear view of one another. In typical habitats – rocky hillsides among heather, peat mosses, moorland edge, grassy and marshy ground – the country is usually fairly open. If the cover grows too high, the birds move their lek elsewhere, though in suitable conditions they, like the Ruffs, return to traditional grounds year after year.

Some observers think that there is a hierarchy among Blackcocks but others take the view that all the cocks are equal; defending, as it were, a symbolic territory within the arena.

The Blackcock's displays on the lek include hissing calls, flutter flights, wing-beating, running and jumping; and rivals are engaged on the territorial boundaries. One of the most spectacular displays is a posture with the head thrust for-

ward. The scarlet combs are inflated, the black feathers of the lyre-shaped tail tilted forward in a stiff semicircle, with the white undertail feathers erected behind and overtopping them. Distended throat pouches increase the size of the neck and also affect the sound the birds make; for the performance is accompanied by a bubbling *rookoo* phrase which can be heard up to three kilometres away. When females arrive on the lek the birds may lower their heads even further, drag their spread wings along the ground and give a more congested form of the *rookoo* phrase. (This call is illustrated in Chapter 7.)

These are extraordinary contrasts in lek behaviour: the Blackcock, large birds with prominent visual displays, a far-carrying 'song' and well spaced out on their lek; the little Ruffs, grouped together and silently manoeuvring in their multicoloured individual splendour.

The street pigeon provides a final example of variety in display. These half tame pigeons of our cities, like the specialized captive breeds and the homers, are all descended from domesticated wild pigeons. Their wild relatives, the Rock Doves, are now only to be found in Britain in a few remote areas such as the west coast and islands of Scotland.

The wild birds are uniform in their colouring: a light blue-grey with two black wing-bars. Some of our Feral Pigeons show this clear-cut pattern but others are chequered, light or dark; some are red, some white. Whether on the Isle of Islay, however, or in Trafalgar Square in the centre of London, the glossy purple and green neck feathers are the same. And so are the bowing, strutting, circling, pursuing movements of courtship, accompanied by the *rookety-coo* call, neck feathers puffed out and vibrating.

Here and there in the middle of the large flocks in city squares you can almost always notice a few males who suddenly stop feeding and go into this courtship routine for the benefit of a female feeding nearby. Unlike the Ruff and the Blackcock, however, pigeons on the whole are faithful birds, rearing and caring for their young together and sometimes remaining mated to the same partner for several years.

In cities they nest in any convenient cavities or on ledges of buildings, often quite close together, and the call which invites the partner to the nest is loud and clear. Courting, too, will take place on any ledge big enough to allow the male to make his display movements, as well as on the ground. For these birds are accustomed to make use of different levels for their activities. They roost separately, though often quite near another bird or communally, as accommodation permits. They choose ledges on large buildings or perch on brackets and drainpipes under the eaves of houses.

On the Isle of Islay where we went to study the wild Rock Doves and compare their behaviour with their city relatives, the nests and roosts are on ledges in the small caves of the low cliffs along the Sound of Jura, a narrow sea channel between the two islands. At dawn, from a rowing boat on the Sound, we watched the Rock Doves fly out of their caves, turn in a swift movement and fly fast and low inland to the fields to feed in their daytime flocks. On their return they would stand around idly on the outer ledges of the cliffs.

From time to time a male strutted, bowed and *rookety-cooed*. To us it was odd, at first, to hear the familiar calls in such a setting. It was as if we were suddenly addressed by someone with a cockney accent when our ears were attuned to expect the soft speech of the Western Isles. But this was a human not an avian response to the environment.

The Feral Pigeons, let loose in urban surroundings, found their ancestral habits adequately adapted for their new habitat. They treated buildings as rocks and caves for their domestic affairs and overnight accommodation, and the streets and squares as their communal feeding grounds. Over the years man has helped them by accidentally or deliberately strewing food in the streets. His relationship with them seems likely to continue since the habitat he has created suits them so well.

These descriptions represent only a few and almost random examples of the great variety of display in avian species: the different combinations of sound and vision; the adaptation of these communication systems to the habitat; and flexibility in the use of the same habitat by different species.

3 The Sounds Birds Make

While I am writing these lines, a Great Tit is ringing its *zizibee* outside my window, a House Sparrow is chirping in front of its nest under the roof and a male Blackbird is singing softly in the bush nearby. Their voices are still just as much music to my ears as when I knew nothing about the sound-spectrograph, the origin of species and behavioural research. That may be a comfort to those who are afraid of losing their enjoyment of nature if they read further. *Gerhard Thielcke* (translation)

In the languages of people all over the world there are special imitative words to describe bird sounds. Among the English onomatapoeic assortment, chirp, chirrup, cluck and twitter are applied to a multitude of avian mutterings. Most of them are very old and related to equally ancient words in other Germanic languages. So our tradition must go back in time to the early Common Germanic tongue and perhaps beyond. Sometimes the names of birds are imitative. The Cuckoo and the Chiffchaff elected themselves into this group by the clear, syllabic structure of their most frequently heard utterances. This bird naming habit is reflected in languages quite unrelated to our own such as those of Africa.

In English, at least, these bird words rarely have any other meaning. We might say, in somewhat dated phrases, that someone is chirpy this morning, or, insultingly to the birds in my view, that someone is all of a twitter. But these are metaphors and not such dead ones that we are unconscious of their origin. What we often do, with little sense of metaphor, is to apply these words, among others, to the utterances of a human baby. This points to the common factor in the communication systems of the bird and the baby. Both have to depend on wordless sound combined with gesture to express their needs, desires, anxieties and pleasures. Both effectively communicate only in the present tense.

In speech we use different intonations – rising or falling or level tones and combinations of these – different basic pitch, and changes in voice quality to amplify the message conveyed in the words. We speak loudly or softly and with varying degrees of emphasis. In addition we use meaningless sounds like 'Oh' and 'Ah' whose message is conveyed solely in the tone of the voice. Then there are expletives whose meaning, such as it is, may be socially regrettable but whose real function is to serve as a vocal release of pent-up irritation or sudden shock.

Birds and babies have only these non-verbal resources at their disposal: their languages are declamatory, exclamatory and emotive. Within totally different frameworks, their use of sound provides some interesting parallels, to be discussed in Chapter 12.

For the moment the question is – what range of sounds can birds produce to meet their needs and what do they hear? In any communication system whether mechanical, electrical or organic, there must be a transmitter and a receiver with some connecting link between them. In the case of an open or 'broadcast' system the link is the earth's atmosphere through which the electromagnetic waves from a broadcasting transmitter, or the sound waves emitted by the avian or the human voice, have to travel. The information that can be carried in the message is restricted by limitations at any point in this chain. In birds both the transmitting and the receiving equipment are extremely effective.

Sound Production and the Sense of Hearing

The avian method of voice production is different from ours and is by no means completely understood. Very briefly, birds have a unique sound-producing organ called the syrinx at the lower end of the windpipe, just where this divides into the main bronchial tubes which lead directly to the lungs. Thin membranes, adjustable like the skin of a drum, vibrate as air from the bird's respiratory system is pushed outwards through them and are the actual sound source. Pairs of muscles inside and outside the syrinx steady the whole voicebox and control the tension of the membranes, thus affecting the characteristics of the sound.[1]

The number and complexity of these muscles varies between different groups of birds and broadly corresponds with their vocal ability. The simplest form of syrinx is found in ostriches, storks, vultures and cormorants, all considered to belong to surviving families of primitive groups of birds and not noted for their vocal achievements. The most recently and highly evolved bird group, the Oscines or true songbirds, have the most complex syrinx in terms of musculature. However, while variety and musical quality of sound is more frequently found among the Oscines than in older and more primitive groups, and their use of vocalizations is more subtle, there are many

[1] See section on 'Voice production' (page 231) for a more detailed discussion.

species among them which seem not to employ this vocal potential as fully as others.

There are also some remarkable singers, like the two lyre-bird species, which do not have quite such extensive muscular equipment. These elegant birds of the forests in eastern Australia dance and sing their elaborate displays in circular clearings which each male constructs on the forest floor. Beautifully decorated tail feathers arch, like the spray from a coloured fountain, over the bird's back and head while he delivers a stream of sound which mingles musical and non-musical notes and mimicry of other species.

Because hearing is easier to assess by observation and experiment than voice production, more is known about the birds' receiving equipment. As we might guess from our response to their sounds, which fit comfortably within the limits of normal human hearing, the range of pitch or frequency for which their hearing is adapted is more or less the same as ours. Within this range birds, on the whole, are most sensitive to sounds with frequencies between 2000 and 4000 Hertz: somewhat higher than those used in our vocal and instrumental music and roughly equivalent to the highest octave on a piano. Many of the notes songbirds produce lie within this range and although they are sensitive to lower pitched sounds, below 1000 Hertz, few species make musical sounds at these frequencies.

The Hertz, or cycle per second as it used to be called, is simply a unit of measurement expressing the number – that is the frequency – of vibrations of a sound in one second. It is the frequency of the vibrations that sets the pitch of the sound: the higher the frequency, the higher the pitch.[1]

Birds have an acute discrimination of variations in frequency. This, too, we should expect from the minute pitch differences that we detect between some of the notes in their songs and calls. They also locate sounds with considerable accuracy. Owls are specially adapted for this – as they need to be for hunting in darkness when they locate their prey by hearing alone. Birds do not, it seems, make use of ultrasonic frequencies as bats do. Some cave-living species have a form of echo-location, like the bats, but the frequencies they emit for this purpose are within the human and avian auditory range (see Chapter 5).

Birds are also very sensitive to faint vibrations. It used to be

[1] See 'Definitions of terms' (page 221) for a fuller explanation of the relationship between pitch and frequency.

thought that this was the result of acute aural perception, but it is now known that the sense of touch not of hearing is involved. Special receptors on the body, wings, and legs can pick up the faint vibrations – of, for example, an enemy approaching on the ground or landing near their sleeping perch. Even sounds can be partly received through these sensitive points.

In one aspect of hearing birds have the advantage of us. Or rather, they have a considerable advantage in the comprehension of the sound signals that they themselves have evolved. They are capable of a far more accurate separation of sounds arriving in rapid succession, or, to put it another way, they have a better time resolution – probably as much as ten times better than ours. Many sounds which we hear as single notes, or perhaps as a vibrant noise, are now known to consist of a sequence of separate sounds and can be perceived by a bird in this way.

The visual equivalent of this ability would let us see a moving film as the series of still pictures from which it is composed. Aurally it means that more information can be conveyed in a short sound signal. This is probably why even the most extensive bird songs seem so brief to us. The bird with its speeded-up time sense must feel as if it had sung its equivalent of an operatic aria.

The tape-recorder, with the facility to reproduce a recording at slower speeds, enables us to appreciate how complicated in their time and frequency structure many bird sounds are. Recordings played at half or quarter speed reveal a new world of sound which the most perceptive of human ears had only guessed at. But even with this advance on our unaided perception, further tools are needed to reveal fully the detail, and the potential for subtle variation, contained in deceptively simple calls.

The Sound-spectrograph

The most important tool is the sound-spectrograph, adopted during the 1950s from the electronics engineers and the phoneticians as a laboratory tool for ornithological work. Not only has it made the analysis of bird sounds possible but it enables us to share the resulting information with people who cannot have access to the recordings. Other analysing equipment is used for special purposes but the sound-spectrograph has held its place as a machine capable of analysing effectively the most significant factors in a wide variety of bird sounds. It presents the results in permanent visual form for the kind of study and comparison of sounds that cannot safely be done by ear alone.

The diagrams, called sound-spectrograms and now, more frequently, 'sonagrams', can be read by anyone willing to spend a little time on learning how to do so. After that it is possible to 'auralize' an unknown sound, at least to the extent of knowing what type of sound it is, from the sonagram. For anyone interested in bird sounds this is a skill worth learning. Increasingly, articles in bird journals include sonagrams and the new handbook, *The birds of the Western Palaearctic* which is to appear volume by volume over a number of years from 1977, illustrates sounds in this way. Sonagrams have become the international written language for bird sounds.

The machine works like this: a section of the original recording is first copied onto the reproducing unit of the sound-spectrograph. The copied recording is then reproduced over and over again while the machine scans it to detect which frequencies are present. The recording, of course, has to be as clear and free of unwanted noise as possible to ensure an accurate picture of the bird sound itself.

The result of each scanning cycle is traced by a stylus on special paper clipped to a revolving, vertical drum. It is not unlike a barograph but rotates much faster – the process takes only a minute or two. After each band of frequencies has been traced, starting from the lowest, the stylus resets itself to trace out the next one. On the earlier, more slowly rotating models, it was exciting when you had at last recorded a long-wanted sound to watch the stylus gradually building up the traces into the shape you had predicted but often with some extra, unpredicted detail.

A commonly used sonagram format, suitable for many bird sounds, displays frequencies up to 8000 Hertz and has a time span of 2·5 seconds but frequencies up to 16000 Hertz can be analysed on many standard machines and some machines have longer or expanded time scales. Figure 1 introduces the sonagram format. The framework shows the scales. The horizontal line is the time scale marked out in tenths of a second. The vertical line is the frequency scale and is normally marked for every 2000 Hertz. These are shown in kiloHertz to get rid of the unwieldy noughts. This frequency scale is a linear one: that is, it gives equal space to each kilo-

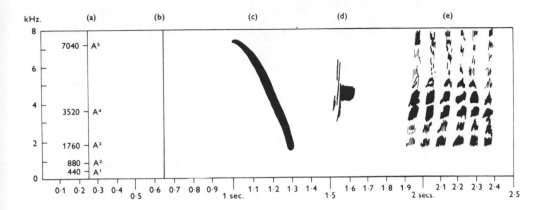

Hertz band. But the relationship of frequency to pitch is not linear. So the A above middle C on the piano (the tuning A of the orchestra), with a frequency of 440 Hertz, is very near the bottom of the diagram and each octave above that – marked on the vertical line in Figure 1 (a) – occupies more and more space on the sonagram. The fourth A at 3520 Hertz is the highest A on the piano and the whole of the top half of the sonagram, between 4 and 8 kiloHertz, covers just about one more octave – the one immediately above the last octave on the piano. This visual spread on the sonagram at higher frequencies is not necessarily a disadvantage for the study of bird sounds since so many of them, at least among the song-birds, lie in the middle or upper part of the sonagram where greater detail is revealed.

Within the framework in Figure 1 are stylized traces illustrating four types of sound – a click; a gliding note, musical in quality and descending in pitch; a clear, ringing, single note (like the *pink* call of the Chaffinch) and a rough, rhythmic sound with no definite musical pitch (like a Great Tit scolding). The non-musical sounds, the click and the scold (b) and (e), cover a wide range of frequencies. Notes with a musical quality and identifiable, fairly steady pitch lie within a well-defined band of frequencies, like the main component of (d). Unbroken upward or downward sloping traces, as in (c), are heard as notes rising or falling in pitch if the gradient is gentle. If it is very steep the sound has a less musical quality and is difficult to pitch: it is a kind of semi-musical click or twang.

The volume of a sound (strictly, the intensity of the various frequencies of which it is composed) is indicated on the original sonagram by the degree of blackness of the trace.

1
Interpreting a sonagram. Vertical scale shows the frequency in kiloHertz; horizontal scale shows time in seconds. (a) Frequency of A in treble octaves; (b) trace made by a single click sound; (c) musical note gliding downwards in pitch; (d) musical note of steady pitch with an abrupt, consonant-like start; (e) rough unmusical *churr* like someone rolling 'rrs'.

But this is not precise and is difficult to reproduce accurately in published sonagrams. In any case we are dealing with birds and often with recordings made in the open. Irrelevant factors, like the bird turning its head away or a gust of wind, may affect the volume of parts of the recorded signal.

All the four types of sound shown in Figure 1 can be produced vocally by a bird. There are many others, with numerous variations and combinations which loquacious species employ in their highly diversified repertoires of sound signals. Not all bird sounds, moreover, are vocal. There are many 'instrumental sounds' as they are usually called, produced by the bill, wings, or tail feathers, and some of these are just as significant as vocalizations in communication.

The rest of this chapter gives a few examples from this gamut of sounds.

Instrumental Sounds

One of the easiest to hear of the instrumental sounds is the *drumming* of a woodpecker. It punctuates the musical warblings of the woodland songbirds in spring with the loud, reverberant insistence of a drill. In England, Scotland and Wales (there are no woodpeckers in Ireland) the principal drummer is the Great Spotted Woodpecker, an adaptable bird that has invaded gardens, visiting bird tables and hanging on nutbaskets. We have even had one hammering on the window frame: a startling alarm clock at 6 a.m.

The Great Spotted Woodpecker has black and white distributed in a bold pattern over the head, back, wings and tail, with a red nape-patch on the male and red undertail flashes in both sexes. All this is dramatically displayed in the back and side views that are presented as it clings to the trunk or large branch of a tree. The sound is made by hammering with the beak against the wood. Specialized in bill shape and muscular development for hacking at a tree trunk to carpenter the nest hole, these birds use a ritualized, speeded up version of the same movements to make a sound signal. Both sexes drum.

They have more than one type of drumming but the longest form – 12 to 16 raps in just over half a second – fulfils many of the same functions as song does in the songbirds. A paired Great Spotted Woodpecker male, hearing drumming within his large territory (even if it comes from a recording played to test his response), will investigate this possible rival. As a rule an unmated male does not try to chase off a drumming rival but retires to his customary tree and looses off his own drum rolls.

The same signal serves paired birds throughout the breeding season. It is heard most frequently at the beginning of the various stages of the cycle: choosing the hole, building the nest, egg-laying, hatching and fledging of the young. The male may drum at any time if the female is out of the territory for too long. For this type of drumming the Great Spotted Woodpecker prefers a hollow tree or branch, thereby adding resonance to the sound and amplifying it sufficiently to carry for about a kilometre – quite a distance for a bird no larger than a Song Thrush. The obvious and unanswerable question is – does the bird 'know' that this is what it is doing?

One explanation could be that as drumming gradually evolved from its primary hacking function into a signal, certain birds in a population chose trees that were good sounding boards for their drumming, either by chance or possibly because they liked the sound. By extending the range of the signal this could have helped them to maintain a larger territory with a lower expenditure of time and energy and so possibly favoured their breeding success. With a bird's proven sensitivity to slight differences in pitch and tone-quality, and good aural memory, subsequent generations, having heard the signal from their nestling days, would tend to choose a tree that 'sounded right'.

The signal of the Lesser Spotted Woodpecker, sparrow-sized relative of the Great, does not carry so far. But this bird, too, is a fine drummer. Although not as common nor as widely distributed as the Great, it can be heard in woods and old orchards, especially in the south of England. It has a longer roll, lasting well over one second, somewhat different in pitch and quality of sound. The master drummer of Europe, however, is the Black Woodpecker. Many travellers in the forests of central and northern Europe must have heard this majestic, peremptory sound. A single roll of 35 to 43 strokes lasts for about $2\frac{1}{2}$ seconds and can be heard two kilometres away. But then the Black Woodpecker is twice the size of the Great.

Figures 2 and 3 illustrate the differences between the drum rolls of these three species. The sonagrams have been traced to bring out the characteristic shapes of the strokes without the surrounding shadows produced on the original sonagram

2
Drumming of
Black Wood-
pecker.

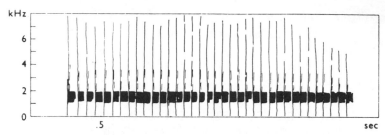

3
Drumming of
(a) Lesser Spotted
Woodpecker; (b)
Great Spotted
Woodpecker.

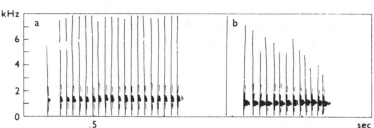

by reverberations from the wood. This technique is often employed in scientific papers and many sonagrams in this book have been prepared in this way. Used with discretion and experience, it has value in highlighting the signal pattern by removing irrelevant background noise.

Drumming is not the only signal in the woodpecker repertoire. They are vocal birds with a number of musical, as well as noisy, calls. The third resident in Britain, the Green Woodpecker, whose feeding habits in particular differ from the other two, has several melodious notes and phrases. These include the *yaffle* which has provided a nickname for this bird. It is a loud, ringing phrase like a slow, musical laugh. The Green Woodpecker drums only rarely. Nevertheless for most species, this woodpecker sound speciality, derived from their primary adaptation as carpenters, is an integral part of their communication system.

Another instrumental sound, important in aerial display, is made by the Common Snipe. Confusingly, this is also sometimes known in English as drumming though the sound bears no resemblance to the drumming of woodpeckers. It is not percussive in origin or effect but has a throbbing character.

The Snipe displays by circling upwards and then diving down at a slant. As it does so, with tail well spread, the air rushing over the extreme outer pair of tail feathers causes them to vibrate. These are much stiffer than the inner tail feathers, narrow on one side of the shaft and broad on the

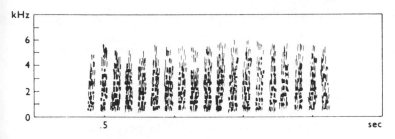

Snipe: sound
produced during
display dive by
vibrating outer
tail feathers.

other – a suitable modification for sound production. The
airstream over them is broken about 11 times a second by
quick wingbeats, thus producing the throbbing effect.

The noise has been variously described as a siren and 'a
booming note like the bleat of a kid'. The German name for
this sound is *Meckern* (bleating) and this captures its tremu-
lous quality. It can be heard over long distances. On the
moors and marshland where the Snipe lives, the strangeness
of the sound is emphasized by the variation in pitch and
volume caused by the speed of the bird's movement; the
sound-waves taking fractionally different times to travel to
the observer's ear (like the siren of a police car travelling at
speed). Recordists sometimes compensate for this effect by
following the bird's dive with a hand-held reflector and
microphone. Figure 4 illustrates the Snipe's drumming.
The sound from the regularly interrupted airflow through this
simple instrument of vibrating feathers shows a very complex
but well-defined time and frequency pattern.

A totally different sound effect from tail feathers is heard
in the Peacock's display (described in Chapter 2). The long
plumes bearing the 'Peacock's eye' – highly elaborated tail
coverts – can be seen to sway in the wind and vibrate. But
their movement is virtually noiseless. The sound comes from
the shorter, stiff feathers of the tail itself. These are snapped into the shape of a smaller fan. They touch and
rattle delicately as the Peacock vibrates both tail and coverts.
The sound is almost like the whispering of stiff grasses. While
the display is primarily visual there might well be an extra
stimulus for the female in the associated sound.

The wing is another sound-producing instrument. Most
people have heard the throbbing, sometimes whistling, wingbeats of flighting ducks and geese. The wing music of the
Mute Swan as it flies low overhead is particularly powerful
and, since these swans do not call in the air, undoubtedly
acts as a signal for other members of a flock. The wing sound

of the Whooper Swan is distinctively different and may be only incidental music: this species takes its name from a call which it makes in the air as well as when it is on the water.

In some species wing sounds are a prominent part of a display. One of the Flappet Lark species of Africa has a repeated pattern of wingflaps. This species belongs to the same family as our Skylark and rises in display flight in much the same way but with these rhythmic wingflaps which are as loud as or louder than the songs of the Skylark and audible at a distance of several hundred metres. Figure 5 shows the individually characteristic pattern of a Flappet Lark recorded in the Serengeti. A brief vocal song has also been heard from the Flappet Lark but observations so far suggest that this is uncommon. While the bird sang the audible wingflaps ceased. It seems likely, therefore, that the flapping display is the Flappet Lark's primary long distance proclamation of its

5
Flappet Lark: sound pattern of wing-flaps in aerial display (a lark in the Serengeti National Park, Tanzania; Bertram, 1977).

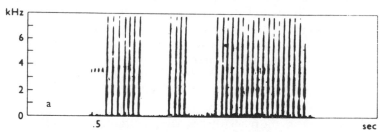

presence and rights of ownership in a territory.

There is a special interest in this display for it seems that while the flapping pattern is consistent for each bird, there are individual, local and regional differences in these 'wing songs'. Figure 6 illustrates some variations recorded in different parts of Africa by two observers, working independently. This kind of variation between populations or between races of the same species – a series of local 'dialects'

6 (a)
Flappet Lark. Geographical variation in wing-flap patterns: (1) Zaria (Nigeria); (2) Sumbu; (3) Bulaya; (4) Kundabwika Falls–all in Zambia (Payne, 1973).

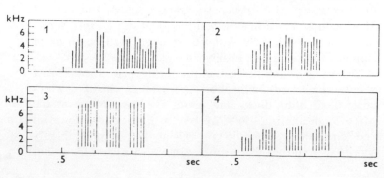

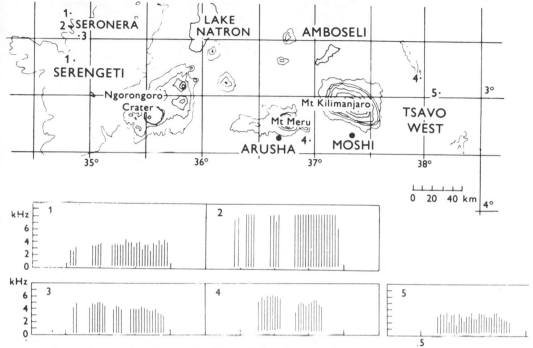

- is better known in songs and a few calls but it occurs in some
instrumental sounds as well. The drum rolls of the Black
Woodpecker in the Netherlands are of a different duration
from those in West Germany. In North America the Common Snipe, though belonging to the same species as the
Snipe of Europe, has a distinctive structure of the tail feathers,
and slower wingbeats. The tempo of the sound-sequence is
correspondingly different from that produced by the birds in
Europe. (Local and regional differences in the vocalizations
of various species are discussed in Chapters 7 and 9.)

    A more familiar example of wing sounds in display is the
wingflap of the Woodpigeon. This is part of an otherwise
silent display flight. The bird spreads its wings widely in
flapping flight with slower and deeper wingbeats than usual,
and at certain stages of the flight often makes a loud clapping
noise with its wings. Then it glides for a while and sometimes
repeats the action in the course of a single flight from one tree
to another. Comparable flights have been described for other
pigeon and dove species including the Rock Dove.

    There seems to be no external 'moving part' of a bird's
anatomy that is not used by one species or another for sound
production. Which part is put into service depends on the

6 (b)
Flappet Lark.
Map of recording
localities (num-
bered) in Kenya
and Tanzania
where the five
wing-flap patterns
shown below it
were recorded
(Seibt, 1975).

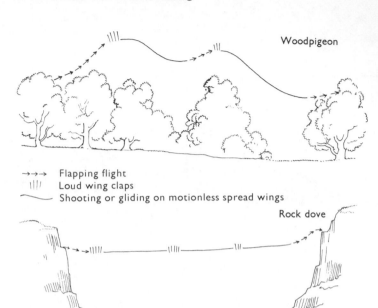

→→→   Flapping flight
\|\|/   Loud wing claps
——   Shooting or gliding on motionless spread wings

habitat and on where, in their three dimensional world, the
birds present their displays. Coots, spending most of their
lives on the surface of the water, are by no means unvocal.
They have a number of short, powerful calls. But one way in
which they drive off other males and attract females into their
neighbourhood is by standing on the nest or any floating
platform and slapping the water with a foot.

A last example of an instrumental sound, accurately
synchronized with both vocalization and other movements, is
the hiss display of the Great Tit. This display is given in
modified forms by other tit species living as far afield as
North America or Asia (where races of the Great Tit species
itself are also found). This extraordinary performance can
often be heard but rarely seen for it takes place in the darkness of the nesthole. It is a defensive display performed when
the tit is alarmed, usually by the appearance of an intruder at
the entrance to the hole.

In the display sequences we observed in one of our house-
living Great Tits, the bird rises from its brooding position
and turns away from the hole. The wings are raised and the
tail fully spread. Then the wings strike downwards with a
sharp cracking sound. This is immediately followed by a
vocal sound – a loud hiss – delivered with open bill. Figure 7

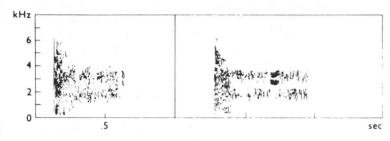

7
Great Tit hiss-
displays. The
first vertical line
in each sound is
the wing-strike,
followed im-
mediately by the
vocal hiss
(Gompertz, 1967).

is a sonagram of the wing strike (the initial vertical line) and the hiss. The bird completes its turning movement and sinks down on to the nest facing the intruder, bill snapped shut, tail still spread, cheek feathers fully erected and eyes staring ahead. In the dark hole this posture is emphasized by the white cheek feathers and white on the outer tail feathers. The whole spectacle, combined with the sound effects, must be alarming to an intruder small enough to have contemplated making an entry or inserting a predatory muzzle, tongue or beak.

There is still much to find out about this display. It is not known with certainty, for example, what kind of intruder provokes it: not, it seems, members of tit species. Patient observation and experiment could provide further answers to this question. The origin of such a display is yet another question but its widespread occurrence probably indicates a very early adaptation of the tits to nesting in holes.

These then are a few examples, mainly from species familiar to us in Britain, of instrumental sounds of birds: sometimes, as in the Great Tit's display, linked with vocal sounds, sometimes serving as the principal component of a signal or the sound element in a visual display. The range of instrumental sounds, however, though considerable, is restricted by the nature of the anatomical structures which are put to incidental use to produce them. Vocalizations are a different matter and it is evident to the most casual listener that their diversity is very great indeed. This is demonstrated in many examples in later chapters but it is worth considering briefly now some points of acoustic interest in these vocal sounds.

Great Tit hiss-display

Vocal Sounds

There is no need to go far afield to illustrate the range. My own aural memory often takes me to a stretch of the Suffolk coast where reed-filled Broads with a few stretches of open water extend right to the shore and peter out in soft sand and shallow pools. Only a bank of pebbles separates them from the sloping beach and the sea. The Broads are surrounded by old, mixed woodland and by grass-covered dunes with gorse scrub. In between, the farmers work their fields almost to the crumbling edges of the low cliffs.

Wherever you stop to listen, sounds from the bird members of several ecological communities are mingled. The ear is dazed with problems of adjustment and selection; the mind bemused but delighted by associations from other, far-separated habitats now all assembled within auditory reach.

Over the fields, Skylarks sing and Lapwings '*peewit*'. Disturbed from a quiet feed on a damp grass track, a Green Woodpecker *yaffles* its way back to the trees. From the woods, which reach right down to the shore, the high-pitched, penetrating songs of Wren, Great Tit and Blue Tit ride over the splash of the waves and the screams of gulls, terns and Oystercatchers. A Pheasant screeches. Then a Yellowhammer strikes up from a gorse bush but the soft, high-pitched *tee* which precedes the lower, vibrant endnote of the song is lost in the general noise (Figure 8).

On the sand, Ringed Plovers whistle away in anxiety and their mobile young squat at the parental alarm call. Sand Martins chitter continuously overhead – their harsher version of the running commentary that their relatives, the House Martins and Swallows, also deliver while insect-catching in the air. From the open water of the Broad there are the sounds of Shelduck and Mallard, and Coots make a clanking call. One or two startled Redshank rise from the water's edge and give their long musical call. They are not really alarmed or the call would have been a short, sharp note. From the reeds, a Sedge Warbler's chattering trills, interspersed with musical sounds, are alternately carried and swept away by the wind.

Among these sounds are some of the noisiest and the most delicate that the birds we know in Britain can make, with many gradations in between.

It is easy to understand why gulls and terns, usually in company whether they are on the wing or in their breeding colonies, and perpetually emitting their signals against a background of wind and water, should have evolved loud, short, shrill or harsh calls, well defined and often repeated. Equally it is evident that within the limitations imposed by a

8
Yellowhammer
song.

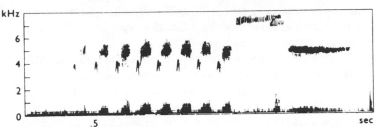

shared sound environment, each species needs a distinctive set of signals. What is more, certain calls at least must indicate not only the species and the situation (danger, food) but the individual identity of the caller. However, there is plenty of space for acoustic manoeuvre even in a relatively short one- or two-note call, uttered as it is in a difficult sound environment. For example recent work on some seabird species has shown that in the raucous clamour of thousands of birds in mixed breeding colonies on the great 'bird cliffs', nestlings pick out the calls of their own parents (see Chapter 8).

Penetration of a different kind of acoustic environment is required by the Bittern whose booming note is regularly heard from the reedbeds. This is of a comparatively low frequency for a bird, with its maximum energy around 500 Hertz. Heard close to, or on a recording, it is not strikingly loud, but its carrying power is remarkable. Said to be audible up to 5 kms away, it is easily heard at about 1½ kms. You can walk a long way without seeming to get any closer to the source of the sound. Low frequencies, with their longer wavelengths, carry farther and travel round solid objects, while very high frequencies are blocked or absorbed by obstacles in their path. The dense reedbed is no place for pure, high-pitched sounds if the message has to travel farther than the ears of a parent or social companion who is merely out of sight a few reed-clumps away. On the other hand, the chattering type of sound, covering a range of frequencies from low to high, carries for relatively long distances in these conditions.

It is unwise to be too rigid in defining the types of sound most suitable for particular environments. The acoustic properties of natural surroundings cannot be measured with the precision of those of a concert hall. They change, too, with the seasons and the weather. Moreover different types of sound are included in the repertoire of a single species. Also, birds colonize new habitats. In recent years the Reed Bunting, with its suggestive name, has moved into drier habitats – though it is too early to say whether its vocalizations will become adapted in any way. The tolerances are fairly wide and there may be more than one successful solution to an acoustic problem.

In all forms of behaviour too precise an adaptation spells disaster for a species faced with the destruction or diminution of its habitat. Fortunately most species have a reservoir of genetic variation, which, particularly when combined with the power of learning, enables them to avoid catastrophe by adapting to new conditions.

There are, nevertheless, certain obvious differences in the sound patterns of the various ecological communities. If you walk along the grassy tracks beside the Broads, the sounds from the reedbeds on one side and the woodland on the other alert you to these acoustic distinctions.

In the song season, the representatives of the warbler family, whose members are nearly all good and varied singers in their different ways, provide an interesting example. Two of them, the Sedge and Reed Warblers, are primarily birds of the marshes, though the Sedge Warbler commutes regularly to the thorn and briar tangle and water runnels at the edge of the wood. Both are small beige and brown birds, suitably difficult to see. At first hearing, their songs seem to be much alike. They are delivered in long, highly variable phrases, often uninterrupted for a minute or more. But with a little experience it is possible to hear that while clicking, chattering and harsh sounds are main components in both, the Sedge Warbler's utterances are more rapid, often turning into trills, with the more frequent insertion of musical notes.

The Reed Warbler has lower-pitched, slower, individual sounds, repeated several times, and the whole sequence is more disjointed. But as in nearly all species with variable songs, some individuals are better than others and it is often a beginner's luck to meet with one of these, whose performance has a musical quality and virtuosity which surpasses both verbal descriptions and recordings selected to illustrate more characteristic singers. Both species are successful imitators and with their capacity for varied sound production find plenty of models to choose from. But since the imitative notes are tossed into the stream of song, they are unlikely to deceive for long.

The other two warblers, the Willow Warbler and the Chiffchaff – the woodland specialists – belong to a different genus of the same family. They have a singing style and tone-quality totally dissimilar from the warblers of the reeds and marshes.

The Willow Warbler's liquid, descending scale, with its changing rhythm, its crescendo and decrescendo, is a familiar sound in woods throughout Europe as far north as the Arctic Circle. A short phrase, pure in tone and repeated at varying intervals, it carries effortlessly through the wood. It is usually echoed by neighbours in their individually characteristic phrases for, though territorial, Willow Warblers seem to have a preference for plenty of neighbours within earshot.

The Chiffchaff is visually almost indistinguishable from the Willow Warbler. Though not such a northerner, elsewhere in the range it is present in the same woodland communities. The song is often dismissed as monotonous: the steady, repeated *chiff, chaff* which has given the bird its name. But careful listening reveals variation in this apparently simple song structure, as well as some softer notes which are sometimes uttered between the *chiff chaff* phrases (Figure 9). These two warbler songs are discussed, with additional illustrations, in later chapters. The point here is that both consist of musical notes, well within the range of frequencies and sound types which have been found to be characteristic of other songbird species in woodland habitats.

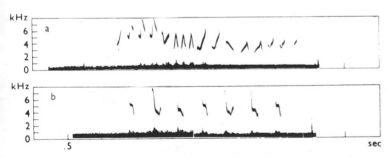

9
Songs of (a)
Willow Warbler;
(b) Chiffchaff.

Nearly all the sounds mentioned so far have been long-distance signals, proclaiming ownership and species identity, variously suited to their sound environment and the living-space requirements of the species. Closer acquaintance, and approach, familiarize the ear with other, more subtle sounds. Everywhere around, dominated by the louder sound patterns but not submerged, are the intimate murmurings of family life whose transmission radius need not (and for safety should not) be more than a few metres. A subdued piping from young Ringed Plovers might be heard on the shore. In the woodland the delicate, shivering, courtship-feeding and copulation call of the Great Tit is just audible from close cover nearby (Figure 10).

10
Zeedling–court-
ship feeding and
copulation call of
the Great Tit.

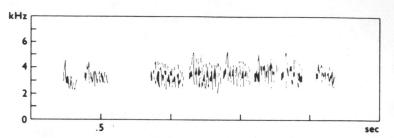

The quiet sounds in the reedbeds are more difficult to pick up. But one sunny July afternoon, tempted out into the marsh by the not too distant babble of young birds on the move, I found a safe foothold along the solid wooden beams of an old duck decoy, now embedded in reeds. Looking down from the far end, I caught occasional glimpses of a brood of Reed Warblers as they fluttered and clambered about in the depths of the reeds. But all the time I could hear the sotto voce *squiks*, *chitters* and random warbling phrases, with hints of adult notes yet to come, that accompanied their exploration of the world outside the nest.

4 Songs

Whan that Aprille with his shoures sote
The droghte of Marche hath perced to the rote,
And bathed every veyne in swich licour,
Of which vertu engendred is the flour;
Whan Zephirus eek with his swete breeth
Inspired hath in every holt and heeth
The tendre croppes, and the younge sonne
Hath in the Ram his halfe cours y-ronne,
And smale fowles maken melodye,
That slepen al the night with open yĕ,
(So priketh hem nature in hir corages):
Than longen folk to goon on pilgrimages . . .
Geoffrey Chaucer

Nearly five hundred years after Chaucer wrote his description of the English spring, we can still accept his list of the environmental, physiological and behavioural factors which, in delicately adjusted interplay, stimulate and regulate the flow of bird song that so clearly delighted him. Nowadays we can explain some of the interconnections; and in a modern scientific study (which would probably have interested Chaucer, for he had a scientific turn of mind) we should use a rather different terminology. This would include photoperiodicity; isotherms and vegetational changes; the enlargement of the gonads, spermatogenesis and the production of testosterone, and reproductive behaviour patterns. But basically, the last and greatest English poet of the Middle Ages, with prodigal richness, has tossed it all into the twelve opening lines of his most famous work. For in a bird's life, song is associated in various ways with the process of reproduction and, in the temperate zones of the world, the peak time for breeding is the spring.

The purpose of this chapter is to consider two aspects of song: its function in a bird's seasonal and daily activities; and the great differences in sound patterns that are to be found between the songs of different species.

Full Song

Full, primary, territorial or advertising song (it has been defined by all these terms) is a complex, ritualized signal, of great biological importance both to the individual and the species. It is distinctive in its proclamatory function and, in most species, in its limitation to a particular part of the year.

It is not always easy to distinguish between the simpler types of song and a complicated call from the sound alone. Some species weave call-notes into their song and even construct it entirely from these notes. So the circumstances and behaviour of the bird are important in deciding whether a particular utterance is a song or not. However, there are some acoustic clues. Even when a song is short, simple and constructed from call-notes, there is usually a firmer pattern in the sequence of sounds, and a greater elaboration than in repeated calls: an obvious grouping of the notes into phrases with predictable pauses between them and a greater regularity of repetition. In highly evolved songs, the qualities of pattern and elaboration are even more pronounced.

I should like to illustrate the functions of full song – as we have come to understand them in many species – by describing its place in the life of the Great Tit. This choice is made, to some extent, because I was a partner in Terry Gompertz' study of this species but also because the songs are familiar to most people and simple in structure. They include notes resembling some that occur in the calls. Although this gives a potentially large number of different sounds, in their songs the majority of Great Tits confine themselves to those between approximately two and seven kiloHertz, each relatively short in duration and, as a rule, musical in quality. The pattern is of two, three or four separate notes or 'elements'[1] though more may be used, combined into a 'motif' which is repeated without alteration a varying number of times. I call this string of repeated motifs a 'song-strophe'. After a pause, the bird will deliver another song-strophe. The number of repetitions in each strophe and the duration of the pauses between strophes seem to depend on the bird's internal state, or the exigencies of the situation, or a combination of both. Within the strophe, the pauses between elements, and between repeated motifs, are virtually invariable for that particular song.

A Great Tit male normally has at least four different songs (song-variants) each based on a different motif. Some birds

[1] The use of the word 'element' avoids the musical implications of 'note' for in the songs of many species non-musical sounds are included. It refers to any unbroken sound trace on a sonagram made from a recording reproduced at normal speed. Slower speeds may reveal that some of these traces are themselves composed of several elements with very brief pauses between them. See 'Definitions of terms', page 221.

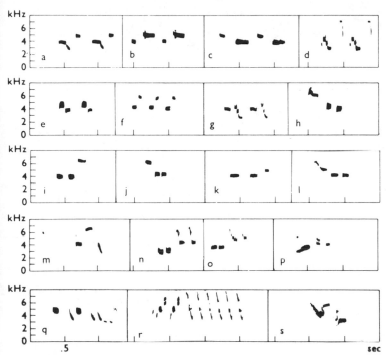

11
Great Tit: 19 different song-motifs showing variation in elements. Fast two-note motifs repeat within each rectangle. Recorded in (b, e–g) Yorkshire; (c, q, r) Hertfordshire; (n-p) southern Germany; others in Middlesex (Gompertz, 1971).

have as many as seven or eight. In a long spell of singing, a bird usually sings one of these for perhaps three to five minutes and then switches to another. Figure 11 illustrates nineteen different song-motifs and Figure 12 the motifs in the song repertoires of five males who held neighbouring territories near our home in the same year. In most situations we found no evidence that a Great Tit is likely to sing one song-variant rather than another; they seem to be interchangeable except when rival males sing against each other (counter-singing). Then the second singer tends to choose from his own repertoire the variant that in motif and tempo most nearly matches the song his rival is singing.

For Great Tits, as for many species, the territory is the heart of the matter at breeding time and song is the proclamation of its importance. As you follow the birds through the year, you learn not only about their vocal habits but also about what is happening in the local Great Tit community.

I begin their year in the late autumn after the long lull when they have had no parental duties. At this time their interest in their territory revives in preparation for the new breeding season in the following spring. Established pairs

12
Great Tit: song repertoires of five males holding neighbouring territories in the same year. Each bird has a study number. Each rectangle shows one (or two) utterances of a different motif: note similar motifs, e.g. (f) and (k); (m) and (w).

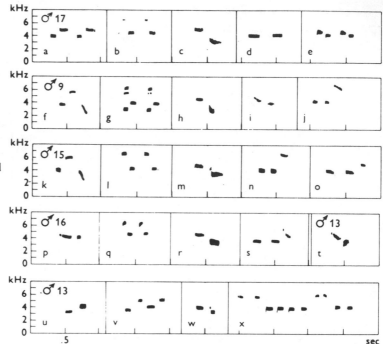

who have survived together from the previous season (they are faithful partners) may have been pottering around the territory since their last brood fledged. This is particularly likely to happen in gardens, which the adult Great Tits seem disinclined to leave for long to join the autumn and winter feeding flocks in the woods. But they have not been seriously occupied with territorial defence during this lull.

The first singing of the new season is heard towards the end of November, or early December, in most years: only one or two of the song-variants at first, rather tentatively delivered. But by early January the male is usually singing them all and flexing his muscles, so to speak, for any trouble to come. If he has old-established neighbours, the boundaries were worked out long ago and none of the birds need bother much. In the context of ownership their songs are hardly more than routine testing of the line to make sure that everything is normal: a social, almost companionable statement rather than a threat. They sing from favourite perches, usually referred to as song-posts, in the centre of the territory and from time to time they 'beat the bounds', pausing on their way round to proclaim their presence.

But branches may have been lopped or shrubs uprooted

during autumn clearances of the garden. In a woodland, trees may have fallen. Rearrangements of the territorial boundary may become necessary. Even more troublesome, a young male may try to edge his way in, to claim a territory of his own. This is when reproductive fighting starts. This term is used to cover any skirmishes associated with reproductive needs: that is, the acquisition or defence of a territory, a mate and a nest.

Such close encounters are noisy, combative affairs, with threat postures and much darting around and chasing in the disputed area. There is rarely any physical contact or injury. Throughout the dispute the males deliver an impressive variety of aggressive calls but these are sometimes interspersed with short song-strophes, emphatically uttered. At the close of the encounter the victor retires within his territory and sings vigorously while the loser utters his *tink* call: a resonant single note, often repeated in groups of two.

During the later autumn and winter, while the male is active and vociferous in territorial matters, the female is an unobtrusive presence. If nothing untoward is happening she behaves as if she were solely concerned with feeding and conserving her energy. However, she quickly joins in reproductive fighting, usually concentrating her attention on the other female, but she is less strenuously vocal than her mate. As in many species she does not normally sing. But if she temporarily inherits full responsibility for the territory from a dead or disabled mate she may produce a weak, harsher version of one of the simpler song-variants.

If an established territory holder has lost his mate, or if he is a young, mateless male, there is a different stimulus for song. This proclamation is not solely aggressive in its message. It also advertises the presence of a potential mate to any wandering female. As a rule, in most species, a mated male sings less than an unmated one. After pairing, Great Tits keep in contact with each other mainly by special calls. But if the female is absent from the territory for any length of time, the male sings.

In April 1975, I had a convincing demonstration of this function of song: a tragic natural experiment, with a happy ending. The back-garden territory holder, colour-ringed Redblack for individual identification, lost his mate when she was already well on with building her nest in one of the boxes.

It had been a quiet year in the local Great Tit community.

The neighbours were known to one another from the previous year and there had been no reproductive fighting, just
a standard daily routine of song: early morning and evening
sessions; periodic outbursts of varying length during the day,
with occasional counter-singing when one of the neighbours
started up; rather more song for several days on end, rather
less for another day or two. During such a mild winter the
weather had little effect on their activities. The amount of
singing diminished as all the pairs became pre-occupied with
nest-building.

Then suddenly I heard long bouts of song from Redblack.
There was only mild and perfunctory counter-singing from
other males indicating that no intruders were present. I went
out to investigate and the situation was soon obvious.
Redblack's mate had disappeared. He was wandering all over
the garden singing in different places. In a human being we
would describe his behaviour as distracted. Next he visited
the nest box where a pair of Blue Tits who had failed to
find accommodation were already trying to take over the
nest, bringing material to complete it. Reddy drove them
off and returned to the box but found nothing to do when he
got there. He sat on a branch and preened, then flew to the
next tree and sang. Then he swooped down and drove off the
Blue Tits again.

This performance was repeated throughout the afternoon
and for several more days. As time went on Redblack moved
outwards, singing farther and farther from the nest-site and
provoking counter-singing from a distant woodland male
into whose territory he must have been intruding. Sometimes
he came back for further fruitless attempts to establish
normal nesting routines. One day he sang much less and was
back in the garden for longer periods. An unfamiliar, un-
ringed female visited the bird table and I caught sight of her
near his favourite song post.

On the ninth day after I had verified his loss I heard one
of his soft contact calls and found him sitting beside a female
on a perch near the table. He waited for her to fetch a nut
before he came for his own. She accompanied him silently
while he sang normally around the garden or called to her
with some of the calls used by paired birds. Then, five days
later, she *zeedled* (see Chapter 3, Figure 10), the sign that she
was ready for courtship feeding or copulaton, and I knew that
all was well with them.

Once the nest is complete and the female is roosting in it,

the routine changes. The male arrives from his own roost in the early morning and sings from a branch nearby. If the hen is late in emerging he stays there, ringing the changes on all his song-variants. He still beats the bounds occasionally.

When the nestlings have hatched, and after fledging, the male is too busy helping the female to feed and supervise them to sing much. For the first week after fledging at least, he leads them to suitable cover which, in garden habitats, may be outside the territory. In any case territorial boundaries tend to be disregarded in this busy phase of the reproductive cycle. From time to time the male uses a short song-strophe to catch the attention of his brood, in addition to the normal rallying call. If there is a second brood the cycle is repeated. But in 1975 Redblack's family tragedy had so delayed proceedings that he was moulting before the first cycle was completed and there was no more song.

In the early autumn after the moult, there is a short period of revived sexual activity, accompanied by occasional snatches of song, but in our experience this vocal recrudescence is less pronounced in the Great Tit than in some other species. After this there is a further song silence until the annual cycle restarts in the weeks before Christmas.

This, then, is the Great Tit's song year. Other species show variations on it, particularly in the time of onset and termination of the song period. Differences in territorial behaviour may account for this variation in the length of the song season. For example Wren song may be heard at almost any time of year though in the off-peak seasons at the end of the summer and again in late autumn, it is less frequent and often the song-pattern is incomplete. Edward Armstrong in his beautiful study of the Wren describes it as 'among the most territorial birds'. Armstrong adds that in areas where the male is sedentary (for there is a considerable movement of Wrens in autumn) it may maintain territory throughout the year.

There is a great deal of Robin song in autumn though it differs somewhat from the typical songs of early spring. Again, Robins hold territory strongly in autumn. The females have territories of their own and also sing. But after pairing has taken place in early spring the female no longer sings. She joins up with the male and a new territorial pattern in the local Robin community is worked out for the breeding season.

The Blackbird starts to sing very late and the song-period is comparatively short: from about mid-February to early

July. The Song Thrush may sing from the beginning of the year or even earlier and go on well into July; a great difference between two closely related species. But this may be explained, as suggested in Chapter 2, by the Blackbird's tendency to use ground displays in settling boundary disputes, and attracting a mate; for pairing, too, has often taken place before the male starts to sing. Nevertheless a male who is widowed during the song season sings almost continuously.

The dates of onset and termination of song, in most species, vary from year to year and in different parts of the country, indicating environmental effects on the bird's organism. Eric Simms, in his book *Birds of town and suburb*, reports from years of observation round his home at Dollis Hill in London that he has heard full song from Blackbirds between December and August. This is a much longer period than in country districts.

Within a species there are differences in the time of onset of full song between individuals, reflecting the influence of the bird's internal rhythm. For song is an acoustic indicator of the physiological state. In some species, the Blackbird and the Chaffinch, for example, changes in plumage or beak colour also show that the bird is coming into breeding condition.

It is now realized that a combination of external factors – changing day length (in the temperate zones); temperature; availability of appropriate food; even, possibly, visual stimuli like budding leaves, affect the physiological development of both sexes. Any phase of the reproductive cycle – the onset of song, pairing, nest-site selection, building, the start of laying the clutch – may be retarded if conditions are unsuitable. So there is a buffer against the dangers of breeding too early in a late spring while an early one stimulates more intensive activity, though birds may be trapped into nesting by a 'false' spring.

The sedentary habits of resident species allow time for this variation in the length of any phase of the cycle. The position is different for the summer migrants. For instance small migrant birds like the warblers may start to sing before they leave their winter quarters in Africa. But this can have no significance for their reproductive activities which only begin when they reach their breeding grounds. These may be anywhere between southern Europe and the Arctic Circle or beyond. The birds are sometimes held up on their journey by cold weather and the shortage of insect food. Once they reach their destination action has to be swift.

No one who has been in the Northern Highlands of Scotland in spring can forget the day some time in early May when the Willow Warblers come in. Each morning one member of the household has been saying hopefully to the others 'I thought I heard a Willow Warbler in the distance in the dawn chorus. Did you?' But no one is quite sure.

Then, all at once, they have arrived. The males come first. They seem to be in every gorse bush, and every birch tree. One after the other they start a floating phrase and repeat it again and again until it sounds as if the whole wood is singing in canon.

Song activity is at a high level, with morning and evening peaks of singing, while territories are being established. It culminates when the females arrive some days later. After this paired males sing less regularly than unpaired ones but with greater variability. Each Willow Warbler has a number of variations in its song repertoire. Figure 13 illustrates five songs from one male. As a rule neighbours have different song variants and, unlike the Great Tits, they do not appear to adjust their variants to each other in counter-singing. In the early days of great territorial activity their song-strophes tend to be short. Later in the season the strophes become longer, lower in pitch, with new elements inserted, and there is a more fluid pattern. Willow Warblers go on singing far into the summer, after breeding is over.

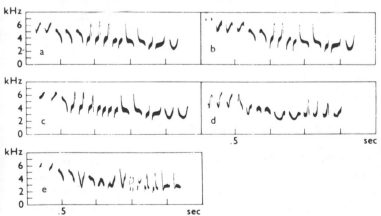

13
Willow warbler song variants: each sonagram shows a complete strophe. All were recorded from one bird on the same day. (a) (b) and (c) are the same type of strophe with a variable number of elements; (d) and (e) are two different types (Schubert, 1967).

So far in this chapter I have referred only to familiar woodland songbirds. But as the earlier descriptions of the Blackcock, the woodpeckers and the Lapwing have shown, many species from other groups, though not songbirds in the systematist's sense, have sound signals with similar functions.

A further, somewhat surprising, example of song behaviour is provided by the Red-necked Phalarope. Like the Lapwing it is a wader, but of a different family. Red-necked Phalaropes are migratory, breeding mainly on the northern coastal tundra, though they may be found further inland. A few pairs nest in Ireland and in Scotland, chiefly on the northern isles. They are small, neat birds, only 18 centimetres long, with a prominent orange-red patch on the side of the neck in their summer plumage. The female is the more conspicuously coloured partner and this in itself suggests that their domestic arrangements are unusual in the bird world where, as a rule, the female cares for the young, with or without the help of her mate, and (unless she nests in a hole, or in a large bird colony) is often cryptically coloured for safety.

When unmated the female Phalarope engages in a number of courtship displays on the water if a male alights nearby. She may stand upright on the water, rattling her wings; this rattling display also precedes a ceremonial flight during which she calls – the equivalent, it seems, of a mate-attracting song. It is she who selects and defends the territory. When she starts to lay, there is a revival of the ceremonial flights and calling. The male follows her and so is shown the location of the nest where he incubates the eggs and cares for the young.

This, and other less extreme examples of role reversal between the sexes, are commonly interpreted as adaptations to a short breeding season and a scarce food supply in a harsh environment; for the female is left free to feed and re-cover her strength for the autumn migration south. Yet there are many species in the same habitat whose behaviour has not been adapted in this way, just as there are some examples of role reversal in less exacting environments. It is an evolutionary puzzle and could be one more example of how widely the special adaptations to any environment can differ.

Examples of the great variety of song behaviour, as of other forms of behaviour, can be multiplied almost indefinitely. We need as much information as possible on these behavioural differences and the factors in the environment which may account for them. There are also many species whose day-to-day song habits are not known in detail and the experienced amateur with time for regular observation can make a useful contribution. Local variations, even in the habits of well-studied species, are of great biological interest.

Red-necked Phalarope male

The Information Content of Song

All the previous examples in this chapter have illustrated the importance of song in the bird's daily and seasonal activities; the domestic functions, regulating the affairs of a particular species. But song has a further function as a proclamation of species identity. A Blackbird, Song Thrush, Robin, Wren, Great, Blue and Coal Tits, a Willow Warbler and a Chiffchaff, to mention only the more common species, frequently hold overlapping territories in the same wood. The confusion would be considerable if they all reacted to each other's songs.

Experienced human observers find no difficulty in distinguishing between the songs. To say that, however, is merely to say that the songs differ. Within the repertoire of each species the variation can be very great indeed. The problem is to discover how so variable a signal conveys such precise messages.

A French ornithologist, Dr J.-C. Brémond, tackled this problem experimentally by a study of Robins in the wild. He started by recording and analysing the songs of a great number of Robins. Then he made a series of field experiments in the territories of as many birds as possible. He set up a tape-recorder and loudspeaker and played back recordings of songs that had been altered in various ways to test the reactions of the birds to each alteration.

As we found with the Great Tit, and as many other researchers have found in playback experiments, the owner in whose territory the loudspeaker is intruding responds to the recorded song of his own species. Usually he begins by singing against it from wherever he happens to be. Then, since the intruder does not go away, the owner flies towards the loudspeaker to investigate, sometimes even attacking it. The intensity of this response to a normal recorded song (the 'control'), measured by the vocal and other behaviour of the individual, forms a basis for comparison with the response of the same bird to experimental recordings.

Brémond's alterations of the song were designed to find out which characteristics of the sound pattern could be changed or omitted and still produce a response from the wild Robins.

In comparison with the Great Tit, Robin song sounds rather complicated. The elements are diverse and numerous. They are combined in varied motifs and a variable number of these motifs make up a song-strophe. In a sequence of strophes it is exceptional for any one motif to be repeated.

Red-necked Phalarope female

This is not surprising for it appears that about 1300 motifs may be used by the Robin species. An individual has a repertoire of several hundred and is apparently capable of increasing their variety by improvizing around them. Figure 14 shows three consecutive song-strophes from a sequence of natural song. The first two strophes each have four motifs. The diversity of the elements, even in so small a sample, is easily recognized.

14
Robin song: three consecutive strophes from a sequence (Brémond, 1967).

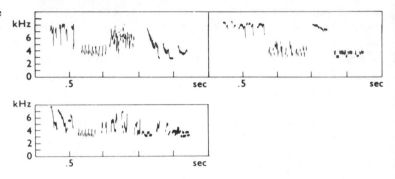

In this seeming jungle of variability, however, the experiments demonstrated the existence of some fundamental 'rules' which provide a structure for the Robin's individual use of the species' repertoire. If too many rules were transgressed, the signal produced no response. If the main rules were kept, a number of other alterations and recombinations could be made without serious loss of effectiveness in communicating species identity.

15
Robin song: extracts from natural song used as a control in experiments (Brémond).

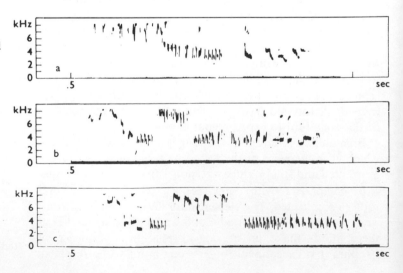

The three main principles in the structure of Robin song that Brémond derived from his experiments are these:

First, that all the consecutive strophes in a song sequence differ from one another.

Second, that in each strophe, all the motifs differ.

Third, that successive motifs should be alternately high and low in pitch: above or below a frequency of approximately four kiloHertz. This can be seen in the strophes in Figure 14.

Some of the experiments are illustrated in the next Figures. Figure 15 shows extracts from the natural song that was played back to the Robins as a control. Three experiments based on it demonstrate the third rule of Robin composition. Selections of high motifs only, and low motifs only, were each made into strophes and separately tested. The results of these two experiments were very similar, with 52% and 56% success rates, compared with the 88% reaction to the control song. But when a strophe was built up from alternating high and low motifs, it produced the same reaction as the control. Parts of these experimental strophes are illustrated in Figure 16.

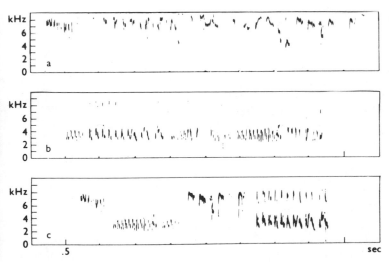

16
Robin song: test strophes made up from natural song with motifs re-arranged. (a) High motifs only; (b) low motifs only; (c) high and low motifs mixed as in natural song (Brémond).

Some other experiments were made with synthesized sounds. A continuous pure tone (a sine wave) was generated electronically and its frequency modulated in regular high and low patterns in the outline shape of Robin song (Figure 17). This had no effect on the Robins at all. Then this signal was cut up into fragments which began to resemble some of the natural song elements (Figure 18a). Next, the elements

17
Continuous sine-
wave (pure tone)
modulated to
imitate the out-
line form of Robin
song (Brémond).

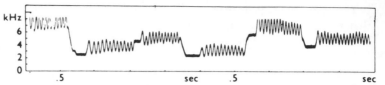

were further altered to give some rhythmic variety (Figure
18 d). These two experiments were of some interest to the
Robins. However, when the frequencies were modulated up
and down more rapidly, and complex tones were introduced
(additional frequencies), the success rate dropped (Figure
18 b). Figure 18 (c) is yet another version. Complex tones were
used, with both irregular rhythm and irregular modulation of
the frequencies. This was the most successful so far. But in the
final test of this series, motifs from all these signals were
strung together, giving a more varied strophe. This was much
nearer the real thing and scored a high success rate with the
Robins.

18
Four synthesized
Robin songs,
generated electro-
nically. First two
motifs of each
(Brémond, 1967).

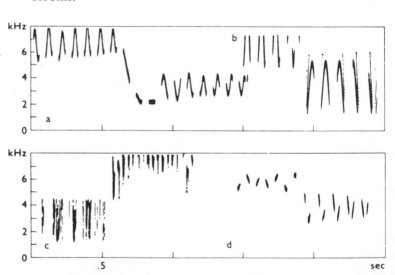

It seems from these experiments that the 'receiving' Robin
follows the overall pattern of the song, attending to a number
of important characteristics which have wide, though definite,
limits of variation. The term 'parameter', borrowed from
mathematics, is used in ornithological work for any one of
these characteristics of bird sounds – duration, frequency,
rhythm, tone-quality and so on – which can be independently
varied. For convenience in description it will be adopted in
this book.

The Robin's song contains a good deal of repetitive information: a useful feature because if some parts of it are lost in transmission the message is still clear. So the diversity of the song masks a simple basic structure which, in Brémond's view, is comparable with that of the Great Tit. But in addition to the main messages more subtle information is carried: for example, certain changes indicate that the 'transmitting' Robin is in a particularly aggressive mood. The fine details of the structure are thought to carry such information as the identity of the singer for other experiments showed that Robins recognize each other as individuals by song alone when they are out of view.

Robin song, then, bears no relation to language in the sense that 'meaning' is associated with particular sounds in the pattern in the way that words are tied to meanings in human language. But there is a parallel to be drawn for the rules of Robin song composition are rules of syntax, as Brémond himself calls them. If a certain order, or structure, is not observed, the result is non-comprehension. It is as if in human speech we were to say 'Is the today cloudy warm very weather but' – only much, much worse, because for a receiving Robin there would be no meaning in the eight separate 'motifs' of that 'strophe' for him to hang on to while he sorted it out.

These experiments also provided some information on the successful separation of species by song. They did so by indicating the possibility of breakdown if these signals were less subtly varied than we now know them to be. In the course of the experiments with simplified, synthesized versions of the Robin's song there were some reactions from other species. The best interpretation of this seemed to be that the simplified signals contained elements which corresponded fairly well with elements in the repertoire of these species.

The most frequent cause of confusion was the song in Figure 18 (a) which produced only a moderate response from the Robins themselves. This put a Blackbird to flight, uttering the call reproduced in Figure 19 (d). This call usually occurs when a Blackbird is startled or disturbed. The same song induced mild reactions of territorial defence in some Nightingales and they also imitated it. Wrens, too, sometimes responded, though only hesitantly unless they had themselves been singing not more than a minute before, when they appeared to take the signal seriously as a territorial challenge. Figure 19 (a) and (c) illustrate elements from Wren and

19
Song motifs from the natural song of (a) Wren; (b) Robin; (c) Nightingale, with elements resembling those in the synthesized Robin songs (Fig. 18). (d) Alarm call of Blackbird when startled (Brémond, 1967).

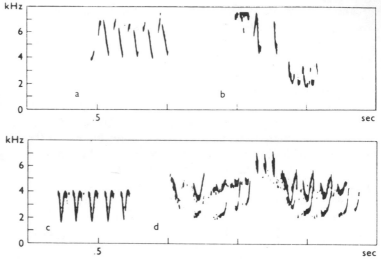

Nightingale song which resemble the synthesized elements. Figure 19 (b) shows other motifs from a natural Robin song for comparison.

It may seem surprising that the Robins themselves, and the other species concerned, responded at all to simplified or distorted versions of sound signals which normally act to prevent waste of energy in attending to irrelevant information and are detailed enough to indicate even individual identity. Probably, however, emergency action is taken on first hearing if the resemblance to the species' own song is close enough to arouse suspicion. A human analogy may be forgiven. We do not stop to question the identity or motives of an intruder in the house. We take immediate action.

The answer to this puzzle is becoming clearer as research proceeds. Experiments like those with the Robin have now been carried out by Dr Brémond and other workers with a number of species and in each case so far several parameters are important for species recognition. These identifying characteristics differ in different species but the principle seems to be the same. Because a number of parameters are carrying the clues to species identity, one or all of them can be varied within certain acceptable limits and the basic message is still conveyed.

However, these signals must not only be recognized by members of the species concerned but also quickly rejected as irrelevant by other species. Some recent work of Brémond's on Bonelli's Warbler (a rare visitor to Britain but common in

Continental Europe) has led him to suggest that while the signal has to include just enough of the 'right' clues if it is to be recognized, it must not include certain 'wrong' ones. This could be important for species with somewhat similar songs that share the same habitat. The song of Bonelli's Warbler, though variable, consists of repeated elements forming a slow trill and in this it resembles part of the song of the Wood Warbler. These two species occur together in many parts of Europe.

The experiments showed that some parameters in the songs of Bonelli's Warbler could be varied considerably – the duration of the trill, for example, was extended beyond that of any natural song so far recorded and still produced a response. But some other changes were unacceptable. When the frequency of the signal was transposed upwards, bringing it into the normal range of the Wood Warbler's trill, it was rejected by the Bonelli's Warblers (and provoked a reply from some Wood Warblers). This parameter, then, is one that could be critical for separation of these two species. Lowering the frequency by the same amount, on the other hand, was acceptable.

I have described these studies at some length for two reasons. In the first place, they have thrown light on two interesting questions: the way in which information is encoded in song and the safety mechanisms which ensure that the code is not broken by other species. Secondly, the studies illustrate the technique of playback experiments with birds in the wild which will be referred to again.

The technique sounds simple but needs great care if the results are to be valid. The normal behaviour of the birds must be completely familiar to the observer, to avoid misinterpretations. Ideally, as much as possible should be known about the circumstances of the individual birds tested. Careful siting and camouflage of equipment, and the observer, is important. No bird should be subjected to a lengthy playback session, for this uses up its energy at a time of year when it is under heavy pressures. In any case its response will diminish and the test become scientifically valueless. Equally, if it is tested too frequently, a bird gets accustomed to the experience and no longer reacts.

During much of our work on the Great Tit, the one male we could never try out with playbacks was our then back-garden resident – the subject of Terry Gompertz' radio programme 'A lifetime of Johnny'. He was with us for nearly ten years. In that period he spent most of his time within earshot of unpredictable Great Tit sounds that issued from the tape-recorders in the house, with songs and calls delivered in improbable sequences and often at the wrong time of year. He very quickly learned to ignore them all.

Song Patterns

The variety of song patterns in the full songs of different species is obvious from the few examples I have already given. From the point of hearing of the human listener anxious to identify bird songs it is bewildering.

While a musically trained ear is, in general, an asset I do not believe it is an essential qualification for learning bird songs. Responsiveness to sound and good discrimination of pitch variation and tone-quality, which can be improved by experience, take the dedicated listener a long way. A few guide lines, however, to add to verbal descriptions and listening, can focus the memory of musical and non-musical alike. Some sort of classification is of interest to the learner and the research worker and I think that, for many people, a grouping according to the general pattern of the song is the most practical beginning.

Dr Poul Bondesen, of the University of Aarhus in Denmark, has published one such classification. He worked it out in far greater detail than can be quoted here but he made a broad division into three groups. In illustrating these, and their main sub-divisions, I have chosen from his examples only species which are referred to in the present book.

Group 1

The STARLING *Group*: SOUND COMPOSITION
(a) Continuous non-musical song with no consistent division into phrases. The birds often sing in chorus. Melodic motifs exceptional (i.e. many of the elements are noisy rather than musical); existence of mimicry doubtful. E.g. Fieldfare with 'spasmodic' staccato sound composition. Sand and House Martins with 'flowing non-spasmodic sound composition'.
(b) Melodic motifs often form part of the sound composition; more or less distinct mimicry. E.g. Starling.

Group 2

The CHAFFINCH *Group*: NON-FREE COMPOSITION
(a) Non-continuous songs with distinct patterns. Monotonous motif song. E.g. the Grasshopper Warbler and Savi's Warbler with regular repetitions of a single element, forming a trill; Chiffchaff: rhythmically combined elements; Great and Coal Tits: uniform, repeated motifs.

(b) Song-strophes not made up of precise repetitions of the same elements or motifs. E.g. Chaffinch, Yellowhammer, Willow Warbler, Redwing, Robin, Wren.

Group 3

The SKYLARK *Group*: FREE COMPOSITION
The song seems continuous. There is often a kind of regular rhythm through the song, and phrases of varying length. E.g. Skylark, Nightingale, Blackbird, Song Thrush and Mistle Thrush; Sedge, Reed- and Garden-Warblers.

Blackbird

Dr Bondesen uses various parameters to make many fine sub-divisions, particularly in the last main group: for instance, the presence or absence of precise rhythms; variations in tempo or intensity in the course of the song; the amount of repetition of elements or motifs and how clearly these are separated by pauses.

These are all features worth noting as an aid to memory and as keys to future recognition.

Ring Ouzel

I want now to return to this question of specific differences in song patterns from the birds' point of hearing as well as ours. The Thrush family is a good example and six species from a single genus (*Turdus*) are illustration enough. They are the Blackbird, Song Thrush and Mistle Thrush, Fieldfare, Redwing and Ring Ouzel.

The woodland species are the Blackbird, Song Thrush and Mistle Thrush: all territorial birds. There are distinctive differences in their songs as well as a certain family resemblance in the quality of voice. For beginners there can be some confusion. When Terry Gompertz was trying to help such listeners in the Radio 4 series 'Birds in their element' she said, 'I think it's probably a fair description of the Mistle Thrush's song to say that the tone-quality of the voice is a cross between that of the Blackbird and the Song Thrush and the material of the song, though much, much simpler, is nearer to the Blackbird.'

The Redwing and the Fieldfare, our two winter visitors from the north, mostly flock in open fields while they are in Britain, though in their breeding areas they nest in parks, gardens and open woodland. Fortunately both species are on their way to becoming residents. The Redwing is breeding in increasing numbers in the Highlands of Scotland. The song is a quiet, mainly musical strophe repeated at intervals, and varied. It can sometimes be heard, though not at its best, before the migrant Redwings leave us in spring. In Scandi-

Mistle Thrush

Song Thrush

Fieldfare

Redwing

Six thrush species drawn to the same scale

navia and in northern Scotland it is one of the gentle sounds of summer in open woodland and scrub.

As for the Fieldfare – well! In the hard winter of 1962–3 we had the unusual experience of a Fieldfare living in the garden, driven by hunger from the snow-bound fields. It lingered on after the snow had virtually disappeared and one early spring morning we rushed to the window to identify the source of a weak, squeaky and appallingly ugly cackle. It was, of course, the Fieldfare, tuning up his song before departure. Even as we heard it later the same year in city parks in Sweden, there was not much improvement. Among the members of a musical genus the Fieldfare rates low. But this is a gregarious bird, given to chattering parties in trees and noisy communal roosting, which we can hear in Britain in winter. Above all, it tends to nest in colonies, so it has less need of a strong territorial song.

The Ring Ouzel has to contend with a totally different situation. It is a solitary bird of the high moorlands and mountains. The song is simple: a few repetitions at a time of some quite complex and varied elements. The pauses between utterances are often quite long. As the Ring Ouzel perches, perhaps, on a rock jutting out of the heather, these clear, musical notes easily cut through the sound of the hill streams near which it likes to nest. Though not powerful, the separate, staccato quality of the sounds arrests attention and carries them far in the moorland silence.

At the head of some of the short, finger-shaped dales of the North Yorkshire moors, it is possible to be within simultaneous earshot of the farmland Blackbird at the bottom of the steep slope and the Ring Ouzel at the top. Then, though the songs bear no resemblance in any other way, something that I can only call a 'thrush quality' is apparent in the individual sounds from the two birds. Electronic techniques are not yet good enough to reveal such subtleties of tone-quality but I believe that their detection by the superior analysing equipment of the human ear and brain is neither illusory nor directed by prior knowledge of the family relationship.

As a last example of diversity in song patterns, and species distinctiveness, I have chosen a totally different type: the long, almost mechanical, vibrating sounds of two warblers of the *Locustella* genus: the Grasshopper Warbler and Savi's Warbler. This sound, often described as 'reeling' from its resemblance to the winding of an angler's reel, carries over great distances and, in the case of the Grasshopper Warbler, is difficult to locate.

The Grasshopper Warbler is quite common in Britain and many parts of Europe and fairly catholic in its choice of habitat. My strongest memory is of one perched on a wire fence along the Ridgeway above the Vale of the White Horse in Oxfordshire. With open beak and head turning this way and that (which produces the ventriloquial effect) it delivered an almost unbroken sequence of whirring sound for more than ten minutes. But I have heard it in marsh and reed country too. This is where it shares the habitat with Savi's Warbler which is a swamp and reedbed specialist and has recently recolonized suitable sites in Kent and Suffolk. Since these two species overlap in part of their range, they (like Bonelli's Warbler and the Wood Warbler) must be able to reject each other's signals. The reeling of the Grasshopper Warbler has a different distribution of energy in the broad spectrum of frequencies and a different rhythmic beat from that of Savi's Warbler. The difference can be seen on the sonagrams (Figure 20 a and b) and even more clearly heard in slowed down recordings. Without a bird's fine discrimination of the elements in rapid sequences of sound, signals of this type could not carry the essential information and ensure species separation.

Grasshopper Warbler

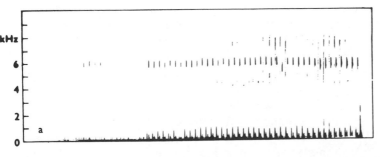

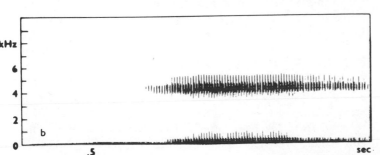

20
Songs of (a)
Grasshopper
Warbler; (b)
Savi's Warbler.

Song in Other Situations

References to other use of full song have crept into the discussion of full song in its main, territorial context. For instance, during reproductive fighting, the Great Tit delivers a few song motifs amidst the flow of vituperative-sounding calls on which it mainly relies. The Wren behaves vocally in much the same way. In many species the song is terse, incomplete, harsh and almost strangulated: a different delivery altogether from the territorial proclamations. The Robin's fighting song is a good example of this.

Wrens sometimes use song as a rallying signal on a cold winter evening when small companies of them assemble to roost together, tightly packed for warmth in a very small space. According to Armstrong, this song 'is usually of a rather jumbled pattern compared with the normal phrase'. Even so, he considers, it might not be distinctively different for other Wrens from the territorial song. In that case, as he points out, the normal message of song for other males has changed from 'Keep out' to 'Come along'.

The Great Tit's occasional quiet song-motifs when rallying fledglings are less difficult to account for. The young have learned in the nest to associate these sounds with him and, like his mate, would be attracted towards him by this use of song in a family context. On the whole, in our experience, a Great Tit was more likely to use song, in addition to the normal rallying and contact calls, in tense situations: for example, the critical period immediately after fledging, or when gathering the brood together at roosting time. But these observations are not easy to quantify and in this, as in so much else, individual birds are likely to vary in their habits. There are similar intimate uses of song in many species: in particular when a male displays at a nest site (as the Wren does) to impress the female with its suitability.

Many writers have reported song in abnormal situations: for example when a bird has been disturbed, or is startled. Some of these might be explained as a reaction of defiance, bringing them within the range of the song messages as we understand them. In others, a state of general excitement resulting from an unexpected stimulus might account better for the use of song. Sometimes, of course, it is possible that a bird may simply be confused and utter the wrong signal in error: a kind of avian Spoonerism. A Wren often sings when released from the hand after it has been ringed. It is difficult to say whether this is defiance, excitement, fright or confusion, but it is probably a way of releasing tension.

A number of other utterances are often referred to as 'songs' and subsong is a term used to define some of them. These songs differ in their sound patterns from the full songs of the species and are uttered in quite different contexts. Perhaps the only characteristic they have in common is that they are quiet fairly continuous sound-sequences, covering a wide range of frequencies; often without a definite rhythm and audible at a distance of only a few metres. The singer is usually in cover so that the circumstances are difficult to observe. This is why statements about them are hedged around with probabilities and possibilities even more than is usual in discussion of bird vocalizations.

Specific occasions for some types of subdued song are known: occasions on which the signal communicates directly. Courtship and nesting ceremonies are among these. As well as the quiet warblings and twitterings of songbird courtship, the excited state of the bird is revealed in movement: a shivering of the wings too rapid to be called fluttering. The *zeedling* of the Great Tit (referred to earlier as its courtship-feeding and copulation call) is one of these signals (Figure 10). In sound it resembles neither the song nor any of the true calls. Though more highly stylized, it is closer to the other forms of quiet song or warble in this species. In this borderline area, especially, the label of 'call' or 'song' is unimportant except to the human observer trying to clarify by functional classification.

An invitation to the partner to enter the nest has to be delivered vocally by birds that nest in holes or cavities. The Feral Pigeon gives a long, vibrant coo which resonates over the city rooftops or issues from the depths of the Rock Dove's communal nesting caves. It indicates the location and identity of the calling bird. We found that we were soon able to recognize the individual nest-invitation coos of our pigeons.

The sounds of the small songbirds at the nest site (other than song) are much less audible than those of the pigeon and this is likely to have evolved as a safety measure. We could only check that the nest invitation call (or song) of the Great Tit occurred in the wild by placing a microphone right under the nest-box. We had been introduced to the sound by a solitary hand-reared male, a foundling, who regarded Terry Gompertz as his mate. He persistently invited her to enter various small spaces in the house and even nest-boxes under other ownership in the garden. The Great Tit nest-invitation, quite different from their song, is a kind of staccato warbling, giving us an impression of insistent urgency. It may be delivered in long bursts of sound especially if there is no response. Other species, such as the Wren, are described as uttering from the nest very subdued chittering sounds which bear no resemblance to full song.

With some species it may be difficult to separate the sounds of these communicatory quiet songs from other, apparently messageless forms of subdued singing. It is these non-communicatory signals that are usually referred to as subsongs.

21
Chaffinch subsong showing chirps and rattling sounds (Thorpe, 1958).

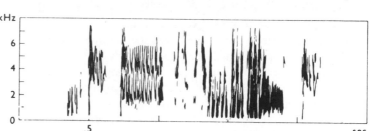

The Chaffinch was first studied extensively by Professor W. H. Thorpe and his colleagues in Cambridge. A passage of Chaffinch subsong is illustrated in Figure 21. Professor Thorpe describes the elements of which it is composed as 'first, a variety of chirping and cheeping notes and secondly a series of mechanical sounding rattles of varying pitch.' The simplest form of Chaffinch subsong can be heard from young birds in their first autumn: mainly the chirping notes, fluctuating in pitch. It may be uttered by females as well as males. A good deal more subsong can be heard in the spring from adult Chaffinches as well as the young. Interestingly, for a species that is not normally imitative in its full song, notes and phrases from other species may appear in the subsong.

In young birds, at least, subsong seems to be a form of practice for full song: the extreme frequencies are gradually discarded and some of the elements begin to take on the shape of elements in the full song. Figure 22 (a) shows a transitional stage in subsong and (b) a strophe from the full song of a Chaffinch for comparison. The Blackbird, Song Thrush and Mistle Thrush are also thought to use subsong as practice for full song.

Much subsong, however, especially in the autumn and the late spring and summer, does not have this function. In hand-reared birds and in the wild, whenever good observation of

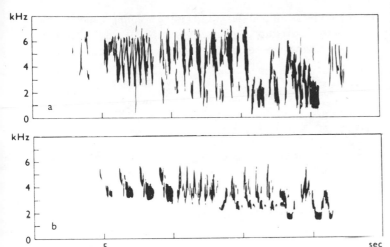

22
(a) Chaffinch sub-
song in transition
to full song; (b)
strophe of Chaf-
finch full song for
comparison
(Thorpe, 1958).

the singer is possible, it seems to be a solitary, unforced
activity, indulged in by adults as well as the young.

In the Great Tit, we called this version *Whispered song*. It
is sung by adults of both sexes though the male's is more
mellifluous. It is very similar to the random warbling of the
young Great Tits. But the youngsters use it more frequently,
and often in excitement as well as in relaxation. For them, it
is the usual accompaniment to exploration of their surroundings. It is first heard while they are still begging for food
from their parents: a begging note suddenly 'breaks' into a
sound of higher frequency and wanders off into an astonishing
little glissando.

Warbling can be stimulated by sounds from other birds,
music (as in the response of our first hand-reared female to
the Haydn sonata) or even frying bacon! Anything with
plenty of high frequencies was liable to start them off and
could raise them to a state of wing-shivering excitement. In
more relaxed moments the birds seemed just to be experimenting with sound.

The Great Tit has another, rather different, form of subdued singing. We called it *Intense quiet song*. This, too,
appeared to be a solitary performance. All Terry Gompertz'
observations suggested that it is given only by males (both
adults, and juveniles in their first spring) and that 'it is
associated with a degree of sexual excitement which has no
other outlet'. The bird crouches with bowed head and
shivers its wings: a combination of movements similar to
those of the courtship feeding and pre-copulatory displays.

But the sound is quite different from the *zeedling* which would accompany courtship displays. A section of this song from one of our hand-reared males is shown in Figure 23.

23
Intense quiet song of hand-reared male Great Tit.

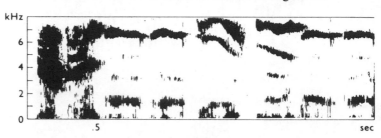

All these last examples of subdued forms of song seem, then, to have no function in the bird's communication system. Like some of the elaborations of full song to be discussed in Chapter 11, much subdued singing appears to be unrelated to any primary biological requirement. It may be that for these birds, the use of sound is a satisfying experience in itself.

The communicatory signals of birds transmit a limited number of simple messages. Full song, and its equivalents in other territorial species, carry only a few of these; the special song-forms of courtship and nesting, a few more. The nature of the rest of the messages is the subject of the next chapter. The prolific variety of expression in which these messages are encoded, however, is one of the most fascinating aspects of bird vocalizations. But the potential variety is greater still. In the songbirds, at least, the subdued songs give evidence that a further rich fund of raw sound-material underlies the formalized, communicatory signals in the repertoire of each species.

5　Moods and Events

I sometimes amuse myself by imagining an intelligent visitor from another planet arriving on this earth just before the differentiation of the human stock – say somewhere about one million years ago. If such a visitor had been asked by an all-seeing Creator which group of animals he supposed would the most easily be able to achieve a true language, I feel little doubt that he would have said unhesitatingly, 'Why, of course, the birds'. And indeed, if we now look at the birds together with all the mammals other than man, we have little hesitation in saying that the birds are by far the more advanced, both in their control of their vocalizations and by the way in which they can adapt them collectively and individually to function as a most powerful communication system.
W. H. Thorpe

One dull but mild day in mid-February 1975 when all the garden birds were pretty active and vocal – the general tempo of life speeding up rather early because of the mildness of the winter – Redblack the Great Tit arrived on the bird table, in a hurry. There was no food on it at the time; I was close to the window and a visiting dog was standing nearby gazing hopefully at us both. Redblack's mate was present but not fussing. He uttered a couple of loud calls as he stood poised on the table and then made straight for the filled nutbaskets which hang on separate poles a couple of metres from the table. To my ear and eye he was in a vile temper.

Now, Redblack was evidently hungry. He could have been irritated by a number of obvious things – the absence of food on the table (he prefers and expects it to be there for him); my nearness (though tame he is not keen on this); the presence of the dog (less likely); or by his mate getting in the way of his immediate concerns. But for any or all of these he was more likely to have 'sworn' mildly with one or other of the versions of the *churring* call.

Instead, he used a call belonging to the category that Terry Gompertz and I called 'war-whoops', normally only heard in close encounters between rival males. I suspected, therefore, that he could see, though I could not, the male Great Tit from the next territory who also visits the baskets and table. Strictly speaking, these are on Redblack's property. But with Great Tits, as with many species, so long as intruders of the same species behave discreetly and are successful in the timing of their comings and goings, we found that their visits are tolerated by the territory owner.

Redblack's rival confirmed my suspicions about his

presence by appearing as soon as Redblack had flown off. His silence and delay while Redblack was in occupation of the basket suggest that he had got the message of the war-whoop.

Each male Great Tit is likely to have one or more variants of these highly aggressive calls; and there appears to be a great variety of them in the repertoire of the species as a whole. Strolling through an unfamiliar wood one is likely to hear very strange sounds; but their general character, and observation of the situation, with two males whooping away from adjacent trees and posturing aggressively if they catch sight of one another, quickly puts the calls into the war-whoop category.

These calls can be heard most frequently from the early autumn onwards during close encounters between rivals and they are a prominent part of the 'vocal score' of reproductive skirmishes. They are strongly rhythmical, with a mixture of high frequency sounds and noisy or clicking elements. These have a satisfactory consonantal effect which adds to our impression that the bird is spitting with fury. Some typical war-whoops are shown in Figure 24.

24
Great Tit aggres-
sive calls: war-
whoops. Each
example is a
complete call. (b)
and (c) from one
male. All recorded
in same Middlesex
garden (Gompertz,
1971).

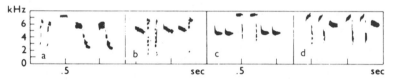

The nut-basket episode between Redblack and his neighbour illustrates the difficulty of interpreting observations. Even in less artificial situations than that of a bird-table, several factors – visible and invisible, internal as well as external – may be influencing the behaviour of an individual at any moment.

It also illustrates the 'call problem'. Within one species, the same message may apparently be carried in different sound signals, as in the variety of war-whoops. As far as Terry Gompertz was able to discover, the war-whoops are interchangeable in meaning, though perhaps usefully marking individuals. New variants are often heard even in our local population.

On the other hand slightly varied messages may be encoded in the same type of sound signal. This is then likely to differ in some of its parameters: rhythm, intensity, tempo, duration, or the addition of extra elements. Such calls are referred to as 'intergrading calls' and Great Tit *churring* is one of them. Different versions of this are heard, for example, in reproductive fighting; scolding; situations provoking mild annoyance or frustration; or – two rather stylized types – when the mate's company is desired. Some of the gradations are illustrated in Figure 25.

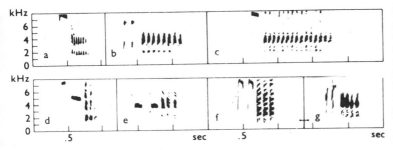

25
Great Tit *churrs*: some gradations and special forms. (a–b) used in territorial skirmishes; (c) scolding; (d) excited food-foraging; (e) seeking contact with mate – all from same male (Johnny). (f) Seeking contact with mate; (g) situation tricky but not dangerous – both from another male.

The use of the same call in different situations is also not uncommon. In some cases it is possible that minor changes in one or more parameters have been missed, so that the call is in reality an intergrading one. Where this is not the case, careful analysis of the situations may indicate that they could evoke the same mood or emotion in the bird. The message, in other words, is a generalized one and its interpretation depends on the context.

Before these subtle differentiations are tackled, it is helpful to think about the main categories of calls and their messages. As detailed studies of the sound-repertoires of various species have accumulated, sub-categories and other refinements have emerged. Almost any species that has been thoroughly observed turns out to have a larger number of distinguishable utterances than had been supposed. But experienced observers now know more or less what to expect.

It is also known that the habitat, social organization and habits of a species are likely to suggest explanations for the presence or absence of certain types of call in the repertoire. Broadly speaking, a fairly similar list of call messages has been made for all the species studied so far.

First of all – and these are useful preliminary clues to their possible significance – certain calls can be heard all the year round, others only seasonally. Some are used by both sexes; others by males only or by females only.

At the simplest level there are cries of injury and, we may suppose, panic – usually harsh squawks such as bird-lovers whose gardens are also haunted by cats have heard when the lucky bird escapes without a tail or the unlucky one does not. There are alarm calls when a potential predator appears overhead. Among the songbirds these are often clear, shrill whistles, difficult to locate. Many species, however, have additional calls for other dangerous or stressful situations and can express degrees of disturbance down to what appears to be only mild anxiety.

There are aggressive calls supporting, or replacing in close encounters, the aggressive message of song. Again, some species have a number of such calls, others just one or two, delivered with varying intensity. In both cases the messages seem to indicate gradations between fierce threat and cautious assertiveness.

Another group of calls is associated with flight and may be uttered immediately before take-off or in the air. Undoubtedly these have some significance for keeping contact with companions. But there are also social and contact calls which are normally delivered from a perch or on the ground.

Paired birds have further calls associated, for example, with courtship, greeting or loss of contact. Their nesting and parental duties require a vocabulary of their own, but the number and nature of these calls differ according to the nesting habits of the species. For instance, a fairly small bird with a nest in a hedge or in undergrowth would not have time to deter a predator by the hiss-and-wingflap type of display that the hole-nesting tits have evolved (page 46). Fight or flight are the only possibilities. In more open habitats, however, some species have an alternative strategy. Leaving the nest before the predator gets too near, they feign injury and scuttle or flutter away from the nest, drooping a wing and sometimes calling distressfully, to attract attention to themselves.

For small species whose young are helpless when hatched, and cared for in an open nest for two weeks or so, the less said at the nest site the better. As a rule there are only *sotto voce* cheeps and grunts between parents and nestlings, or parent and parent, as they arrive and depart – no sound that carries far. The risk is quite great enough in the later stages when begging calls from well-grown young may betray the position of the nest. Blackbird nestlings can be very noisy at this time though I have observed a late brood in an ill-concealed nest on the house wall, which was silent throughout. But many of the smaller open-nesting species have more discreet, less directional signals.

Male Golden Plover
in distraction display

In contrast, young Snow Buntings are said to call loudly when in their nest under a stone but little, and softly, after they have fledged. The larger ground-nesting species like gulls or geese, and especially those that nest in colonies, can afford to have elaborate, noisy ceremonies associated with their nesting affairs. These and other species such as the waders – or the farmyard hen – have young who are mobile, even if they are unable to fly, very soon after hatching. Vocal signals from both parent and chicks help to keep the brood safe, together, and doing what they should at the right time.

These are the main categories of calls. The vocal repertoire of young birds and the associated parental calls are more fully discussed in the next chapter. In this one I want to give some examples of adult calls from several species and to relate these tidy categories to the living birds who still pose us puzzling problems as we try to learn more about their form of communication.

Alarm, Anxiety and Aggression

I have grouped these calls together for purposes of discussion because they are terms describing human emotions and we cannot do more than guess at a bird's mood from its actions. There are many situations where one mood apparently shades into another. When a Great Tit delivers a scolding *churr* at an owl perched on a branch or at a passing cat, is it anxious, aggressive, or a bit of both?

At the extremes there is little doubt. At one extreme there are, for example, the Great Tit war-whoops or the Robin's fighting song; at the other, the 'predator overhead' alarm signals. Many of the woodland songbirds have very similar alarm calls (Figure 26). They are long, single notes, starting and tailing off almost imperceptibly; high pitched and very pure in tone. These characteristics give them safety value for

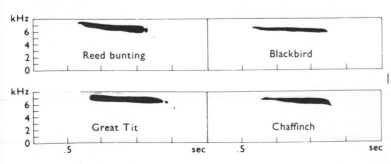

26
Calls of four different species given when a predator flies overhead (after Marler, 1959).

Jays, too, crouch
and give a hawk
alarm note

the bird who is first to spot the predator: together they ensure that the signaller is extremely difficult to locate.

I remember an excellent demonstration of this. As we came into the room where our first hand-reared female Great Tit lived uncaged, an aircraft flew over and could be seen through the window. Immediately the tit uttered the alarm call. She was nowhere to be seen and our ears gave us not the slightest clue to her whereabouts. In the open, one is more accustomed to taking a little time for precise location of a bird by sound but in an enclosed space the effect is very curious.

Birds, with their similar hearing apparatus, locate sound in the same way that we do: a comparison of the sound waves arriving at the two ears. We automatically turn our heads when trying to find the direction of a difficult sound in order to increase the difference between the sounds each ear receives. For when a sound comes from one side, it takes a fractionally longer time to arrive at the ear on the opposite side. We then have three different ways of analysing the sound. If the signal is sharply discontinuous and preferably repeated, we can perceive this minute difference in arrival time, at any frequency. With low-pitched notes, the pulses of which they are made up are 'out of phase' as well. This, too, helps to locate the sound. For high-pitched notes, the head acts as a barrier so that the sound is louder in one ear than the other.

There is, however, a critical range of frequencies in between (depending on the size of head, and therefore the distance between the two ears) where neither of the last two methods is fully effective. So the easiest type of sound to locate is one in which all three methods can be used: it is short, repetitive and complex, that is with a mixture of high and low frequencies. The most difficult to locate is precisely the type of sound that these vulnerable small bird species have evolved for their alarm calls.

It does not matter if they, too, cannot very easily locate the caller. Their instant response is to dive for cover, or 'freeze' where they are: flattening their outline in such a way that they look as little like a bird as possible. The overhead predator, or 'hawk-alarm', calls appear to be inborn, as is the crouching response. This is not a reaction that a bird has time to learn and to perfect. Nor is there time to work out what the predator is. I once caused two hand-reared nestlings to crouch in the nest-box while I was feeding them, by accidentally flicking a dish cloth across their field of view.

The additional advantage of a similarity between the signals of so many species is obvious. Whatever bird is the first to call the alarm, members of other species respond. This is one of the clearest examples of inter-specific communication.

This is another point worth bearing in mind about calls. They do not all necessarily function to keep species separate from one another in the way that song does. In situations connected with territory or breeding it is advantageous that the calls, like the songs, should be distinctively different from those of other species. But on occasions of danger or in joint enterprises such as mixed feeding or migrating flocks, communication between species is an advantage.

It is not likely that birds are predisposed at birth to respond to the calls of any species other than their own. But experience of these calls on communal occasions teaches them to recognize the significance.

This can be illustrated from other types of alarm or 'scolding' calls. Figure 29 shows the calls used by several species when mobbing owls. The presence of a perched owl creates a great disturbance in the small bird community. Their reaction to its static presence on a branch instead of overhead, however, is to approach and call, not to take cover.

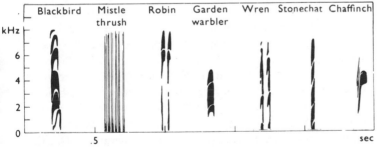

27
Calls of birds from several families given while mobbing an owl (Marler, 1959).

The sounds they make are readily located and must be recognized by other species, for when somebody starts the vocal onslaught there is soon a noisy mob of several species, as birds that must have been occupied elsewhere, well out of sight, continue to arrive on the scene. The reason for this performance, incidentally, remains obscure. The owl is normally totally unmoved by it and only temporarily prevented from surprising a single victim. But the response of the small birds is so strong that it can be elicited by a crude stuffed model of an owl. Aerial mobbing of a predator in flight, however, is often more successful in driving it away.

The same calls are given to announce the appearance of a

prowling cat. Again, the chorus is taken up by all the species present though in deference to this mobile enemy they sometimes stay hidden. The cat's progress can be traced by the intensity of calling along its route. But I have seen a ground-feeding Jay, whose presence as a potential nest predator provokes the same vocal response from the small birds, directly attacked as well by a couple of courageous Blackbirds who made dive-bombing swoops right over it. In all these situations, of course, the potential predator is located so that no bird in the vicinity is unaware of its presence, and any young birds can learn to identify their enemies by sight.

The Blackbird has an interesting range of calls associated with alarm, anxiety and aggression. It has a very aggressive call which, oddly, is similar to the overhead predator alarm call in Figure 26 though it is higher in pitch. This is used in combative territorial situations by the dominant bird and I have heard it delivered on the bird table by the resident male when he had just driven off an intruding rival.

There is the *chook* call, associated with situations in which the bird seems to be uncertain or anxious, and the more musical and emphatic *duk* or *pook*, directed at owls and ground predators, which is illustrated in Figure 27. These very similar calls are delivered as single, well-separated notes. If the bird is even more worked up, as it may be in owl mobbing, it may also utter a more rapid sequence of *chinking* elements.

Chinks are the familiar Blackbird sounds so often heard at dusk and particularly at a large roost, when territory holders and intruders are working out the problems of dominance and spacing in these communal gatherings. *Chinking* can be heard again before the birds leave in the morning. In fact this call seems to indicate a generally aggressive or assertive mood, to judge from the variety of situations in which it is used.

The alarm rattle referred to in Chapter 4 (Figure 19), given when the Blackbird heard the modified Robin song, is likely to be heard if the bird is suddenly startled or is involved in ,a chase. But this rattle sometimes follows a period of *chinking* when excitement rises very high.

The Chaffinch provides a good example of a multi-purpose call. One form of the *spink* or *pink* call is shown in Figure 27. Like the Blackbird's *chink*, it is given by both males and females. Three distinct gradations in the sound have been recognized. The form in Figure 27 is a staccato, musical note. In owl mobbing and in fighting during the breeding season, it is repeated in rapid sequences. Uttered singly or in groups of two, it is also used as a social call by birds wanting contact. There is a coarser-sounding form which is heard in winter fighting, and a shrill form associated with escape but also given in courtship by newly paired males. In the latter context it probably reveals the conflicting tendencies of approach and escape characteristic of some courtship behaviour (see Chapter 2).

Many people find it difficult to distinguish the Chaffinch *pink* from the rather similar Great Tit call, the *tink*, which is also uttered singly or in twos. In fact the Great Tit note has a more ringing tone. However, a Chaffinch giving the social form of the *pink* note near a house, where the roof provides an echo, may sound more like a Great Tit than it does when calling in a wood.

Tink calls from five Great Tit males are illustrated in Figure 28. These have a degree of individual variation, detectable by tuned-in human listeners. However, the call always shows a characteristic outline on sonagrams, different from that of the Chaffinch note and also different from any other Great Tit call-notes. It is the most stylized and emphatic form of the intergrading *pee* calls: distinguishable from them by sound and message.

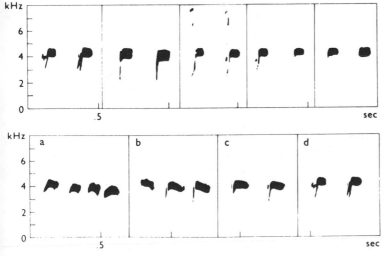

28
Great Tit aggressive *tink* call from five males.

29
Four Great Tit calls from the same male (Johnny): (a–c) gradations of *pee* social notes of which (c) is the most assertive; (d) aggressive *tink*.

Some of the gradations of *pee* calls are illustrated in Figure 29. These were all recorded from the same bird –

Johnny, scientifically known as Bluewhite, from his individually coloured leg-rings. The first two sounds are purely social calls, used in keeping contact; the third occurs when the bird is mildly assertive and the last is the *tink*. This is the very opposite of a social call for the message is definitely aggressive. Unlike the social calls it is normally given only by males. It can occur as an alternative to song in aggressive song-contexts and is often heard around the territory in autumn before song has reappeared in the repertoire.

Rival males have long *tinking* duels both during and independently of reproductive fighting. At the end of a fight, the victor sings and the loser *tinks*. This call is also heard in situations of exploration and uncertainty. A hand-reared male *tinked* his way round a room in the house to which we had just admitted him, as if cautiously taking over an extra bit of territory. At the same time he displayed aggressively at other males he could see through the window. A wild bird newly establishing itself in a territory will do exactly the same thing.

All this evidence suggests that there is a definite relationship between song and tinking and the internal state of the bird. In a dramatic natural experiment, we were recording a singing male on a Yorkshire farm when he was suddenly startled by a gunshot. He stopped singing immediately. Then, after a brief silence, he started up again – with *tinks*.

Keeping in Contact

Discussion of the calls of alarm, anxiety and aggression has already introduced a few of the social contact signals and revealed that some vocalizations such as the Chaffinch *pink* seem to bridge these artificial, though useful, categories. And why not? There is often an overlap in the situations, or a rapid transition. Contact may be sought or assertion required within a short space of time.

This is particularly evident in the vocal behaviour of birds in large flocks. Lapwings, for instance, sort themselves out on alighting with a 'conversational yet peevish-sounding chorus of *peee, peeyip, peeyi, yi yi . . .*' as K. G. Spencer describes it in his book *The Lapwing in Britain*. A different, long drawn-out call, also used in alarm, starts up the flight at dusk to the fields where the flock will spend the night.

The chatter of Fieldfares and Starlings at communal roosts and the peevish-sounding chorus of the ground-flocking

Lapwings probably indicate a mildly aggressive assertion of individual rights to occupy a comfortable living space. Even these gregarious birds, like the less communally-minded Blackbird with its aggressive *chinks*, require an individual distance appropriate to the situation and the species.

At Wicken Fen in Cambridgeshire, one sunny afternoon in early September, I heard what must have been a vast concealed gathering of Starlings who were obviously feeding on berries deep in a tangled marshy and wooded part of the Fen. From a distance it sounded almost like the uproar of a Promenade Concert audience at the Albert Hall. Close to, it became an ear-stunning mixture of squawks, chatter and twitters, with whistled notes from near but still invisible birds suddenly penetrating the cacophony.

Is this competitive, or co-operative signalling, as they scrummage around and gorge themselves on the abundant crop, or sheer gregarious excitement? If it were possible to distinguish all the separate sounds, threat, aggressive and short-flight calls might be identified by an experienced listener; for in flocks there can be a multitude of individual encounters of different kinds. But when a group of Starlings are singing together there are often no overt signs of aggression.

However, much flock behaviour is obviously companionable. The intricate manoeuvres and long-distance movements of airborne flocks are at least partly regulated by sound-signals. By night, observers stationed along the regular migration routes can tell from the calls what species are flying unseen overhead. The magnificent formation-flying of geese to the accompaniment of their honking calls offers, to my mind, a deeply moving experience of social co-operation. This is crystallized in the passage by Aldo Leopold that I have set at the head of the last chapter in this book.

Then there are the less cohesive and temporary flocks of small songbirds. These assemble for the common purpose of exploiting the seed, nut and berry crops of autumn and winter, and dawdle along through scrub and woodland, with individuals delayed by the discovery of a particularly rich picking! Yet flight and social calls help to keep the flock safely and companionably together in a slow but steady progress. Such flocks usually include a number of species: for instance, an assortment of the true tits, Long-tailed Tits, Goldcrests and perhaps a Nuthatch and a Treecreeper or two. It is evident that while the calls of each species are different they are understood by other members of the flock.

Many of the finches, such as Linnets, Greenfinches and Goldfinches, are much more given to flocking than the highly individualistic tits and they are less sedentary in their habits. Living in more open habitats, they generally have to move about very freely to exploit suitable food resources and are often to be heard and seen in graceful, undulating flight, in company with varying numbers of their own species.

Goldfinches have increased in numbers during this century, in Britain, and the increase was spectacular between 1969 and 1974, particularly in suburban areas. It is now a much more common experience in gardens to hear their musical flight calls as a small party arrives to feed or drink. (In dry areas water is often a better way of attracting a variety of birds than food.)

Linnets, quiet in voice as well as plumage, and with a twittering flight call, are also musical visitors to some gardens, in small feeding parties. They may sit in full view for a quiet preen on a bare branch – as birds adapted to naturally more open country they seem to make little effort at concealment – before twittering into the air on their way to the next destination.

In upland country of northern Britain and in Ireland a dull-brown coloured finch of the moors, the Twite, takes over from the Linnet. It is sometimes called the Mountain Linnet, but winter visitors from Scandinavia can also be seen along the east coast. Like the other finches it is a great vocalizer while in the air and a number of different calls may be heard. But the 'flight call', given all the year round by both sexes, is the one most closely linked with flight and take-off.

It might have been supposed that such a basic type of call, uttered apparently automatically whenever a bird undertakes so fundamental an activity as flight, would be a completely inborn signal. But it appears that this is not necessarily so. Recently the Twite has been studied in Norway, Scotland and Ireland by Professor Peter Marler and Dr Paul Mundinger from the United States and they have found out some interesting facts about this call.

In these far separated populations, the call is similar in pattern: if Twites from these three countries were to meet, they would almost certainly respond to each other's calls. Nevertheless there were some slight differences: for example, calls recorded in Scotland were higher-pitched than the Irish ones. The elements in the calls of the Norwegian Twites, recognized on other grounds as a different race, had a greater range of frequencies than those of the British race.

Within each breeding population (several were studied in Norway) there was a consistent pattern. But even so there was individual variation in certain parameters. It was found that the calls of paired birds matched each other almost exactly (Figure 30).

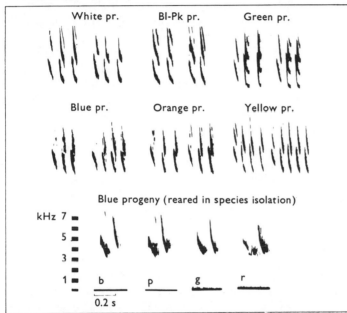

30
Flight calls of six breeding pairs of Twites (males on left) and a group of siblings, progeny of Blue pair, reared in isolation from other members of their species from the late nestling stage (Marler and Mundinger, 1975).

The value of this close-matching of calls could be seen from the behaviour of the pair. In the breeding season the female identified her approaching mate by his flight call and responded with a different call of her own, indicating that she was ready for courtship and copulation. Moreover, the Twite does not appear to be very territorially-minded as far as ownership of ground is concerned. Apart from the actual nest site, the male's main concern is to defend the female wherever she happens to be. Although the nests are well-separated so that each pair has a fairly solitary home base, food-foraging may take place at a distance from it. This means that Twites have to pass through each other's territories, often under escort from the local resident. Immediate individual recognition of birds in the air must be helpful in this semi-communal way of life.

There are only two possible explanations for such a marked resemblance in the flight calls of paired birds. Either each seeks out a mate with a similar call or they modify their calls after pairing. The second explanation seems the more likely. In this study, the only direct evidence came from the four nestlings, reared in isolation from other Twites, whose calls are also illustrated in Figure 30. These resemble each other but are completely different from the calls of the parents. However, Dr Mundinger had already demonstrated that other finches undoubtedly modify their flight calls to match those of breeding mates, or flock-mates of the same sex. So it seems likely that Twites do the same.

Of the species that are known at present to modify their calls one is the European Siskin, a woodland finch with a preference for conifers, whose numbers in Britain have been increased by afforestation. Except in the far north, the Siskin is mainly a winter visitor but it is now breeding more frequently in the south as well. It is worth looking out for this Blue-Tit sized, yellowy-green bird feeding acrobatically even in broadleaf woods for it favours birch and alder trees in winter. The other two are American species – the Pine Siskin and the Goldfinch, a smaller and slightly less gaily-coloured relative of the Goldfinch of Europe.

This doubling of functions, with a flight-call also serving as a signal between paired birds, raises a wider point about the varying size of sound repertoire observed in the species that have been well studied. I said earlier that a fairly similar list of messages has been found in each. This is true. But the total number of distinguishable signals shows a much greater variation. For, as we have already seen, some species have several signals within each category of messages.

Signals associated with alarm, anxiety and aggression are rarely absent from a species' repertoire. It is in the social calls and in communication between paired birds that there seems to be a greater variation in the number of signals. This does not mean that there are no social and courtship messages; only more – or less – economy in their vocal expression.

It is not safe to generalize about why this might be so. A few examples indicate that no single explanation of repertoire size is likely to be adequate. The Twite for instance has an unusually small one. Perhaps this is because in its open moorland habitat it can rely to a large extent on visual information. So the evolution of individual identification in the flight call has been an economical dual-purpose use of an essential signal. Of the other finches with a similar adaptation one is

known to have a larger but not very extensive repertoire. None
of them are truly territorial birds. So it may turn out that
ownership of territory, as well as the type of habitat, is a
factor affecting size of repertoire.

The Chaffinch, the Wren and the Great Tit, all with large
repertoires, have fixed territories. But habitat and territoria-
lity are not the only variables. The strongly territorial and
somewhat unsociable Robin has very few sound signals:
virtually only the hawk-alarm; the familiar *tic tic* directed at
owls, cats, humans and other disturbances; the compressed
fighting song and a combat call in real beak-to-beak encounters. The flexible and variable full song seems to do duty
in most marital situations where many other species have a
number of special calls.

The Starling has no territory other than the nest and spends
most of its time in company with its fellows. It has a suitable
range of signals for danger from the environment and for
regulating communal relationships: threat, aggressive, flight
and flocking calls. But, as with the Robin, its variable, complicated song seems to have an all-purpose use in communication with the female.

The Great Tit, on the other hand, although it sings often
in family contexts, is also prolific in its basic social call notes
and the numerous combinations in which they are used.
Besides the *pee* notes illustrated in Figure 29 there is a softer
and higher-pitched *tsee*. *Tsees* and *pees* can be used separately
or together as social calls, almost always associated with
movement and flight. When used between paired birds they
appear to be no more than a routine contact, indicating
present location and movement. One of the forms of *churring*
referred to earlier is prefixed by *pee* notes and given by either
sex when thwarted of the company of its mate. The male will
use it, for instance, if the female refuses him entry to the nest
hole. *Pee-churrs* are individually identifiable even to human
ears. Either member of the pair will deliver a light, chattering
churr, as if from a miniature Magpie, when contact is temporarily lost. Besides the *zeedle*, which is associated with
courtship-feeding and copulation and is used by both sexes,
the female has another call in the breeding season to attract
the attention of her mate. She utters begging notes exactly
similar to those of the young tits when demanding to be fed.
The Robin does this too. These begging calls are sometimes
used before the female Great Tit solicits the male for courtship feeding but also when she is separated from him.

Both mates have a beautiful call of five to nine notes (an elaborate, standardized group of *pee* notes) which we named the *duple* call because of its two-beats-to-the-bar musical rhythm (Figure 31). This sounds almost like a song motif but the elements are different, the call is never repeated in long sequences and is usually uttered very softly. It is used for contact and in greeting; during nest building; by the male when he brings food to his mate or the young on the nest, and in rallying the fledged brood.

31
Great Tit *duple* call used by paired birds and in rallying fledglings.

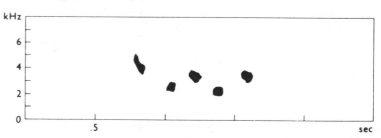

All these examples of variations in the size of call repertoire and of communication between paired birds have been taken from the songbirds. So were most of the examples of alarm, anxiety and aggressive calls. There is some justification for this. The vocalizations of a number of species have been studied so that there are sufficient to provide a basis for comparison. Also, the songbirds are attractively vocal and it has been possible to choose from among them species which readers can easily observe for themselves.

However, the calls of non-passerine species[1] are equally interesting, if often less musical, and I should like to give examples from two of them of the use of sound signals in pair relationships.

The Lesser Blackbacked Gull is mainly a summer visitor to Britain and Ireland. It is a little smaller than the more common Herring Gull with which it often associates and can be seen round most of our northern and western coasts. However, the range is expanding and there is now a sizeable colony at Orfordness in Suffolk. It has a preference for islands and is more willing than the Herring Gull to move away from the shore to found its breeding colonies on inland moors and bogs.

[1] Passerines are members of the large order of the 'Perching Birds', the Passeriformes. This order includes the true songbirds (the Oscines). All the other bird orders are collectively referred to as non-passerines: these include ducks, geese, gamebirds, gulls, owls, waders and woodpeckers.

The colonies can be very large. A famous one at Walney Island off the Lancashire Coast contains about 10,000 pairs and about the same number of Herring Gull pairs. The clamour of raucous calling can be imagined, with the birds indicating their intentions to each other by sounds as well as postures, and defending their high density accommodation against rapacious neighbours who have little sense of responsibility for any but their own eggs and chicks.

Gulls do not sing to attract a mate. It would hardly be practical in the colonial din. Pair formation starts with a visual search. But the call of territorial ownership from a solitary male indicates to any unattached female flying low over the colony that here is a potential mate. Lesser Black-backed Gulls pair for life and each year special displays help to maintain the pair bond and ensure the smooth progress of their nesting affairs. These are comparable with some songbird displays but adapted to the open, ground-nesting and colonial habits of the species.

For example, the female demands courtship feeding from her mate with begging notes, as the female Great Tit sometimes does. Before they copulate both the male and female gulls toss their heads and give the begging call. When they are deciding on where to site the nest within their territory, the male has a cat-like mewing call which he utters as he leads his mate to a suitable place. They stand on the site together and give a rhythmic *choking* signal, the highly descriptive name for this sound.

From then on they frequently go through the same performance, especially after they have had a brush with a neighbouring pair. So the ceremony is both a warning to outsiders and a mutual confirmation of their own relationship.

The *mewing* and *choking* calls, head-tossing, or the presentation of further nest-material, are used later on when one of
the pair returns from a feeding trip to take over incubation
duties from the other. *Mewing* also acts economically as a
'come here' signal to the chicks to return to the nest after a
danger alert which left them crouched wherever they happened
to be.[1]

Geese, with their more peaceable temperament, have a
different version of the same problem as the gulls: how to
maintain family companionship within their orderly flocks.
All the true geese have a noisy ceremony which, in its varied
forms, helps to regulate their social relationships. It has been
most fully studied in the Greylag, the wild progenitor of our
domesticated geese.

This is known as the 'Triumph Ceremony' from its German
name, *Triumphgeschrei*. The ceremony was first studied in
Germany, at the research station then directed by Konrad
Lorenz, and it has continued for many years to arouse the
interest of research workers. The unravelling of a complicated
pattern of behaviour has led, as so often, to much discussion
about its origin and interpretation, but this can only be
hinted at in a short summary. As Dr Helga Fischer describes
it, the Triumph Ceremony combines ritualized sounds and
movements from other contexts. Though there are reminders
of threat behaviour, the display seems to be assertive rather
than aggressive, and reassuring for the displaying birds.

Vocally, there are two distinct types of sound known as
rolling and *cackling*. These accompany the two sections of
the typical display. In this form, it helps to establish and
maintain the bond between the faithful Greylag partners.
The first section is initiated by the male. He rushes off with
extended wings as if in attack. The display may be provoked
by a genuine intruder but it can also take place in the absence
of one: the symbolic attack is still delivered, accompanied by
the rolling call, though it is less intense. The male returns to
the female who advances to meet him with neck extended
forwards and slightly upwards, also giving the rolling call.
Then, facing each other and lowering their heads, they
deliver the cackling call.

[1] The behaviour of the Lesser Blackbacked Gull has been described
and illustrated in 'Signals for Survival' by Niko Tinbergen and Hugh
Falkus, with drawings by Eric Ennion. The book is based on the prize-
winning TV documentary film with the same title which was made in
the Walney Island colony. It was first shown in 1969.

The display may vary not only in intensity of sound and posture but in the balance between *rolling* and *cackling*. This probably indicates variations in the conflicting moods or tendencies that these signals convey.

Sometimes in autumn and winter, there is a kind of communal Triumph Ceremony. Groups of geese – they may be pairs, families, or assemblies of different species in a mixed flock who have wandered too close together – face each other with outstretched necks in a chorus of *rolling*. This is a way of peacefully ensuring a suitable spacing out on the feeding grounds. The ceremony ends with intensive cackling within each group.

Rolling, a call used only by adult birds, is interpreted as a conflict between attachment to a companion and escape. On its own, it is used with assertive posturing by young males in an early stage of pair formation; by brooding females, and in arguments between two ganders who regularly consort together. These homosexual pairs may also give the full Triumph Ceremony.

32
Greylag Goose.
(a) Greeting call
from day-old
goslings (Kear);
(b) *cackling* of
adult which
develops from
gosling greeting
call; (c) *rolling*
call of adult. (b)
and (c) are used in
the Triumph
Ceremony
(Fischer, 1965).

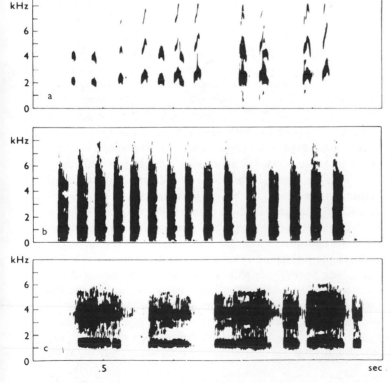

Cackling develops from the greeting call of the goslings given as early as their first day of life. This is a soft, repeated single-element call uttered with the neck stretched forwards in the same position as the adult when cackling. It is a specialized form of the gosling contact call. It can be triggered by any disturbance in the environment or, if a gosling has been separated from the group, on rejoining it. The gosling will greet parents or siblings with this call and, like cackling, it seems to be a reiteration of friendly intentions. A recent study in Sweden indicates that the goslings establish a rank order among themselves and possibly that those of lower rank offer more greetings than the dominant members of the group – a form of social propitiation.

So, analysed in this way, the Triumph Ceremony is seen to be a mixture of calls and postures which convey assertive, deterrent and reassuring messages. Figure 32 illustrates the goslings' greeting call; *rolling*, and *cackling*.

Two Unusual Calls

Whether they form part of elaborate displays or are used on their own, most calls carry straightforward messages associated with moods and events that are commonplace in the lives of nearly all bird species. But here and there unusual sound signals have evolved, linked with specialization in habits or habitat.

One such is the *churring* food-call of an African species, the Black-throated Honeyguide, which has the Latin name of *Indicator indicator*. Both the popular and the scientific name point to the profitable habit that these birds and some related species have evolved. They indicate the whereabouts of bees' nests to more powerful species such as honey-badgers and man who can open this source of food for them. In fact this is mutually beneficial, for while the honeyguides' helpers enjoy the honey, the birds feed on the wax. Possibly this behaviour evolved when the honeyguides, finding that badgers robbed bees' nests, began to utter the call, by association, on catching sight of the animal. The mammals in their turn learned that the calling honeyguide would lead them from quite a distance to a nest. The bird usually falls silent as the little procession reaches the nest and perches nearby until the nest has been plundered and it can feed on the broken bits of honeycomb.

The other example is of a call that enables the species using it to fly in total darkness – unlike owls which rely on at least minimal light. These species detect obstacles in their vicinity from echoes of the call reflected from solid surfaces. This is somewhat similar in principle to the echolocation of bats. But bats use very high frequencies, well above the range of human and avian hearing and the insect-eating species among them can even locate their tiny prey as well as navigate in this way.

The echolocating signals of birds, at frequencies audible to man, have evolved independently in species belonging to two different orders and living on different continents. They are the Oilbirds of South America and Trinidad and some of the swiftlet species of South-east Asia. The Oilbirds are related to the nightjars and feed on nuts, whereas the swiftlets are basically insectivorous: the only common factor in the way of life of these echolocating species is their habit of cave nesting and roosting.

The swiftlets are smaller relatives of the swifts of Europe and, cave-dwelling apart, have similar habits. They cannot walk or perch but cling to the surfaces of the walls and ceilings of the caves. The rest of their time is spent in the air where they catch their insect food. It seems likely that all swiftlets have acute vision in dim light, for species with and without the echolocating call have been seen feeding in semi-darkness. But they are not truly nocturnal birds and in general they leave the caves in their thousands in the morning and return there to roost at night so that most of their food is found in daylight.

They have been studied for some years, both in the field and experimentally, by Lord Medway and recently he has collaborated with Professor David Pye of Queen Mary College, London, in a detailed analysis of the sounds. The echolocating call is used only when the birds are in flight. It is delivered in bursts of sharp clicks, sounding at times like a rattle; for the rate of delivery varies from 3 to about 20 a second. The clicks cover a wide frequency range from 2 kiloHertz up to as high as 15 kiloHertz and, in all but one of the species studied so far, each click actually consists of two separate pulses of sound, each lasting about two-thousandths of a second and separated by only 15–16 thousandths of a second. The exception is the Black-nest Swiftlet, formerly called Low's Swiftlet after the ornithologist who first identified it. In this species the click seems to be a single pulse of sound, longer, with a narrower frequency range and with a lower maximum speed of delivery. However, on closer analysis, this single clicking sound appears to have several peaks of amplitude – in other words it is a multiple pulse of sound: and in this it resembles the clicks of the Oilbirds. It is not yet known how the clicks are produced but from various observations it is assumed that they are probably not produced in the syrinx. Figure 33 shows the clicks of the Black-nest Swiftlet and the double clicks of one of the other species, the Mossy-nest or Grey Swiftlet.[1]

33
Echo-locating calls of cave-dwelling swiftlets of South-east Asia. (a) Blacknest Swiftlet; (b) Mossy-nest Swiftlet. Note extended time scale of these two sonagrams (Medway and Pye, in press, adapted).

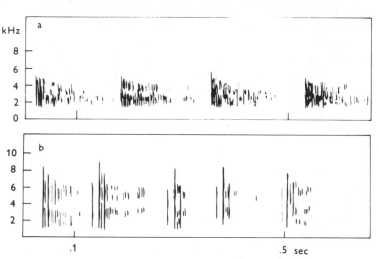

Experiments with captured birds in a specially constructed chamber in the Sarawak Museum showed that the Swiftlets can navigate without calling as long as there is any light. But the moment the light was switched off they started to click again. Other experiments suggested (as the frequency range and duration of the sound pulses also indicate) that the signal would not be precise enough for hunting small insects and that it works only at fairly short range. In the massed noise of clicks and echoes in a cave with so many birds simultaneously on the wing, it seems improbable that an individual bird could detect the echoes from its own clicking over longer distances.

The advantages that the echolocating swiftlets gain from their call appear to be two. They can nest and roost in the

[1] There has been a recent reclassification of the swiftlets. The Black-nest (Low's) Swiftlet formerly had the Latin name of *Collocalia maxima* and should now be called *Aerodramus maximus*. The other species illustrated here, formerly *Collocalia salangana*, should now be called *Aerodramus vanikorensis*. The work on the echolocating clicks of the swiftlets has supported the reclassification of this group of birds.

deepest recesses of large caves gaining greater safety from predators and extra accommodation. And, in the all-the-year-round twelve hours of darkness of their tropical home, they can exploit distant feeding grounds by day because they are able to make the journey back to the caves and enter them after dark. Field observations have shown that the species without the locating call tend to nest near cave entrances where some light penetrates. They all roost betimes and fall silent. But the inner recesses where the echolocating swiftlets live are a babel of sound far into the night, with chattering at roost and nest and a continuing stream of traffic as more and more birds, returning from far afield, rattle their way in to join their roosting companions.

6 The Early Stages

When the chick in the egg chirps within the shell, thou givest him the breath within it to sustain him. Thou createst for him his proper term within the egg, so that he shall break it and come forth from it to testify to his completion as he runs about on his two feet when he emerges. Akhenaten – *Hymn to Aten, c.* 14th century B.C.

Physiologically speaking, Akhenaten's interpretation has been confirmed by modern research on birds such as the domestic fowl whose young leave the nest soon after they emerge from the egg. In these species (precocial, or nidifugous, species to the scientific ornithologist), the young are hatched well covered in down; their eyes are open and they can stand up within a few hours.

Two or three days before hatching, the embryos of wild Mallard Ducks, and of our domesticated ducks that have been bred from this stock, push their beaks through the inner shell membrane into the air space at the blunt end of the egg and start breathing with their lungs. When this has happened, they can make vocal sounds.

Two-way communication between brooding parent and the unhatched offspring is also possible, for it has been shown in the domestic chick that the embryos can hear low-pitched sounds at about 12 days, half way through their incubation period. The embryos of Laughing Gulls are known to respond to a particular parental call from about the same stage of development. By the time domestic chicks hatch, they can hear up to about 800 Hertz, or around a soprano's high A. So from quite an early stage, it seems, sounds form part of an embryo's environment. These include its own heartbeats, breathing, bill-clapping and, later, its vocalizations, as well as all the noises from parents and the other eggs in the clutch that can penetrate eggshell, inner membranes and fluids.

In the last few years studies have been made of the embryos of domesticated fowl and ducks, wild ducks, gulls and quails, with the help of sensitive microphones, tape recorders and instruments for recording pressure, and heart and breathing rates. Sounds made by the embryos themselves, and their reactions to naturally occurring and experimentally produced sounds from outside the egg, indicate the development of acoustic safety-mechanisms which will protect the chick 'as he runs about on his two feet when he emerges'. And he needs them.

The hole-nesting species of duck such as the Goosander, or the Mandarin Duck, and some of the waders, may keep their young fully sheltered for a day or so. But for many precocial species it is literally a matter of life or death that the hatchlings should be mobile almost immediately. Yet they must keep together, within easy reach of warmth and safety under their mother's wing on land, or in close convoy with parental protection on water. This disciplined situation requires both physiological maturity and good communication. The last few days, and even hours, in the egg are very important for subsequent success.

Red-legged Partridge and chicks

The first hazard is the timing of the hatching process itself. Many bird species, of course, start to incubate only when the clutch is nearly complete and this prevents an unduly long period between the hatching of the first and last eggs to be laid. But the results are not very precise. In species that lay large clutches there could be serious losses among the young birds if hatching were spread over more than a few hours. Since all the eggs of a clutch hatch at approximately the same time in many of these precocial species, the obvious question to ask is how such synchronization is achieved.

It may be that the same answer does not hold good for all: species differ, for example, in the time interval between 'pipping' (when the embryo first perforates the shell) and its emergence from the egg. The Herring Gull's egg pips as early as 64 hours before hatching; the Coot's about 24 hours; the domestic fowl's only 12 hours and the Japanese Quail's 10 hours. The start of lung breathing in relation to hatching time is equally variable. However, it is now evident that the timing of the final stages of development within the egg is not a fully automatic process. To some extent, at least, it is under external control. The embryo is responsive to stimuli – including sounds – from outside the egg and it is becoming clear that these affect its development. Such stimuli can play a part, therefore, in the synchronization of hatching, even if

the process has evolved somewhat differently in different species.

The hatching sequences in the Japanese Quail and the Bobwhite Quail of North America have been studied very carefully, at the Psychological Laboratory in Cambridge, by Miss Margaret Vince and her colleagues in the Medical Research Council Unit. Though the two species vary slightly, an interesting story has been pieced together from observations and experiments on them both. These delightful birds, incidentally, spend most of their lives in outdoor aviaries on a farm just outside Cambridge to which the young from eggs successfully hatched in incubators in the laboratory are returned.

First of all, contact between the eggs of a clutch has been shown to be important in synchronizing the hatch. If the eggs are kept in individual isolation from about 48 hours before the expected hatching time, the hatch may be spread over a day or two. But if they are in the same incubator they all hatch within a couple of hours of each other.

In the course of development the embryos produce various sounds and vibrations: beak-clapping, limb movements and head-lifting, as well as the regular rhythms of heart-beat and breathing. All these, presumably, might act as stimuli for neighbouring embryos. After lung-breathing is established, they add cheeping calls. But there is one sound, which starts at about this time, that has been shown to be an especially important mutual stimulus. This is the 'click'. It has been known for a long while that a clicking sound – nothing to do with the pipping of the shell, or the later cutting of it – can be heard from the eggs of many species and indicates the imminence of hatching. It is not a call, nor indeed a vocal signal at all, but occurs in the course of   breathing.

In the quails, a long period of relatively silent breathing, with infrequent soft clicks, is followed at about 12 to 15 hours before hatching by loud, regular clicking and this continues until just before the chick emerges. Although the eggs of a clutch do not click in unison it appears that this form of communication between them affects the speed of development of the embryos during the final stage before hatching.

The loud clicks are produced as part of a new and complicated breathing pattern. They accompany a very rapid additional exhalation in between normal breaths and their onset more or less coincides with a quicker breathing rate.

This, too, is maintained almost up to hatching, when the rate falls again.

The Cambridge experiments have demonstrated that the development of quail embryos can be speeded up by playing click sounds to them, even if they have not yet reached the clicking stage themselves. In other words the silent-breathing phase can be shortened if required. This does not necessarily harm the chick though there is some evidence that chicks whose hatching time has been artificially brought forward may be a little late, for example, in getting on to their feet after hatching. Other experiments showed that it was also possible to slow up development, though only slightly. For instance when eggs with a difference of 24 hours in their previous incubation time were put together, there was a two-way adjustment of hatching time: the less advanced speeding up and the more advanced slowing down. An average hatching time was achieved which meant that individual embryos made the minimum adjustment to hatch simultaneously.

Whatever alterations are made in the experimental situation, the duration of the clicking period is more or less the same. It seems likely, then, that in the quails this phase of click-breathing is very important for their development and that it cannot be unduly shortened. Its onset among slightly more advanced embryos in the clutch probably stimulates the

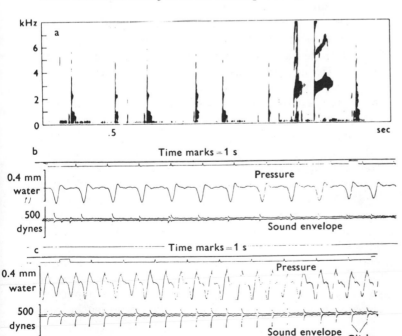

34
Sounds in the egg. (a) Clicks and calls from a quail embryo shortly before hatching (Vince); (b) Bobwhite Quail $9\frac{1}{2}$ hours before hatching: regular breathing of medium amplitude and very soft clicks; (c) $2\frac{1}{2}$ hours before hatching: rapid breathing of high amplitude and regular loud clicks (Vince, 1969).

others to enter this phase and from then on minor adjustments, right up to the final stage of breaking the shell, could ensure a synchronized hatch. Figure 34 illustrates click-breathing and the clicks and a call from a single embryo.

During this period, a great many other things are happening besides the count-down to hatching time. The male keeps in contact with the female during incubation and may share in it himself. So the embryos should be able to hear any communication between the parents. This consists of very soft sounds, mainly from the female, inaudible to an observer just over a metre away. In the laboratory, microphones in the nest record these and other low frequency sounds: cheeps, the female's heart-beats and her shuffling as she moves about on the eggs. So there is plenty of sound, and the vibrations from movements, to affect the rapidly developing embryos.

It is known from observation of the nest behaviour of several species that the parents, in turn, respond to the calls, beak-clapping and movements of the embryos. It seems, for instance, that embryos call within the egg if it is cooling off and this stimulates the parent to brood them. Again, a domestic chick embryo that has been signalling distress for some reason will stop calling if the hen clucks. (These interactions are not only with the parents. In a Herring Gull colony, the embryos answer when the adults are calling overhead after a disturbance.)

In 1952 Eric Simms made a pioneering and successful attempt to record all the calls of the Stone Curlew, a large bird related to the waders that breeds on bare ground on open country. He observed a pair from their arrival in early spring until the young left the nest some 48 hours after the first of the two chicks hatched. One May morning, the microphone picked up faint sounds from one of the unhatched eggs, alternating with calls from the mother; probably the first parent-embryo dialogue ever recorded in the wild. This was exactly what Eric Simms had hoped for because he had already heard similar dialogues from Lapwings and Little Ringed Plovers – two of the wader species in which he was especially interested.

At the pipping stage, then, or perhaps earlier, the adult birds might be said to begin their change of role from that of 'cook', carefully rotating, turning and incubating the eggs, to that of parent, actively controlling a responsive brood of youngsters. Such a period of interaction is an important preparation for the hazardous stage that follows hatching.

Yet another safety-mechanism is being built up during this time. Some duck embryos can distinguish their mother's calls from those of other species from about five days before they hatch. It is not that they ignore other signals: their heart-rate goes up when different maternal calls are played to them. But as soon as they hear the maternal call of their own species they answer with an increased rate of beak-clapping. This, of course, could mean that there is an innate response to the vocalizations of their own species. But other experiments have demonstrated that when eggs have been individually isolated the young birds, both in the egg and after hatching, are much less competent at distinguishing the maternal call of their species. Even the cheeping of their siblings and their own vocalizations are necessary for them to develop a normal capacity to discriminate.

It looks as if information may be carried in the genes which provides a general framework for the recognition of the vocalizations characteristic of the species. But unless there is the right amount and the right kind of stimulation at the appropriate time, the sensory equipment of the young birds does not develop properly. Their responses must be tuned up with the help of stimuli from their surroundings. If this has occurred they can respond to their species' sound signals. Since they need to use their sound-communication system immediately after hatching, their initial experience in the egg may be vital for their survival.

After Hatching

From the moment of hatching, in the precocial species, visual signals are added to the communication system and the young birds start on a new learning programme.

The phenomenon of 'imprinting' has become familiar to anyone who has read much about birds. A brood, or an isolated bird, will become imprinted to humans, or almost any moving object presented to them during a 'sensitive period' after hatching. They will go wherever they are led, as if following the natural mother. This is the result of our experimental breaking of a safety mechanism. In natural conditions the first thing the hatchling normally sees is its mother and the chances of imprinting to the wrong model are practically nil.

Vocalizations are another safeguard both for the protection of the young birds, and for their social integration with other members of their species. As bird-breeders know, closely related species may sometimes be induced to foster the young of others and such cases are known in the wild (apart from the Cuckoo and some other species which habitually lay their eggs for fostering). This fostering is more common among ducks and geese than in most bird families. But, in general, in the wild, birds are hatched by their own parents so that they see and hear them, and their siblings, in this important early phase when they are learning by imitation and experience.

During the period of dependence, the young precocial birds are kept under continuous parental control. Nearly everyone must have seen family parties with tiny, almost wingless ducklings or goslings waddling flatfootedly towards the water and buoyantly bobbing on the swell as soon as they reach it. Flotilla formation is a matter for each species.

On the gravel-pit lake where I watch the Great Crested Grebes, I am also entertained by the sooty brown bunches of Tufted Ducklings tagging along after their mother and, especially if there is any danger, responding to her low grunts by gathering close to her flanks or scattering to cover if it is near enough. The Greylag Geese, on the other hand, who have taken to nesting by the lake quite recently, prefer the line-astern formation, with a parent at either end and the goslings in single file between them. When they are all on the banks one parent continually scans the surroundings while the other feeds with the goslings, and after a time they change the watch. If I approach too closely there is a signal for a slow, unpanicky descent into the water (unless someone gets stuck on the steep bank).

The Grebes, with their one or two young, have less of a management problem. When small, the young are carried pick-a-back, concealed between the raised wings of the parent, their tiny, striped heads sometimes poking forwards like back-seat passengers. They are fed on the water by either parent and can often be heard giving their shrill whistling call not only for food but for transport. As they get older they are encouraged to become fully self-propelling and there are noisy squabbles when an over-large youngster tries to scramble aboard and is shaken off by an unwilling parent.

The sea-going Eider Ducks have another way of organizing the young: the crèche system. Females cannot feed themselves while incubating and after the eggs hatch some of the mothers go out to sea to recuperate. Mixed broods are supervised by several females, among whom may be mothers who have not abandoned their own offspring but take on extra responsibility. In the summer of 1975 I had my first sight and sound of this – about 30 Common Eider ducklings, convoyed by five females, slowly paddling along near the mouth of the Ythan Estuary just north of Aberdeen. The observation point was some distance away, high above them, facing the steep dune slopes of the Sands of Forvie on the other side of the Estuary. Many seabirds nest there and my guide from the Culterty Field Station of the University had been telling me of the recent appearance of four young Fulmars, possibly the start of a new colony of this rapidly spreading species. So, when I singled out of the general noise a low-pitched *ug-ug*, puzzling to me but reminiscent of a conversational Fulmar note, I asked him about it. It was the shepherding call of the Eider ducks to their charges: obviously a penetrating and far-carrying sound.

The calls of ducklings and goslings have been specially studied by Dr Janet Kear at the Research Centre of the Wildfowl Trust at Slimbridge in Gloucestershire. In this large collection which includes most of the 140 or so species of this worldwide family, the Anatidae, comparisons between species have been possible on a scale which could not have been achieved with recordings made solely in the wild.

As visitors to Slimbridge know, most of the birds live outdoors in large pens or move freely round the grounds. Spectacular species such as the Red-breasted Goose, or the softly coloured Ne-ne or Hawaian Goose (almost extinct until it was successfully bred in captivity), are to be met on the paths. In the autumn flocks of wild geese arrive from their northern breeding grounds to winter in and around the Trust grounds along the banks of the Severn Estuary.

For recording, the newly hatched and very young birds were brought into the laboratory and their calls of contentment were delivered from the comfort of the experimenter's lap where they also had the company of a sibling.

These calls are single-element sounds, uttered in sequences, and in some species turning into a trill with increasing excitement. In very young birds, clicks, like those of the embryos, often precede the call elements. Contentment, or pleasure calls, as some authors have named them, are frequently heard from most species of ducklings and goslings and are all fairly similar. They are given during feeding, preening and exploration and seem to have a social function in keeping the brood together. The greeting call, described in Chapter 5, in the Greylag goslings is a special version of these contact, or contentment calls.

If a youngster is out of contact with the rest of the brood it delivers its *isolation distress call*: a slower series of loud single notes. Temporary relegation to the laboratory floor was enough to produce this call in one-day-old birds. Variations of the distress note are given when the birds are hungry, cold or wet.

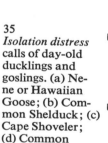

Figure 35 illustrates the isolation distress calls of day-old hatchlings of four species: two ducklings – the Common Eider of Europe and the Cape Shoveler of South Africa; a Ne-ne gosling and a Common Shelduck. This last species is readily seen around the coast of Britain and belongs to a group that is intermediate between geese and ducks. The adult plumage is very striking: green neck and head, orange bill, and bold bronze and black bands against the white of the rest of the body. The sonagrams in Figure 35 show that the Eider duckling has an unusually low-pitched distress call. This seems to be characteristic of the voices of all Eider species, adults as well as young.

35
Isolation distress calls of day-old ducklings and goslings. (a) Ne-ne or Hawaiian Goose; (b) Common Shelduck; (c) Cape Shoveler; (d) Common Eider (Kear, 1968)

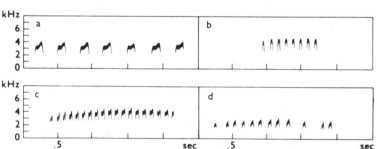

Another call, made by goslings and cygnets (for the swans, too, are members of the same family), has been named the *sleepy call*. As the name implies it is commonly heard before resting periods and at roosting time and may help both to assemble the brood for rest and to stimulate the mother to brood them. But sometimes a gosling gives it while moving about and feeding. If so, the youngster is likely to be found sitting down shortly afterwards, which suggests that the call is a spontaneous reaction to tiredness.

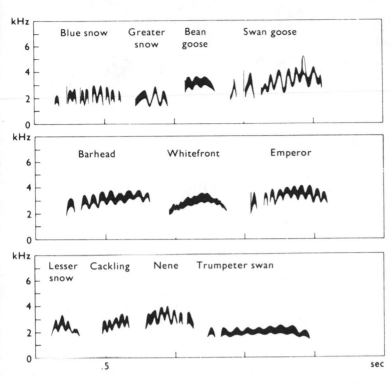

36
Sleepy calls of
geese and swans
(Kear).

In form, the sleepy call – a soft trill – looks rather like a series of pleasure notes joined together, so it is possible that in terms of the gosling's internal state the calls are related and the sleepy call indicates comfortable exhaustion. Figure 36 illustrates sleepy calls of ten species of geese and swans.

The sleepy calls are rather variable, even within a species. But the distress calls appear to be much more constant and characteristic. The form of the elements and their frequency range tends to be fairly similar in closely related species and less so in distantly related ones. So in this large family whose relationships are complicated and still puzzling to the systematist, these calls may provide additional evidence in remaining cases of doubt.

All these calls were recorded from ducklings and goslings only one day after they hatched. As the young birds develop, additional gradations in the sounds, and intergradations between types of call, indicate more complicated responses to their needs and situations.

The chicks of another precocial species, the Domestic Fowl, have a somewhat similar range of calls though they belong to

37
Some domestic chick calls. (a) From very young chicks under brooding hen; (b) *withdrawing trills* followed by *thwarting notes*: a frequent sequence when chicks are exploring and find something unfamiliar; (c) *isolation distress* call from a lost chick and *roosting trill* from sibling which helps it to locate the brood (Guyomarc'h).

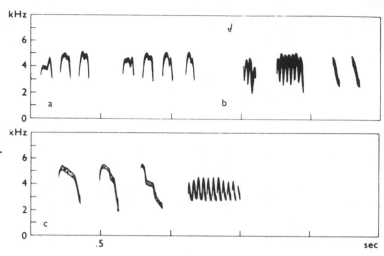

a different order from the Anatidae. The behaviour, of the species has been much studied in Britain, North America and Continental Europe. Figure 37 illustrates some of the calls in their interesting vocal repertoire. (a) shows part of the series of short sounds which the chicks produce at roost or under the broody hen when they are only a few days old. These calls stimulate the hen to crouch over the chicks and lead to rest. (b) shows a very common sequence of calls made when the chicks are actively exploring. If they see an unfamiliar object, or if they are slightly afraid or are touched, they utter *withdrawing trills* followed by *tension* or *thwarting notes*.

These calls were recorded at the University of Rennes in France where domestic fowl have been studied for many years by Dr J.-C. Guyomarc'h in the open air conditions that are natural for these farmyard birds. The significance of some sounds, however, needs to be confirmed by simple experiments in controlled conditions and this was done, for example, in the study of roosting behaviour.

On one occasion the light was put out when most of the chicks were already roosting and calling sleepily – a signal to any scattered members of the brood to join them. However, one chick was stranded in the sudden darkness and immediately gave its isolation distress call. By day, the only effect of this call would have been a temporary slowing down of the group's activity to enable the wanderer to catch up. But in the darkness one of its siblings responded with a long trilling call – an effective localizing signal. The lost

chick stopped its own calling for several seconds and began to
move in the right direction. After several exchanges of isolation calls and location trills the lost chick was safely back
in the group (Figure 37c). The location trill is very like
the maternal roosting call though higher in pitch than the
adult sound. The maternal call is given when the hen gathers
the brood together for the night.

Nestlings and Fledglings

Young birds that are cared for in the nest for a more or less
prolonged period after hatching – and this includes all the
songbirds in Britain – are known as altricial or nidicolous
species. They have a completely different pattern of development from the precocial species. When they are first hatched
their eyes are closed, they have comparatively little protective
covering in many cases, and are dependent on the nest and
intensive parental care.

Much less is known about the behaviour of the small
altricial species in the egg and their hearing has not been
studied at that stage. But clicks have been heard from the
eggs of many species and, as with the precocial species, seem
to continue for a time after hatching. Though the downy or
mossy lining of some types of nest (and the walls of hole
nests) must insulate the eggs to some extent from sound
as well as cold it is possible, at the very least, that altricial
embryos are affected by the movements and soft calls of the
incubating female and the loud songs and calls of nearby
adults of their species.

Immediately after hatching, while the young are still
being brooded, the sounds from songbird nestlings are mainly
quiet cheeps. But as the nestlings gain strength the food
begging-call characteristic of each species becomes more
clearly defined and quite noisy. However, a wide range of
calls in altricial young before fledging is neither useful to them
nor desirable. It would merely draw even more attention to
the nest – especially dangerous if it is an open one.

In the Great Tit, the begging-call is a series of complex
elements with several bands of frequencies from low to high.
This makes it an easy sound to locate: an important factor
after the young birds have left the nest but are still being fed
by the parents. The rhythm is uneven, with faster notes at the
beginning and the emphasis and volume increases during the
phrase (Figure 38). The volume and number of phrases also

38
Food-begging
call of young
Great Tit. Arrow
indicates element
used to form the
location call.

39
Contact call of
young Robin
(Brémond, 1968).

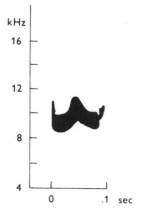

increases, and the pauses between them diminish, with the stimulus of the parent's approach. The chorus in the nest dies away as each youngster in turn has its gape stuffed with food.

Among birds such as the Blackbird and Song Thrush that build open nests in hedges and bushes, the young fledge before they can manage more than a fluttering stumble through the air. They are parked in low bushes or thick undergrowth for a day or two and are stealthily fed by the wary adults. Until they begin to move about more freely they keep fairly silent. The young Robin, for instance, gives only a high-pitched short call which is not very easy for human observers, at any rate, to locate and quite different in form from its begging-call (Figure 39).

The greater safety of nests in holes allows a longer stay and the fuller development of the young. Young Great Tits fly well, if a little unsteadily, to a perch above ground as they fledge from the hole one by one. By this time their begging call is quite a powerful signal. It is not as loud as the begging of young Great Spotted Woodpeckers, among the larger birds, which once attracted me towards them from a distance of about 100 metres. But it is very effective when a Great Tit parent returns from a food-finding trip only to discover that the active little fledglings have moved to different parts of the tree and have to be relocated by sound.

Nevertheless, after fledging, the young Great Tits make considerable use of a different version of this call. It acts more directly as a location call and seems to indicate separation

from siblings or parents – a form, perhaps, of isolation distress call. As soon as a parent arrives to round up the lost fledgling which has been calling in this way, it switches to the normal begging notes.

The location call is, most commonly, four notes – each like the arrowed element of the begging-call in Figure 38. But the sounds are evenly spaced, on the same pitch, and equally emphasized. The call is uttered without the wing-shivering that accompanies food begging. One spring morning, when we had some hand-reared tits which were almost due to fledge, we heard this signal from the room where their box was kept. We found that one of them had come out of the box on its own, probably accidentally while clambering around the hole, and was clinging precariously to a microphone cable.

Unlike the majority of the precocial species the tits and most other songbirds do not begin to feed themselves for about a fortnight after leaving the nest. In suburban areas the Great Tit broods are usually led to the nearest patch of thick and high leafy cover where they can get lost and be retrieved in comparative safety for a week or so. But as soon as they are really strong on the wing they are taken on longer tours. Sometimes as many as four or five broods come through our garden in a day; the fledglings begging noisily, the parents giving their *pee* and *duple* calls and occasionally *churring* as they try to feed and marshal the adventurous youngsters. Familiarity with the begging calls of each brood makes it possible to distinguish them from slight differences in the tone-quality of the sound: though such distinctions must be treated with care unless the broods are colour-ringed (as ours were) for there are other differences in the sound according to the age of the brood.

Gradually, as the young Great Tits learn to feed themselves, the output of begging calls diminishes though they are still delivered as if absent-mindedly, when a parent approaches, by a youngster that is already busily feeding, or food-exploring, with the staccato *pit* and *spick* sounds that accompany this activity.

About this time the rough quality of the call begins to change and it may switch, occasionally, into the first musical glissandos of the juvenile subsong (described in Chapter 4). Soon the young tits are giving the *tsee* and *pee* notes, like the adults. They are already churring: a short, distinct *churr*, during foraging (Figure 25d); and the scold *churr* (Figure 25c) which they learn from their parents to direct at dangerous animals like Jays, cats and humans when they come too close.

This is more or less the extent of the young Great Tits' repertoire until the autumn, when the males begin to use the territorial calls as they try to find a place for themselves somewhere in the adult community.

Their vocal apprenticeship, however, has a long time to run. The males have yet to develop their songs which they do during the next winter and spring. The process of song development has now been experimentally studied in a number of songbird species. Although some species do not seem to have to learn their song, in most cases learning has been shown to be very important.

Song Learning

The duck embryos' recognition of their mother's call improved when they had normal 'ear training': regular exposure to the call itself and the other natural sounds in the nest. In much the same way young songbird males of many species appear to need auditory experience in their first weeks of life as well as further experience – in the following spring – of songs from adults of their species, if they are to perfect their song.

The story of song development is a complicated one and differs from species to species. All that can be described here are a few of the key points from more than twenty years of scientific detective work in many countries.

The Chaffinch was one of the first birds whose song development was thoroughly studied by modern methods and the species continues to be a favourite among ethologists for many purposes. It is a common bird, widespread in Europe, and hardy. Its song is varied in detail but because it is a well-structured phrase, with sections in which the elements are of different types, deviations from the basic form and variations in the elaboration of detail can be detected and considered separately (Figure 40). There are further sonagrams of Chaffinch song variation in Chapter 7.

This was crucial in the classic work by Professor W. H. Thorpe and Dr Peter Marler at Cambridge during the 1950s, when the Chaffinch was studied in the wild and in the laboratory. The first stage in the song-study had been to find out that young Chaffinch males developed their song by a

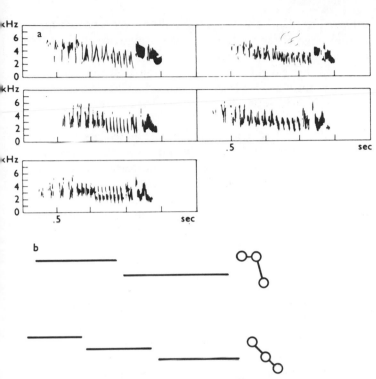

40
Chaffinch songs:
(a) typical strophes
recorded near
Cambridge in area
from which the
nestlings used in
learning experi-
ments were taken
(Thorpe, 1958);
(b) diagram of
two typical
Chaffinch stro-
phes. The lines
represent the main
sections and the
circles the single
elements of the
end-phrase
(Marler, 1956).

gradual process of refining it from their juvenile subsong in
the early spring of their first breeding season; that is, when
they are about nine months old (see Chapter 4). By the time
they are doing this, the adult Chaffinches around them are
beginning to sing again. The adults themselves sing incomplete songs at first but in a few days their repertoire of two
or three variants is fully re-established. Some individuals
may have only one variant; a few, as many as six.

The young birds take much longer to achieve fully-formed
strophes and go through a stage when their song is extremely
variable, with the final flourish missing or indeterminate.
Gradually a youngster begins to produce a strophe which
resembles one from a neighbour's repertoire. Sometimes he
copies from more than one neighbour or combines a trill
and an end-phrase taken from different strophes among the
models he has available around him.

Once the repertoire has crystallized after this period of
choice it does not seem to change significantly in successive
years, and there has been no evidence that Chaffinches in the
wild learn new songs after their first season. But without this
apprenticeship at the right stage of their development, they

cannot form their song properly at all; for the second, experimental stage of the study was to deprive young birds of this normal auditory experience.

Chaffinches caught during the autumn after their hatching were kept together, but isolated from older Chaffinches. When they came into song the following spring, they produced strophes of the correct pattern, with three main sections and a final flourish but their version was slightly less elaborate than normal song. If, however, young birds were taken from the nest at the age of five days and hand-reared in individual isolation, their songs in the following spring were very inadequate. The division into sections was vague, and all the elements tended to be of about the same frequency range instead of a gradual descent. The end-flourish hardly existed. Figure 41 shows the songs of some of these birds.

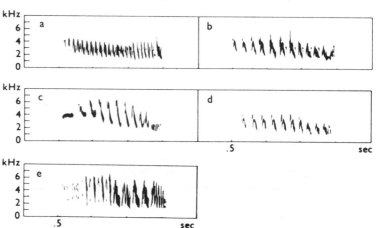

41
Songs of young Chaffinches reared in isolation: (a–d) individually isolated birds; (c, d) birds which were also visually isolated from other Chaffinches (this seemed to make little difference to their song-development); (e) a bird isolated with one companion (Thorpe, 1958).

When nestlings taken from different nests were hand-reared in isolation from older Chaffinches, but kept together in groups, the result was different again. They were still unable to produce strophes that resembled normal song in the wild, though the structure was a little firmer, with an occasional squeak as an end-flourish. But they apparently used each other as models. This was so effective that their song could only be described as communal: each bird conforming almost exactly with the jointly established patterns.

The argument from these and other experiments is that two periods of learning are involved. Young birds, although they do not themselves sing in their first summer, 'remember' some features of normal song from the adults around them.

This would explain why young Chaffinches caught in the autumn did much better than those taken as nestlings. Full elaboration of song is only achieved during the second learning period in the following spring when the youngsters are performing for the first time, as well as listening to their neighbours.

In spite of this capacity for learning there are limits on what a Chaffinch finds acceptable as learning material. Experiments at tutoring them with recordings showed this clearly. For example a song-strophe of the correct length and approximately the right number of elements at the right pitch was not imitated, probably because the sounds were too pure. (They had been produced on an organ.) The song of a Tree Pipit, however, was copied by one of the hand-reared, isolated birds. But he condensed the Tree Pipit's longer phrase to the standard duration of a Chaffinch strophe.

One way of interpreting all this evidence has been to pro-pose that there is some form of genetic control – the mecha-nisms of which are not yet understood – over the range of sound-patterns that are acceptable to the young bird, within the much wider range of auditory stimuli provided by its natural environment. This supposed pre-set range is some-times called the 'auditory template'. In the Chaffinch it probably consists of a preferred band of frequencies and types of element and the tendency to form strophes of a certain length. It is just a sketchy outline of the right kind of song. Subsequently, different forms of learning contribute to the full development of both recognition and performance.

Other workers, particularly from North America, have carried these studies further. They have been especially interested in the 'sensitive period' for song-development and in how the bird learns to control its own vocalizations. Like babies learning to talk, birds have to establish nervous and muscular control of the vocal organs. This comes with prac-tice and with feed-back from listening to the sounds that they themselves produce (motor learning).

Some of these experiments have involved deafening birds at various ages.[1] Such experiments have shown, for instance, that Chaffinches deafened while they were still practising their songs in their first spring produced only simple songs as their final versions. Even a young male that had almost crystallized its song when deafened, began to deviate further and further

[1] See Chapter 12 for comment on experimental techniques.

from normal song: he had not yet, it seems, established it by motor learning. The earlier in life that the birds were deafened, the simpler the songs they produced the following spring. On the other hand birds deafened at two or three years of age continued to sing more or less normally.

Taken together, these experiments confirm that vocalizing, and monitoring the results aurally, is necessary for song-learning, as well as the experience of hearing the normal song from adults. Similar results were obtained for many, but not all species that have been tested in this way. The reasons for these differences are not always clear but may be due, at least in part, to the different ways in which species develop their songs. The experiments have not provided any information on the relationship between genetically-coded information and learning processes; for the deafening of song-bird embryos has not been undertaken and the extent of learning that might take place in the egg is not known.

In another type of experiment, designed to find out more about the sensitive period for learning, a young male Chaffinch was castrated in January before it had started to sing for the first time. It was kept in isolation from other Chaffinches until March of the following year. It had therefore neither sung nor heard song until it was more than $2\frac{1}{2}$ years old. It was then brought into singing condition by the injection of a male hormone, which is linked with song-behaviour in the normal bird.

Within a few days this bird began to sing subsong and to fashion song-strophes just as a young bird does. Recordings from two strophes of wild Chaffinches, chosen for their difference from those the captive bird seemed to be developing, were then played to it daily for some time. It incorporated components from these into its own strophes. But a year later, although offered other variants, the bird retained its previous repertoire with little change. This experiment by Dr Fernando Nottebohm suggests that the sensitive period is not necessarily related to age. This bird produced new sounds of its own and imitated others, well beyond the age at which learning usually ceases in the Chaffinch in natural conditions.

Such experiments, then, and comparisons with other species, indicate that the sensitive periods for vocal learning vary in different species and are not necessarily absolute. They also show that the periods during which a bird is capable of learning new material by imitation, and of translating this into performance by motor learning, may not always coincide.

Species with more flexible song-patterns than the Chaffinch, or a greater disposition to imitate other species, present us with further questions and some of these are discussed in Chapter 10. Meanwhile a further example, the story of song-development in the Coal Tit, offers both comparisons and contrasts with that of the Chaffinch. The Coat Tit's song has the same structure as the Great Tit's, though it is higher in pitch and the elements are different in form, producing a thinner sound. Repeated motifs of two or three elements form strophes of varying length and each male has up to six song-variants, each with a different motif. As in the Great Tit, some variants are shared with neighbours, others are not.

Song-development in the Coal Tit was recently studied in Germany by Dr Gerhard Thielcke of the Max-Planck Institute for behavioural research at Radolfzell–Mögginen in West Germany. Birds were taken from nests at ages between 10 and 14 days and hand-reared. They were isolated from wild-living Coal Tits at all the relevant times. When their sexes were known, two of the males were kept together in a sound-proof room with two females. Each of the males developed five song-variants: of these, two were shared, two were not and one had some common features. None of the songs resembled those of wild-living birds. Figure 42 shows a wild Coal Tit song and some of the songs of the hand-

42
Coal Tit songs:
(a) a wild Coal
Tit; (b-c) shared
variant of hand-
reared males B
and G who were
kept together in
isolation from
other Coal Tits;
(d-h) other variants
of birds B and G
and of isolated
bird R (Thielcke,
1973).

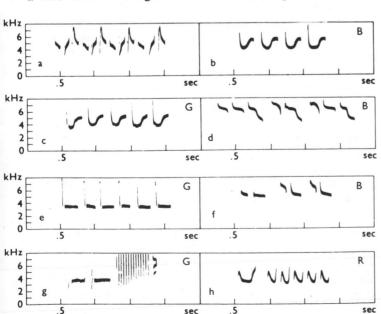

43
Comparison of
songs and alarm
calls from wild
and hand-reared
Coal Tits. (a)
Song of wild Coal
Tit; (b-d) songs of
hand-reared birds
B, G and R; (e)
alarm calls of wild
Coal Tits recorded
near the Bodensee
in Germany; (f)
in the Alps; (g) in
the Black Forest;
(h) alarm call of
hand-reared bird
B and (i) of bird R
(Thielcke, 1973).

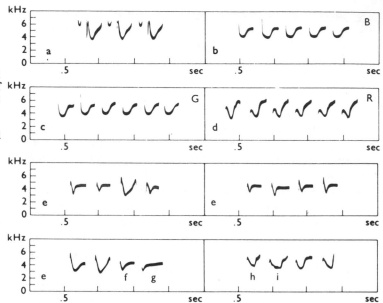

reared birds. However, some of the elements in these songs
were similar to elements in Coal Tit alarm calls. These were
strung together to make a song-motif. Figure 43 illustrates
resemblances between the elements of one of the shared
song-variants of the hand-reared birds, and wild Coal Tit
alarm calls.

When the songs were played back to Coal Tits in the wild
they ignored all but one: a shared song-variant which most
closely resembled the local version of the rather variable
Coal Tit alarm call.

These young Coal Tits, then, in the absence of natural
models for song-learning, included an apparently innate
signal (the alarm call) in their aberrant songs. But even in
isolation they developed a full complement of song-variants,
including individual motifs as well as motifs shared with
their captive companions.

We had a hint of a similar predilection for the individual,
unshared motif in the Great Tit when a foundling male was
brought to us from Central London at the age of four weeks,
after it had been hand-reared by its kindly rescuers since it
was about ten days old. During its song-practice period in
the early spring of the following year, it started by working
away at two perfectly normal three-note motifs; but these
were quite unlike any of the eleven song-variants that it could

hear around our house in Middlesex. Perhaps these were patterns 'remembered' from its early days of life. Possibly, therefore, 'remembered' patterns (if this is what they are) take precedence in learning practice over the readily available models of the present. Some of the latter, as we know, are added to the Great Tit song repertoire during the rest of the young bird's first song-season.

Remembered patterns; patterns that are learned when a bird is already a young adult; aberrant patterns contrived in the absence of natural auditory stimuli or models for imitation: all these patterns conform to a greater or lesser extent to the type of song characteristic of the species concerned. Yet, the failure of wild-living Coal Tits to recognize the signals of the isolated birds underlines the importance of learning in maintaining the stability of communication by song within a species.

It is difficult for professional workers in this field, and for anyone who has studied the evidence, to believe any longer that there is a straightforward answer to the old controversy over inheritance and learning, or 'nature and nurture'. It does not seem possible to separate the components of behaviour into neat sections labelled 'inherited' and 'learned'; the interactions are too complicated. Even where innate factors are certainly involved, the full development of their effects may still depend on influences from the environment and on some measure of learning by imitation and experience.

These studies of the way in which young birds come to identify and to produce the sound signals of their species are helping us to understand biological and psychological processes of great importance.

7 Dialects

Wide seas, unfordable and unbridged rivers, impenetrable forests, impassable valleys, lofty mountains, deserts, marshes and artificial political frontiers divide speech communities; but seas and lakes carrying coastwise shipping along shores well supplied with harbours, fordable streams or deep rivers well furnished with bridges, good canals, mountain passes and wide roads link communities together and make the spread of new expressions and new speech fashions quick and easy. *Simeon Potter*

Very little imaginative effort is required to apply this passage to bird communication. The topographical features that hindered, and to a considerable extent still hinder, human social interchanges are barriers that also effectively isolate populations of many bird species. On the other hand, unbroken stretches of one type of habitat allow free movement and a continuous network of contacts between neighbours.

It is true that seabirds ply up and down the coast or far out over the oceans and that migrants may travel thousands of miles over sea and desert. In this sense topographical barriers are meaningless for some species, and these are in contact with other members from widely separated home bases. But, while breeding, even the most mobile birds are tied to one locality. Moreover that locality is often a traditional one to which the same birds return year after year.

Sedentary species, such as many of our resident garden birds, spend most of their lives within an area of perhaps a few square kilometres and are easily turned back from further exploration by a high ridge between valleys, a wide river or a treeless plain. Even a road or a field may separate them into communities that rarely intermingle.

Whether birds are mobile or sedentary by normal habit, the sound signals they use during the reproductive period are generally the most elaborate and important in their repertoire. During the comparative immobility of this period, local modifications of the signals can be developed by any species in which the young birds have to learn to make them correctly. The young broods of the year are beginning to learn from what they hear all round them. In many species the young adults, fresh recruits to the breeding population, are still learning, too, from the vocal activity of the older members of the community. In this way a tradition can be built up and passed on.

There is still a great deal that we do not know about these

local variations in sound signals which, by analogy with human speech, have been labelled dialects. But the more that is found out, the more prevalent they appear to be, at least among songbirds. They were first widely studied in full song. Now it is becoming evident that some calls, too, vary geographically.

The analogy with human dialects does not work out exactly. Before the increasing geographical and social mobility of our society blurred these speech distinctions, our dialects were confined to one region. Within the region the inhabitants of each town could be identified by their speech, and this is still true to some extent.

This model does not necessarily apply to bird dialects. Species differ, and there are several ways in which dialects are distributed geographically. The Chaffinch was one of the first species whose song dialects were observed. In this species the variations seem to be spread in a kind of mosaic pattern, separated by gaps where the terrain is unsuitable for Chaffinch habitation. Although there are distinct local dialect areas, some of the same song-types can be heard in widely separated parts of the species' range, though they may not have occurred in between. In the words of Peter Marler who conducted the survey of Chaffinch dialects in Britain: 'It is as though all the towns of Yorkshire had been scattered across Britain. Each would be readily differentiated from its immediate neighbours, but would not be distinguished by ear from similar "dialects" elsewhere.' A number of factors contribute to the development of local dialects.

The Chaffinch, like the Great Tit, has the habit of ringing the changes on its repertoire of song-variants during a long bout of singing. The Chaffinch, too, matches its variants with those of a rival when counter-singing. So there is a tendency for a population to come to share a number of variants. Young males holding a territory in their first breeding season learn from their neighbours as they extend their own song-repertoire, thus adapting themselves to the local dialect and preserving its continuity. But, as we have seen in the case of the Great and Coal Tits, birds do not always learn all their songs at this time.

The distance, therefore, that young birds disperse from their birthplace is also important in the development of a local dialect. New recruits may enrich it with a variant they bring with them from a different dialect area which, in time, is widely copied in their new home. Among many of the basically sedentary songbird species, the juveniles are sent packing when they become independent and they wander off to settle elsewhere. In our local Great Tit population we knew of only two young males who settled within hearing range of their hatching place. The father of one of these disappeared towards the end of the breeding season. So the youngster, Yellow-Right, was able to hang around and succeeded in inheriting a small section of the territory which he improved upon as he got on to more equal terms with the neighbouring males. Later he moved to another one nearby. Redblack, who was a son of Yellow's later years, took over our back-garden territory on the death of the owner but only after an apparently territoryless first year during which he occasionally appeared at the bird table.

Mostly, young males of these species have to travel a kilometre or so before they find a living space and some much farther. It depends on the population density and the survival rate of the older birds. A good breeding year, resulting in local over-population, leads to a more than normally wide dispersal and even to the temporary occupation of less favourable habitats. Occasionally a succession of good years sets off an irruption – a large-scale displacement of birds unable to get a living within their customary range of movement who are forced to go exploring far beyond it. In this way, for example, Blue Tits have crossed the channel from the Continent to Britain.

It seems, then, that conflicting pressures are at work. There are good reasons for a strong local tradition to develop, particularly if the population is a fairly isolated one. It was found from the Chaffinch survey that in some of the Scottish glens, where populations are isolated by mountain ridges, there were quite different song-patterns. These are most easily distinguishable in the end section of the songs, particularly the final flourish. These are often broadly characteristic of a population. In southern populations of the Chaffinch, however, far less obvious barriers produce similar vocal borderlines. It takes patient study to find out whether such traditions persist unchanged for decades or just a few years. One report from Westphalia Lippe in West Germany in 1966 mentioned a song-strophe which had been heard in the same places in the Teutoberger Forest and the Egge mountains for 20 years. There are also good reasons for change as birds from areas with a different tradition join an established community or form the nucleus of a new one.

As part of the 'mosaic' effect in the Chaffinch dialect, almost any variant may turn up anywhere. A comparison of the song-survey made in Britain, and some countries of western Europe, with a similar survey in Russia showed that certain variants were to be found dotted all over the map. Nevertheless, though all the variants recorded in Russia could be heard in the west, many of the more complicated song-strophes of western birds were not found in Russia. So it looks as if there is a tendency for the Chaffinch to sing only the simpler variants in the easterly part of its range, which extends far into Asia.

We detected a not dissimilar dialect distribution in the Great Tit in Europe, though this is not supported by statistical data as in the Chaffinch surveys. Certain standard variants – fairly simple two- and three-note motifs – cropped up almost everywhere in the recordings that we were able to hear, and in our own more limited travels abroad. They recurred in recordings from Russia, the Scandinavian countries, Czechslovakia, France and Germany, interspersed with some delightfully different models. The Great Tit who sang the three-note motif which Bruckner took as a theme in his Fourth Symphony probably lived somewhere near Linz in Austria, and certainly before 1874, when the symphony was completed. But a musician heard the same motif quite recently in the Tatra Mountains in Czechoslovakia.

Some years ago many of the Great Tits in the neighbourhood of a Yorkshire farm we often visited had among their shared types a high-pitched, very fast, two-note motif which we neither knew from the southern populations we were acquainted with at that time nor heard elsewhere in the district. Our immediately local population in Middlesex seems to interchange motifs fairly freely across most of the area of a well-wooded golf links and the gardens backing onto it. But the birds of the more extensive woods beyond have for a long time formed a separate vocal community.

Yet our experience of the local population has shown changes in the dialect from time to time – some gradual, one much more sudden. A gradual change starts in one copse or another on the links when a new male appears with a variant which is taken up by others and passed on through the community. For a few years, almost nothing but two-note motifs was heard for a kilometre or so from the house. Then one autumn there was a drastic turnover of territorial males, possibly the result of an epidemic. The new occupants brought some three-note motifs with them and made the local repertoire much more interesting and varied.

I remember listening enviously to some recordings of Great Tit songs from Finland, which offered a plethora of unusual three-note motifs, at just the time when our local population was so drearily pre-occupied with very standard two-note patterns. We paused to wonder whether, if the Finnish recordings happened to be a fair sample from the total Great Tit population, there could be any environmental reason for a preponderance of three-note motifs, as there might also be for the simplicity of Chaffinch songs in Russia. Such speculations could be formulated into questions for future co-operative research.

There is already a theory about the evolutionary value of dialect which also links dialect formation with the environment but in a rather different way.[1] Evidence from some species in North and South America suggests that dialects may encourage mating within a broad dialect area: females may have a preference for males with the type of song they became accustomed to in their own learning period. If this is so, it would tend to keep populations separate to some extent, permitting small adaptations to local climatic or other ecological conditions to emerge in each population. This would probably apply only over fairly large areas and where, though the habitat is still suitable for the species, a distinctive topographical change occurs, such as the height above sea-level, or a difference in the soil and vegetation. In this way song-dialects would be a rather flexible barrier to the mixing of populations, for they would not act so completely that a redispersal to other areas of some members of a population was impossible.

Some recent work on the Chaffinch in Belgium supports this theory. A study of the final element – the end-flourish – in different parts of the country showed that there are a number of local dialect areas and several larger, regional, dialect groups referred to as Low, Middle and High Belgium. These zones succeed one another south-eastwards across the country from the coast, with transition zones between them, and they correspond with different climatic conditions particularly in temperature.

In at least part of its range the Chaffinch has an extra-

---

[1] Proposed by Dr F. Nottebohm. The role of song in the evolution of species is discussed further in Chapter 9.

ordinary song habit, quite distinct from its normal type of song-variation. It adds a short, sharp, clicking sound after the end-flourish. The German ornithologists who first noticed and studied this habit called the sound the *kit*. The point of interest is that it resembles very precisely the *kit* alarm call of three of the continental woodpecker species: the Great, Middle and Lesser Spotted Woodpeckers. (The Middle Spotted Woodpecker is absent from Britain.)

Cases of unrelated species in which similar sound signals have evolved independently are not unknown. But such signals usually differ in their finer details. The close resemblance between the Chaffinch and the woodpecker *kits* looks more like imitation. If this is so, which species was the imitator? The woodpeckers are the less likely. They are definitely not mimics. For that matter the Chaffinch is not an habitual imitator except of its own species, but it does

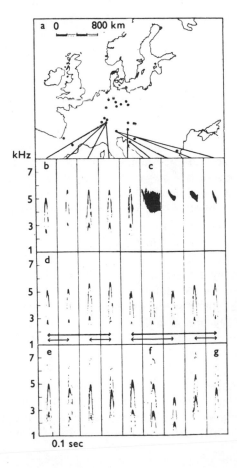

44
Chaffinch songs: (a) map of places in Europe where *kit* is known to be added to song; (b) *kit* of five males; (c) *kit* variants of four males (lines link to recording locations); (d) *kits* from two males (top arrows; *kits* used with song-strophes of the same type are linked by bottom arrows); (e, f, g) *kits* of Great, Middle and Lesser Spotted Woodpeckers respectively.

occasionally copy notes from others (as in the juvenile sub-song). So the best guess is that the Chaffinch took its woodland neighbours as the model for this addition to its song.

Figure 44 shows the localities in which the Chaffinch *kit* has been recorded. There may well be others. Sonagrams of Chaffinch and woodpecker *kits* are shown for comparison. The only significant differences in the Chaffinch's faithful copy are the absence of harmonics above six kilo Hertz and the lack of volume compared with that of the woodpecker. Figure 45 (c) shows other forms of *kit* which are also used at the end of the song-strophe but do not resemble the woodpecker call. Figure 45 illustrates some Chaffinch song-strophes with and without the *kit* and its variants. The last two strophes, (f) and (g), also show another variation that was found in the Dolomites: a double end-flourish.

Chaffinch song-variants are not too difficult to identify in the field once you are familiar with the structure of the strophe and its separate sections though because of the speed at which the elements follow one another, recordings played at half speed are necessary for appreciation of detail. But there is no difficulty in distinguishing between different forms of one of the Chaffinch's best known calls.

As I walk further along the Berkshire lane where I am accustomed to linger with the Skylarks and Lapwings, I come to a stretch where fingers of woodland reach down towards the road from hillside copses. At any time in spring and summer the Chaffinch males, if they are not singing, are likely to be repeating a single, whistling note: the *huit* call. But this is only on one side of the road. From the other comes a more vibrant *hrreet*. The narrow lane apparently acts as a dialect border for this call.

The Chaffinch was the first species known to have a call which varied from place to place: it was noted in the wild as early as 1939 by a German ornithologist, Dr H. Sick. The extreme forms are so different that this call did not have to await the sound-spectrograph for confirmation of its variations. They are so different in fact that it must have required very close observation of Chaffinch behaviour to realize that they were alternative versions of the same call; especially as the range of situations in which they are used is fairly wide. These situations include owl-mobbing (mixed in with *pinks*); after the excitement caused by an overhead predator alarm has subsided; and, sometimes, in courtship. But the call is also delivered monotonously for minutes on

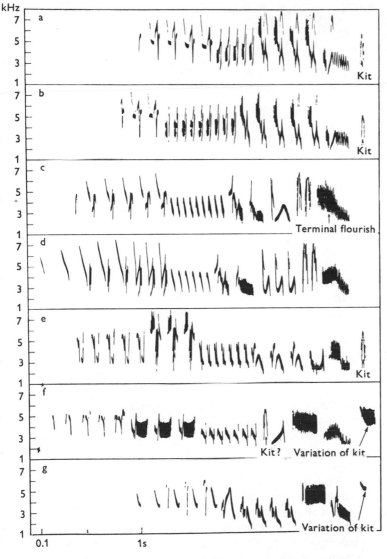

45
Chaffinch song-strophes. (a) and (d) from the same male, (b) and (c) from another male. (a) and (b) are strophes of the same type, (c) and (d) of another type. (a), (b) and (e) have the *kit* at the end of the strophe; (f) and (g) have *kit* variants. Recording localities: (a-d) south-west Germany; (e) Graz, Austria; (f, g) Dolomites (Thielcke, 1969).

end, apparently spontaneously, as song may be. In social contexts its significance seems to be much the same as that of song.

The *huit* form of the call is a musical element, gliding upwards in pitch and coming to an abrupt stop. The Willow Warbler, Chiffchaff and Redstart have calls that sound rather like it but with practice it is quite possible to tell them apart. At the other extreme is the *breeze*, a long vibrato element, resembling one of the Greenfinch calls. In between there are

46
Rain call of the
Chaffinch: some
gradations of *huit*
and *hrreet*. Lines
link the forms to
recording locali-
ties (Thielcke,
1969).

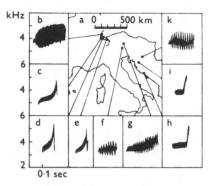

numerous more or less vibrant gradations such as the *hrreet*.

The distribution of these different forms seems to follow much the same pattern as the song. Where any barrier exists there is a sharp dialect borderline. But where there are continuous stretches of good Chaffinch country as, for example, in large continental forests, the borderlines are less clear. A single-form dialect area may be succeeded by an intermediate zone where the same bird is heard to utter the *huit* as well as the *breeze* or one of the intermediate versions. Figure 46 illustrates some of the forms of this call and the locations in central and southern Europe where they were recorded: southern Germany, Austria, northern Italy and Yugoslavia.

As with song-variants, we do not yet know enough about the persistence of a local tradition. The *huits* and *hrreets* of the Berkshire lane have remained constant for several years and round my home in Middlesex one of the vibrant *hrreet* forms has been in use for eighteen years and possibly much longer.

A great deal of attention has been given to the songs of a North American member of a family fairly closely related to that of the Chaffinch – the Cardinal. The Cardinal's songs are particularly interesting, not only in the different form of geographical distribution of the dialects but for other reasons as well. The male is a spectacular bird about the size of a Song Thrush, with rich red plumage, a crest and a stout red bill, made even more prominent by the black which fringes the base and forms a short bib. The female is less brilliantly coloured: mainly yellowish brown, but she has the same red bill and a red tip to her crest.

The gaudy appearance of the Cardinal, like that of the Golden Oriole, is a reminder that not all the common garden

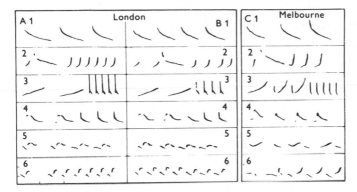

47
Songs of the North
American Car-
dinal: approxi-
mately half the
song-repertoires
of three male
Cardinals from
two locations in
Ontario, Canada,
34 km apart. The
songs in columns
A and B are from
two birds at
London with
territories in
contact, and are
quite similar. The
songs in column C
are from a bird at
Melbourne. Some
of these, especially
in row 1, are
similar to their
counterparts at
London; those
from rows 2 to 6
become increasin-
gly different
(Lemon, 1975).

and woodland birds of the northern temperate latitudes are
as subtly coloured as most of those that are resident in
Britain. The Cardinal is a species whose range on the eastern
side of North America extends from southern Florida over
the Canadian border into southern Ontario and it is still
spreading northwards. Professor Robert Lemon, who has
been studying the Cardinals for many years, found them all
around him on the University campus at London, Western
Ontario, which lies in the same latitude as southern France.

The song consists of well-separated and repeated whistling
notes: either single elements, rising or falling in pitch, or
with a more complicated structure which may sometimes
consist of two or three closely linked elements. Professor
Lemon calls these notes syllables and they are combined to
form song-strophes. Commonly only one or two types of
syllable are used in each strophe. The Cardinals on the
London campus had a total of 14 different syllables between
them and most of the birds used most of them. Each bird
had about ten different strophes, or song-variants, in its
repertoire. Figure 47 illustrates song-variants from two
separate localities in Ontario (London and Melbourne) and
Figure 48 is a sonagram of yet another Ontario variant.

The habit of neighbours matching their variants in counter-
singing has been taken further by the Cardinals than by

48
Another Cardinal
song-variant,
recorded in
Ontario (Dr
W. W. H. Gunn).

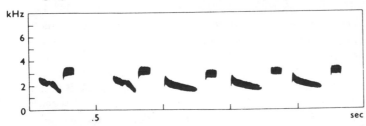

many other species. As a result the number of variants, like the number of syllables in each neighbourhood, is comparatively low and each bird has a high proportion of them in its large song repertoire. In other words there is greater conformity and less individuality in the song-repertoires of the Cardinals than in species discussed so far. There are, however, still possibilities for individual recognition: for example, in slight differences of duration in the syllables.

Cardinals hold rather big territories (about 4 to 8 acres: 1·6 to 3·2 hectares), occupying them for a large part of the year and usually retaining them for years on end: a not uncommon pattern in sedentary species. But, less common, the females sing too. They do so less frequently than the males, except just before they begin to nest, and when the male and female sing together, the female matches her variants with those of her mate even more exactly than he does with his neighbours.

For comparison with the Ontario songs, recordings were made at sample localities throughout the Cardinal's range. These showed that the types of syllable varied considerably from place to place. Some were fairly widespread but as recordings from localities further and further south from London, Ontario, were analysed, fewer and fewer of the London syllables were to be heard. Even in Ohio (immediately south of Ontario on the opposite shore of Lake Erie) London syllables, though still common, were differently combined in the strophes. So these two modes of variation – the basic syllables, and their combination – produced distinctive dialects in each locality and very different ones at opposite ends of the range. Playback experiments at Komoka and Melbourne in Ontario, 23 kilometres apart, showed that the birds were most responsive to a local variant and less so to those from other Ontario sites. A variant from Texas, in the far south, was ignored.

In discussing changes over time within one dialect area, I mentioned new recruits to the population as a fruitful source of fresh variants. One feature of the Cardinal's song points to a further way in which dialects can be modified. A syllable is often slightly altered in form in the course of its repetition in a strophe: it 'drifts'. This was noticed not only in fully developed songs in the wild, but in the early efforts of young Cardinals, reared in isolation from adults of their species, with no opportunity to learn by imitation. In the course of their juvenile subsong they began to shape song-syllables and

to repeat them: a preliminary attempt at a song-strophe.
In the repetition, drift often occurred. In this way a syllable
could be so transformed that it might well become the
starting point for a fresh strophe. Some of the fairly similar
variants in the individual repertoires of adults probably
developed by this process. The songs in Figure 49 illustrate
both drift within the strophe and a close relationship between the syllables of different songs.

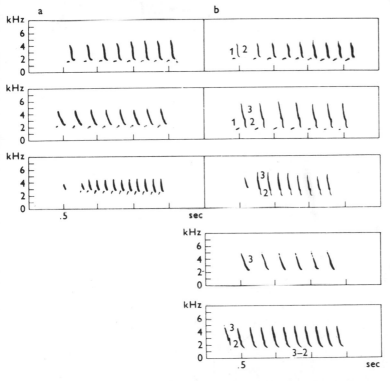

49
Cardinal songs:
the effect of
'drift' on songs of
wild birds when
combined with
separation of
syllable variants
into different
songs. (a) Songs
of a male at St
Mary's, Ontario,
in which the
syllables have the
same overall form
but sound differ-
ent; (b) songs
from London,
Ontario. Numbers
indicate compar-
able parts of a
syllable. Syllables
differ mainly in
the presence,
absence or fusion
of their compo-
nent parts (Lemon,
1971).

So, side by side with the recognized practice of modelling
their syllables and strophes on those of parents and neighbouring adults, the young birds may actively introduce an
element of change into the local repertoires. The Cardinal,
with its repetitive elements in the song, demonstrates the
effect of drift very clearly. But the same process may operate,
less detectably, in the songs and perhaps even the calls of
other species.

In Chapter 2 I described some of the lek displays of the
Black Grouse. There are members of the same family who
do not indulge in this communal activity. One of these is the

50
Whistling Canti of
male Hazel
Grouse. The upper
trace in each
diagram shows the
frequency; the
lower records
fluctuations in the
intensity of the
sound. (a) and (c)
are apparently
from the same
individual; (b) and
(d) from another
individual, both
singing in the
same recording
(S. Palmer,
Swedish Broad-
casting Corpora-
tion); (e) and (f)
recorded in France
by J. -C. Roché
('Guide sonore
des oiseaux
d'Europe')
(Hjorth, 1970).

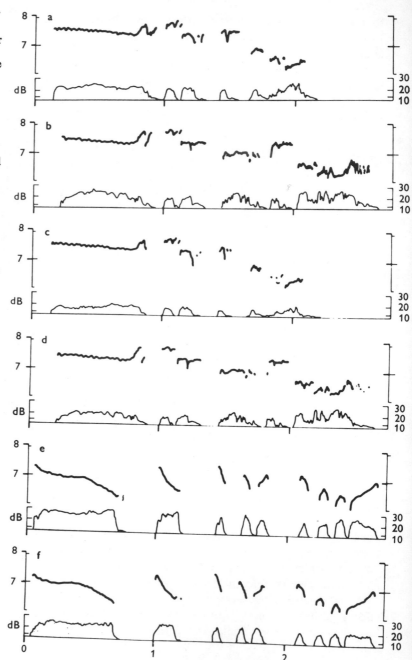

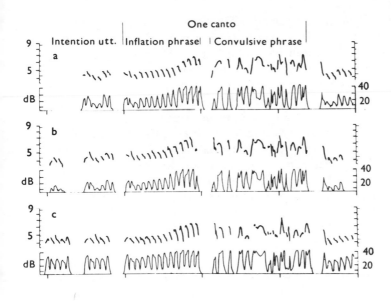

51
Rookooing Canto of Black Grouse from three different cocks. The canto may be preceded by one or more *Intention Utterances*. The elements in these are similar to the first elements in the *Inflation Phrase*. After the last note of each canto, the cock forcefully expels air. In (a) and (c) another canto followed immediately; in (b) an *Intention Utterance* was given after the canto (Hjorth, 1970).

Hazel Grouse. The male and female of this species look almost alike; they are softly coloured, with dappled plumage in browns, greys and black, and have only small red combs. The species was presumably named after the hazel shrubs among which it was supposed to live. But though it inhabits mixed woodland and conifer forest (so long as there is reasonable light, and thick broadleaf undergrowth) the Grouse is far more widely distributed than the hazel. It is found right across Europe and Asia except near the coasts at either end of the range. It has a preference for the higher latitudes, around 60° north, but in Europe it penetrates quite far south into Yugoslavia and Romania. The Hazel Grouse is an all-the-year-round resident. Only change or destruction of habitat, a forest fire, for instance, sets off the small migrating packs that are occasionally seen.

The males hold a territory and are apparently monogamous. One of the ways in which they signify territorial ownership is by 'song'. This song, or 'Whistling Canto' as it is called by Dr Ingmar Hjorth, the Swedish ornithologist who studied the reproductive behaviour of the Grouse family, is a high-pitched melody with five to nine elements of frequencies between 6 and 7·5 kiloHertz. It is often effectively imitated by hunters and the Hazel Grouse whistle in reply.

The particular interest here is that, although little is known so far about any possible regional variations in this

Saddleback

and other non-passerine families, some recordings of Hazel Grouse made in Sweden and France show a marked difference between the canti. The structure is similar but the elements are very obviously different. Figure 50 illustrates four Swedish canti – two from each of two cocks, which vary individually but have similar types of element – and two from France. As a family comparison and contrast, Figure 51 shows *Rookooing* canti from three different Black Grouse cocks, used in their displays on the lek.

These recordings were analysed electronically on a melograph. The upper part of the diagram shows traces similar to those made by the sound-spectrograph. The lower curve follows the fluctuating intensity of the signal: the higher the peak on the graph, the greater the intensity. (See Definitions of terms on page 221.)

The last example of dialect – yet another pattern, the origin of which is known – comes from a small island in the Pacific Ocean, only two and a half kilometres long and about one and a half kilometres across at its broadest point. It lies 100 kilometres north-east of Auckland, New Zealand. Its thick evergreen forests were once inhabited by a passerine species, the New Zealand Saddleback. These extraordinary birds are small and dark, with long legs and a splendid patch of golden plumage in the shape of a saddle across their backs. They also have a soft, red wattle. They are very lively birds, and active over short distances, but a few metres of level flight is all that they can manage at a time.

The previous island population had died out by the turn of the century and, with such limited flying power, recolonization from the mainland was impossible. Indeed the species as a whole was almost extinct. So in an imaginative attempt to conserve it, the New Zealand Wildlife Service took some birds to the island and released them in the forests where their subsequent behaviour has been systematically and continuously studied by Dr Peter Jenkins of the University of Auckland.

One of the most fascinating aspects has been the development of local dialect groups which radiate from the well-spaced-out territories taken up by the first resettlers. On so tiny an island the area covered by each group is comparatively small and Peter Jenkins prefers to call them 'song-groups'. The song-variants differ considerably over the island but within each song-group the birds share similar variants.

The New Zealand Saddlebacks maintain territories all

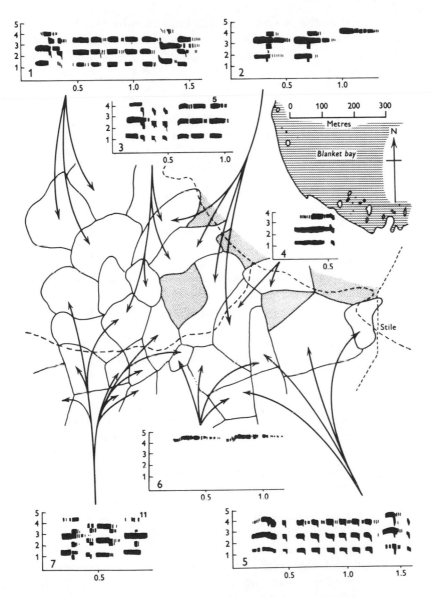

52
New Zealand Saddlebacks. The map shows part of the study area
on Cuvier Island. Boundary lines enclose individual territories and
the branching arrows link sonagrams to each song-group. The song
selected is representative of that song-group. Some birds near
group boundaries sang two of the songs shown (indicated by two
arrows). The upper traces on the sonagrams may be harmonics
or independently generated frequencies. These strongly affect the
tone quality of the sound (Jenkins).

through the year and normally keep them for life. They have an equally continuous and permanent relationship with their mates. They spend all day together, only separating for the night to solitary roosting holes. The territories are proclaimed by loud songs, with a good deal of counter-singing in which the song variants are matched. Little else is needed to keep the territories intact; aggressive encounters are rare and mutual avoidance appears to be the basic principle of the species' social organization. This would seem to be an ideal solution to the problems of a sedentary bird, with limited flying power, in a dense habitat.

Each male has between one and four song variants and analysis of their repertoires showed that all the variants are learned from neighbours wherever the bird first settles: usually in his first breeding year but occasionally later. Unless he happens to take up a territory near his father, the father's songs are not present in his repertoire. When, as sometimes happens, a bird shifts to a territory which lies within another song-group, he modifies his songs to match those of the group he has joined.

In one or two cases three-year-old birds learned new songs. So it looks as if with this species there is little, if any, genetic influence on the song and the tradition is socially or 'culturally' transmitted. There were some cases where young birds made 'mistakes' in their imitation of a song-pattern and retained it in their final version. This is clearly another potential source of song-group, or dialect, change. Figure 52 shows some individual territories in the study area on Cuvier Island, with sonagram examples of representative songs from different song-groups.

This last example of developing dialects draws attention to two matters of great importance in bird vocalizations. First there is the question of island populations. This has fascinated zoologists since Darwin observed the difference that had evolved between the isolated populations of obviously closely related finches on the Galapagos Islands and started his revolutionary work on 'The Origin of Species'.

Unless the nearest mainland is within regular flying distance for the species in question, or there is a chain of islands sufficiently close together for easy movement between them, island populations are isolated from the rest of their species. Small differences in body structure, plumage and behaviour, linked with finer adaptations to the limited habitat, can become established. Vocalizations, too, may come to diverge more and more widely from those of mainland populations. In time some of these more remote island communities may have differentiated sufficiently to be recognized as sub-species of the mainland form. The island Wrens of the Faroes, the Hebrides, Shetland, St Kilda and Iceland, for example, have long been recognized as sub-species. Their songs, though not well studied, seem to show modifications which may distinguish them from each other and from typical Wren songs on the mainland.

Secondly, the young New Zealand Saddlebacks who made a permanent muddle of their song imitations point to another source of variation in species that learn some or all of their songs – errors in the copying chain. So far, three possible sources of dialect variation have been mentioned: new recruits to the population from different dialect areas; drift, and now copying errors. To this I would add, from experience of Great Tits, the presence in a population of particularly 'talented' individuals – birds that produce more than normally complicated, or individually varied, versions of their species' songs. Such versions may not readily be taken up by other birds but sometimes they are, even if the imitations are not perfect. Every sensitive bird-listener is aware of this phenomenon of the good singer in many songbird species though in some it is an elusive quality to analyse.

This brief summary and, indeed, the whole question of dialect variation, introduce topics that need separate discussion and illustration. They are: individual recognition; the evidence that vocalizations offer on evolutionary relationships between species; imitation both within and between species; and the capacity of certain species and individuals for great elaboration in their songs. These topics are the subjects of the next four chapters.

8 Individual Recognition

In contrast to almost all other North American birds, each Song Sparrow sings songs that are different from those of every other Song Sparrow . . . The definite knowledge of Uno's and 4M's songs whenever heard was an important aid to me when listening to the birds from the sleeping porch in the early morning hours, and from my study during the day. It also proved an added source of happiness, for I became aware of character and loveliness to which I had formerly been oblivious. 4Ms' song *A* had a determined, almost grim sound; with *C*, he seemed in a desperate hurry; *G* was light and airy – a charming song; and *K* was the prettiest of all, with the gayest little lilt at the end. Uno's *H* was spirited, and his *C* had a triumphant ring, while *F* was high and clear, of exquisite haunting beauty. Indeed, as far as variety of singing went, it was as if fifteen birds of different species had settled on our grounds.   *Margaret Morse Nice*

Uno and 4M were territorial neighbours, nearly 50 years ago, in a garden in Columbus, Ohio. They were not, of course, relatives of the gregarious, chattering House Sparrows of Europe. On the North American side of the Atlantic 'sparrows' are buntings – members of the same family as the European Yellowhammer which makes the beauty of their songs seem less improbable to us in Europe. It must have been their size and the beige and brown-streaked plumage that led to their naming by the early settlers from Britain.

4M survived for nearly nine years to become world famous among ornithologists as well as readers of Margaret Morse Nice's popular account of her work. For he had settled by the home of a woman who, as an amateur, produced a scientific study of his species that has become required reading for students of bird behaviour.

In all studies that are concerned with the fine details of behaviour, only work with individually identified birds can produce the kind of information that is needed. At first this information is anecdotal – a word that is sometimes used with undertones of contempt in scientific literature and justifiably so if the anecdote makes much of an unusual piece of behaviour for which there is no supporting evidence. Poor observation, over-imaginative interpretation – or both – are immediately suspected. But experienced and cautious field observers know that a single episode can raise questions with wide implications, and open new lines of enquiry. Interpretations are tested by further observation and experiment until a series of anecdotes turns into a consistent story.

This is the way in which knowledge of the behaviour of a

little studied species is gradually extended. 4M and his like who, all unwittingly, have lived their lives under scientific surveillance, have put us in their debt.

This chapter is about only one aspect of the individuality of birds – their capacity to identify each other by voice. Such individual recognition demands two things: sufficient information in the sound signal itself and the ability of the receiving bird to extract it from a song or call carrying other information to which the receiver is also attending.

On the second point, the ability of most bird species to discriminate very precisely between sounds is no longer in doubt. What has to be established in each case is that the birds are using this ability for individual recognition by sound alone and not responding to other clues in a given situation. On the first point, as we have seen, the range of acceptable variation in certain signals, especially song, may be quite wide. But it must not deviate so far from the normal signals as to be unrecognizable. Individual differences, therefore, can only be conveyed by variation in particular parameters or by the elaboration of detail within this acceptable range.

Interest in individual recognition, and experimental testing of its validity, is a fairly recent development. Even where the fact is established it is not always possible, with the equipment we have at present, to work out exactly how the information is carried in the signal. With such varied sound patterns it is also bound to vary from species to species.

The Song Sparrows, for instance, whose songs are highly individual (they share, at most, one or two variants out of an average of 16 in the repertoire of each male) need to learn all the variants of their neighbours if they are not to go dashing off after suspected intruders several times a day. Some recent experiments show that while they do respond a little more strongly to playbacks of songs from non-neighbouring males than to those of their neighbours, the difference is not as great as it has been found to be in some other species – so perhaps they do not manage to learn all their neighbours' variants. Perhaps, too, this form of song repertoire is not well adapted for conveying individual identity.

Great Tits appear to be in much the same case but they and a number of other species with this form of repertoire share rather more of their variants with their neighbours. Individual identification possibly rests on rather subtle distinctions in the form of the elements, in emphasis, and even in the timbre of the voice. Most of these distinctions in the Great Tit can be detected by the human ear, especially on slowed down recordings. Some are shown clearly on sonagrams, others are not. For this particular purpose different types of sound analysis are needed to supplement the sound-spectrograph.

Whatever the distinctions that we can detect, the essential evidence for individual recognition is the response of the birds themselves. In a natural experiment Johnny, our back-garden territory owner for nearly ten years, may have provided some interesting anecdotal information to add to the results of playback experiments. In Chapter 4 I mentioned that he had learnt to ignore playbacks of Great Tit sounds in the house or garden but in the last years of his life we caught him out once, quite unintentionally. It was outside the song season and we were in the middle of a long session of listening to recordings of Great Tit variants including many heard in the neighbourhood the previous summer. As always there had been no reaction from Johnny. After some time we happened to play one of the variants of a long-dead territorial neighbour of his.

Immediately Johnny appeared. We saw him through the window, flying towards the corner of the house. Inside, the song was playing; outside was their old boundary where Johnny had been accustomed to have trouble with this lively and rather pushing rival. He perched on a little willow tree and looked around. Then he seemed to realize that it was all a mistake. At any rate, he took no further action and went quietly back to the centre of the garden. If he had recognized his old rival's song, as his behaviour suggested, Johnny had given us evidence of an aural memory of an individual voice that spanned five years.

Differences between individual versions of the same Great Tit song-variant that show up on sonagrams are illustrated in Figure 53. This displays the complete song repertoires of Johnny himself and of Yellow-Right who took up residence in an adjoining territory some years after Johnny's arrival on the scene. Yellow-Right was the youngster who was born on the territory and inherited it from his father (Chapter 7). So he was within earshot of Johnny's singing from his early life in the nest and in his important first adult spring. He almost certainly learned four of his variants from his older neighbour. Two of them were not sung by any other bird in the district at the time (δ 11 b and d). One of these is discussed,

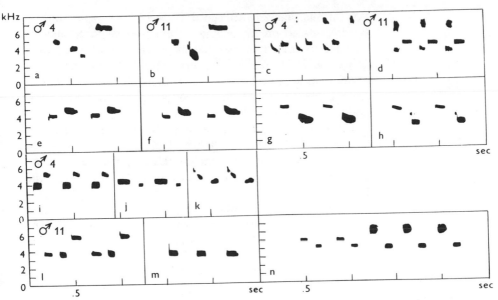

53
Song-repertoires
of two male Great
Tits: Johnny
(♂4) and Yellow-
Right (♂11). The
variants they
shared are (a) and
(b); (c) and (d);
(e) and (f);
(g) and (h).
Johnny's other
variants are (i),
(j), (k), and Yellow-
Right's are (l),
(m) and (n).

for other reasons, in Chapter 11. The remaining two variants that he shared with Johnny (his f and h) are widespread in this and many other Great Tit populations. Johnny and Yellow-Right each had seven variants, three of which were not shared and these are also shown in Figure 53 (♂ 4 i, j and k and ♂ 11 l, m and n).

Some types of song are easier than the Great Tit's to investigate experimentally for individual recognition. One of these is the song of the White-throated Sparrow of North America. This is a common bunting, breeding in open coniferous forest and scrubby forest-edge, right across most of Canada and into some of the more northerly parts of the United States. It is a relative of the Song Sparrow and can be found in some of the same habitats. Their songs, incidentally, are quite different.

The song of the White-throated Sparrow consists of long, clear whistled sounds, fairly constant in pitch and very pure in tone. Comparatively few species use notes of this kind in territorial song, where sounds with a wider frequency range help to locate the singer. However, in the White-throated Sparrow's song, the repetition of the elements and their relatively low frequency must compensate for this to some extent because it was found that the birds located the direc-

tion of the signal with speed and accuracy. The song is typically based on five elements. But the last three may be repeated twice or more so that the song is variable in length as well as in its rate of delivery. This two-note-and-triplet rhythm has led to a Canadian mnemonic of 'I love Canada'. Among New Englanders, the equivalent is 'Old Sam Peabody.'

The songs vary: for example in their overall pattern, in loudness, absolute pitch, change of pitch between elements, and the duration of the elements. Usually there are one or two changes of pitch in the course of each song and in the two commonest basic patterns, one has a rise in pitch after the first note, and the other a drop in pitch after the second (Figure 54). Each male normally has only one song-pattern: more rarely a second which is less frequently used.

**54
White-throated
Sparrows of North
America: the two
most common
basic song-
patterns (Falls,
1969).**

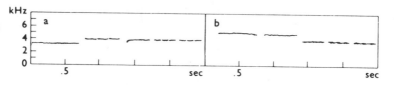

The response of territorial males in the wild to different forms of the species' songs has been investigated by a Canadian ornithologist, Professor Bruce Falls, and his colleagues at the University of Toronto, using techniques similar to those described for the study of Robin song in Chapter 4. The pure tones of the White-throated Sparrow's song can be simulated by an oscillator and variations in the frequency and duration of each element introduced. So natural songs, and artificially altered songs, were used in playback experiments to discover the relative importance of different parameters for species recognition and for recognition of an individual bird.

It appeared that the pitch of the song was important for both. As with the Robin, only a certain range of frequencies was acceptable. An otherwise unaltered song pitched above or below this critical range was not recognized. Individual songs differ in pitch within this range. They also differ in the relative pitch of the elements. The overall pattern of the strophe, the relative timing of the elements, and the relative loudness of the elements, are other characteristics which vary in individuals but remain constant in the performance of each bird. So several parameters could be involved in individual recognition in the White-throated Sparrow.

Other playback experiments were made to test reactions to natural songs from neighbours and from birds recorded some distance away. These experiments left no doubt that territorial males recognized the songs of their neighbours. As a rule they responded to the playback of a neighbour's song only after several repetitions of the strophe. But when a stranger's song was played, they often replied after the first strophe. They also sang more and continued to sing for much longer after the stranger's song had ceased. On one occasion a genuine stranger was attracted by a playback. He approached the loudspeaker and began to sing. At that moment, the male for whose benefit the playback was conducted was being tested with a neighbour's song. But as soon as the stranger started to sing, the territory-holder chased him, ignoring the recorded song of the neighbour.

However, it was found that the location of the singer was important. Territory holders responded strongly to the songs of strangers whatever direction they came from. But if a territory holder heard the song of the neighbour who lived to the south of him, for example, coming instead from his northern boundary, he responded to it as if to a stranger's. It may be that the location of the singer in the 'correct' place helps recognition. On the other hand even if the song was recognized, there might be reasons connected with the security of the territory for reacting strongly to a neighbour who has turned up in the wrong place. These particular experiments could not distinguish between the two possible interpretations of this consistent response.

The advantage of individual voice recognition among small birds who spend much of their time in cover is obvious. Their distance vision is known to be acute. But on many of their daily occasions this ability is little use to them. In the concealing environments vocal individuality could prevent the waste of time and energy involved in searching for the wrong companion, or chasing an 'intruder' who turns out to be an amicable neighbour.

In the last few years a great deal of work has been done on individual acoustic recognition in seabirds. With these species the problem is a different one. On the whole they are fairly large, conspicuous birds. In the air, on water or on land, there are few obstacles to obstruct their vision. But there are other visual barriers. Mist, glare reflected from the surface of the water or rocks, and their own superb manoeuvrability in flight, so that they are perpetually approaching one another from different angles, must all make visual adjustment difficult.

Above all many of these species nest in colonies: tens of thousands of birds on shores, dune-slopes or the ledges of a rocky cliff-face. Anyone who has watched the traffic movements in and out of the great bird-cliffs on the coasts and islands of northern and western Britain is aware of the bewildering number of birds leaving or landing on the rock ledges at any given moment.

The location of the nest by a bird returning from a fishing expedition at sea may be achieved visually, though it must require very accurate orientation. Gannets, for instance, nest 'a beak-stab apart' as one account graphically puts it. But vocal identification between the returning bird and its mate, or between parent and offspring, on the final approach might avoid either embarrassing landings on the wrong site or the starvation of young birds who were continually overlooked. Individual differences in the appropriate calls of adults have now been shown for a number of these species.

The Gannets, magnificent fliers, with black tips to their powerful white wings, nest mainly on offshore rockstacks and islands. They catch fish in spectacular dives, folding their wings as they plummet down from a considerable height above the sea. On the upper slopes and cliff-tops where the nests are sited, the parents share the task of brooding during the long incubation period and then comes another three months or so during which the single chick (more rarely two) has to be fed.

The *landing calls* of adult Gannets were studied in the great colony on the Bass Rock in the Firth of Forth by Sheila and Richard White, working with Professor W. H. Thorpe. It was found that mates certainly recognized each other's calls and did not respond to those of neighbours. There was some evidence that the young also recognized their parents' calls though they were not so obviously responsive to them.

Sonagrams of these repeated, single-note calls revealed no features that consistently identified individuals. But when the sounds were analysed for amplitude[1] variation (changes of loudness in the course of the signal) individual differences

[1] See 'Definitions of Terms' for the relationship between the amplitude of a sound and our perception of its loudness (p. 221).

emerged and these were most significant at the beginning of each call-note.[1] It is not known how well birds perceive variations in amplitude; since these are also variations in time, the birds could pick up the changes in the signal in this way. There may be other parameters, not detected by our present types of equipment, within which Gannet calls differ individually. However, amplitude variation could be a useful component in the signal to ensure individual recognition. Amplitude suffers less than the frequency pattern from the 'train whistle' distortion caused by movement. In a call given on the swift approach flight to the nest it might therefore be a valuable adaptation, and in future it may be possible to test the response of birds to small changes in amplitude.

Amplitude variations, as well as individual characteristics which show up clearly on sonagrams, have been found in an important call given by Sandwich Terns. This graceful species also nests colonially, mainly on sand dunes and shores. While the young terns are still dependent on their parents for food, they start to wander exploratively along the shore in sizeable groups. This, it seems, is where the parental *fish call* functions as a signal to each youngster that its own parent is approaching with food for it. Apparently the parents make no attempt to look for their offspring in a particular place but circle low over the shore giving this call. One youngster will show signs of excitement while the rest take no notice. If there is no response, even when the parent lands, it takes off again and continues to circle and call. It may be some time before the right chick is located.

The relationship between parent and offspring in these communal yet highly individual seabird societies is a very close one and I should like to illustrate it in more detail from studies that have been made in the Zoological Institute of the University of Bern in Switzerland by Professor Beat Tschanz and his colleagues. One of the species that they have

studied for many years is the Guillemot. Young birds were hatched and hand-reared in the laboratory so that their calls and associated behaviour could be more closely observed and the field work was carried out on the bird-cliffs of the Lofoten Islands off the coast of Norway.

The Guillemot is a fairly large bird: about 42 centimetres long. In summer plumage it is dark brown on its upper parts, head and neck, and white underneath. As it sits upright on rock ledges the slender neck and long, pointed bill give it an elegant appearance. The northern race on the Lofoten Islands is almost black rather than brown and a greater number of birds are 'bridled' than in the southern race – they have a white eye-ring and a fine white line extending back from the eye.

There is no nest; the individually marked, solitary egg is laid on the exposed ledges and in crevices of the cliff. Nor is there any spacing out of territories – the distance between one Guillemot pair and the next may be only a few centimetres. Close family relationships ensure that each chick is reared by its own parents and these relationships are largely maintained by vocal signals between parent and parent, and parents and chick.

The chick is dependent on its parents for a long time. It remains on the ledge and is fed by them. On the Lofoten Islands this period was at least 25 days and it may be as much as 40 days after hatching when the chick jumps from the ledge and takes to the sea 200 metres or so below. It is unable to fly properly for about another three weeks and continues to be fed on the water.

As in the precocial species that have been studied its vocalizations begin in the egg. This is cradled on the feet of the incubating parent (both birds share this duty) and covered by the belly feathers. In the later stages of incubation parent and embryo certainly communicate by sound.

The intensity and variation of this activity can be guessed at from the behaviour of Guillemot embryos in the incubator. 71 hours before it hatched, with the shell of the egg still unpipped, chick no. 57 uttered 91 calls in one five minute period. This was while the egg was being turned by the experimenter, Matilde Schommer. On the cliff ledge the incubating parent would also turn the egg from time to time (though probably not for so long a period). In the next hour the chick gave only 13 calls.

The embryos are listening as well as calling. Laboratory

tests showed that during the time in the egg the chicks learn the individual characteristics of their parents' *luring call* (used only to the young). When, after hatching, the recordings of a call that had been repeatedly played to them in the egg, and a new call, were played simultaneously from two loud-speakers, most of the chicks approached only the call they had heard in the egg. If no calls had been played to the eggs the chicks had no preference when offered a choice of call after hatching.

In their first few days of life, when warmth and darkness are important to them, the chicks snuggle among the feathers of the adult birds and sometimes a small beak can be seen protruding between the strong wing feathers, which must act as a comfortable headprop. If a chick has wandered away from this safe hiding-place it will not follow the luring call of a strange Guillemot but responds quickly if the parent calls it back again. Chicks approach a loudspeaker on their cliff-ledge if it is playing the parental calls but not if the calls are those of other adults. A chick has been known to respond to the loudspeaker even if one of its parents was calling, but not as persistently, from further along the ledge.

No chickless adult succeeds in adopting a chick by calling it away from its own parents. But a chick that is left alone for some time in these early days tries to hide anywhere – in a rock crevice or under a strange adult – that offers warmth and darkness. If its own parent returns and gives the luring call the chick answers but until it is warm again the shelter of the strange adult is the stronger attraction. Once warmed up, it responds to its parent's call and comes 'home'. An orphaned chick may be adopted by another adult. At first the absence of the right luring call is a problem at feeding time. But chicks can learn new calls, at least up to the age of 20 days, so an adjustment to the new situation can be made.

Their learning capacity, and their preference for sound over visual stimuli (though they used these as well), was shown in some experiments with the hand-reared chicks. They were first conditioned to a pad where they found shelter and food. Once the pad was established as home they were played a particular call, or even conditioned to the sound of their own names at feeding times; for they were given names as well as numbers for this purpose. When, after this condition-ing, they were presented with a choice between the food pad and their experimental sound they immediately went towards the sound.

55
Luring calls of
three adult
Guillemots: L1,
L2 and L3 shown
on sonagrams
(Tschanz).

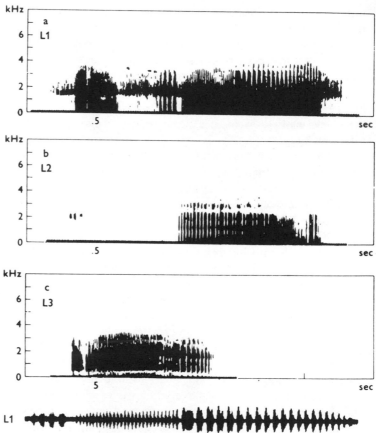

56
The same three
calls from Guille-
mots L1, L2 and
L3 shown on
oscillograms
(Tschanz, 1969).

The luring calls of the adults show individual differences
which probably account for the response of the chicks to
them. Figures 55 and 56 show the luring calls of three adult
Guillemots. Figure 55 shows them in sonagram form.
Figure 56 gives the same three calls displayed on a different
type of machine, the oscillograph. This traces the amplitude
of the signal, and all the frequencies are combined instead of
being separated out as they are on the sound-spectrograph.
The different sections of the low-pitched, vibrant call can be
seen and compared in these two forms of visual presentation.
However, though each call is characteristic of the individual,

there can still be some variation in its delivery. Figure 57 shows oscillograms of the luring call of a fourth adult: each line is a separate version of the same call. But although the signals differ in duration and the first section of the call is sometimes omitted, the basic pattern is unchanged, and quite different from any of the three shown in Figures 55 and 56.

In experiments with calls that were altered in various ways, the ability of the chicks to identify and reject the changed versions indicated that they had an exact memory of the characteristics of the individual calls they knew. But if the only choice presented was between two very considerably altered calls, a chick would select the one that was nearer to the form of the 'right' call.

The parents, too, recognize the calls of their own chick, at the latest when it is ten days old. If in fact they do not do so up to that time (this point is difficult to demonstrate) the chick's own strong response to the parents' calls is probably its main safeguard. It is also less likely to be separated from them in the early days of close brooding. All the calls of the young change during the course of development. In those that differ individually, the individual characteristics become more strongly marked as the chicks get older.

They have several calls, associated with different situations. The *pecking call* is given when they peck at fish or any object

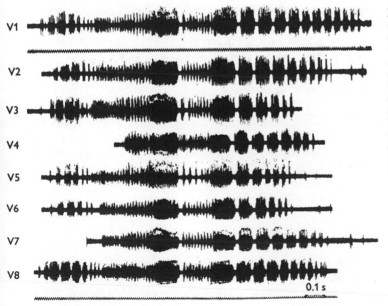

57
Eight versions (V) of the *luring call* of a fourth adult Guillemot. Although sounds are omitted from the beginning and end of the call in some versions, the basic pattern is the same, and differs from the calls in Figure 56 (Tschanz, 1968).

that interests them, such as a small stone. In the laboratory they gave it when pecking at the experimenter's hand. The *contact call* was given when everything was more or less as it should be or when they were snuggling in the hand. But they used it in response to a familiar sound even when they had been placed in unfamiliar surroundings. The *contact-weeping call*, as the Bern workers have called it, is variable – another example of an inter-grading call. It seems to indicate some degree of distress for the hand-reared chicks gave it when in unfamiliar surroundings.

The two calls that differ most obviously between one chick and another are the *weeping call* and the *water call*. Human observers can distinguish individual versions of both of these when the chicks are only four to five days old. The weeping call seems to be a true distress signal. The water call, on the other hand, might be given by the hand-reared birds in any surroundings in response to a familiar sound, or even without any obvious stimulus. From the time they were about three weeks old they were particularly apt to give the water-call in the evenings.

The adults also have a water-call – a special form of one of their inter-grading calls – directed to the young. It is given, for example, when their chick is calling but is out of reach; when it is ready to leap from the ledge into the water, or has done so and landed short. This call is also given as the parent lands on the water near a youngster. If the chick is not its own the adult calls again. When the chicks are on the water with the adults, not far from the cliff, the general noise is considerable. Yet amidst all this sound and movement, the parents and chicks recognize each other's calls and manage to reunite after a separation.

Figure 58 shows sonagrams of the chick calls as given by four hand-reared chicks (including no. 57 whose vocal behaviour in the egg has been referred to already). The pecking call, the contact call and the two forms of weeping call, are each single elements. The water call is delivered in groups of repeated elements. It also has up to five changes of pitch within each element: more than occur in the other calls. The much greater degree of individuality in this and the weeping call is evident on the sonagrams.

Studies of this kind are very demanding. For several years on end, months of field work in difficult conditions are paralleled by months of laboratory work with young birds;

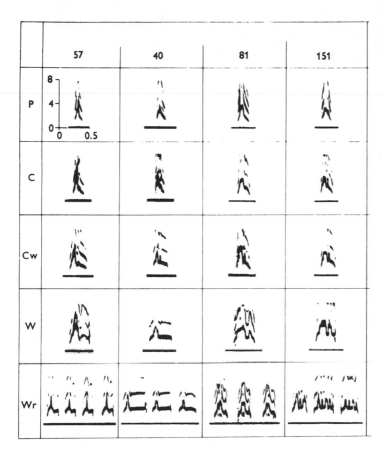

58
Sonagram examples of the calls of four Guillemot chicks (nos. 57, 40, 81 and 151) at the age of 3–4 weeks. P = pecking call; C = contact call; Cw = contact-weeping call; W = weeping call; Wr = water call (Schommer and Tschanz, 1975).

and the analysis of hours of tape-recordings and of numerous sonagrams and oscillograms. Then comes the compilation of the text, tables and graphs in which the findings are presented to the scientific community. A more detailed picture than ever before of the behaviour of a species, or some aspect of it, has been built up. The evidence has been assembled from statistically significant samples; the comparison of the behaviour of experimental groups and control groups; the repetition of observations and tests in the field and the laboratory.

This approach is essential simply because birds are individuals. Within the limits set by the behaviour patterns which ensure the continuity of their species they have their personal vagaries and variations.

So – and I come back to the point I made at the beginning of the chapter – although a considerable number of birds are involved in such studies, all of them in their time were individually known to their observers. Their idiosyncrasies are part of the objective report of the facts. I am glad to have made the acquaintance of Song Sparrow 4M and Guillemot chick no. 57, even at second hand.

9 Far Away and Long Ago

How surely it has been borne upon me that the glimpses of minutes, days or even weeks, which a life of bird-watching as a hobby have given, are inadequate for an interpretation or solution of the deeper problems of evolution, natural selection and survival in the bird world! We need time, time, time and a sense of timelessness. Our pictures of behaviour must be detailed in time equally with those of space.

The social pattern of a species may have to be fulfilled before the cardinal process of reproduction can take place. *Frank Fraser Darling*

It is necessary now to change the perspective and to think about the behaviour of generation after generation of birds on different continents. The Guillemots of the Lofoten Islands, the New Zealand Saddlebacks, the Song Sparrows of Columbus, Ohio, the Chaffinches and the Great and Coal Tits of Britain and Continental Europe exemplify the flexibility and individuality of behaviour in the living bird. But they show us only the present stage in a long chronology.

The subtle distinctions in voice (as in plumage and many other characteristics) which mark each bird as an individual are no more than variations on the theme of its species. This theme both proclaims the species and separates it from all others. It may change slowly with time, for species are not immutable. It may be changing more, and perhaps more rapidly, in some parts of the species' range than in others. But at any moment of time, over extensive areas, the theme is aurally and visually constant.

When we say 'a species' we are talking about a group of animals whose members are capable in the wild of mating and of producing offspring which survive and reproduce in their turn. It is the only concept in the classification of avian relationships with a significance that can be observed in the daily behaviour of the birds themselves. The broader group-ings of species into subgenera, genera and families are based on human judgements. They are an assessment of the degree of kinship between birds: between all living species and the extinct species in the fossil record. They are also, therefore, an indication of the probable lines of evolutionary development.

Human judgements of this kind are rarely unanimous and they are liable to be revised in the light of new evidence – to the confusion of the unwary user of an outdated bird book who discovers that elsewhere a familiar species has had its

Latin name changed and is listed in a different genus or even family. The many revisions of the last twenty years or so have been made largely because the new approach to the classification of living species includes ecological, physiological, biochemical, genetic and behavioural evidence. This approach has modified opinions based on the outward appearance and skeletal features of museum specimens, essential though these characteristics are for primary identification.

The species, then, is the unit on which the evolutionary processes are continually at work. It is not only a question of the extinction of species in which, as we now know very well, man has taken a hand by predation or by habitat destruction. Surviving species retain their identity while remaining adaptable. Yet even so new species are still being formed from them and it is possible to discern some of the intermediate stages at the present time.

The theme of this chapter is the possible role of vocalizations in the continuing separation of existing species and the proliferation of new ones.

While species-in-the-making are evolving from a common ancestral stock, their differences are sharpened by environmental pressures and the adaptations these impose. Visible changes take place in the size, shape or colour of body structures and plumage. To effect and retain these visible changes there are also changes in the controlling gene-complexes. A successful balance is evolved in the genetic make-up of the emergent species between sufficient variability for further adaptations (the evolutionary safety-valve) and essential stability.

Bird breeders make use of the fact that certain closely-related species can interbreed in captivity. In some cases these crosses produce hybrids that survive and reproduce but this does not always happen. Breeding may be possible but the hybrid offspring either die, or are infertile, because the re-combination of genes has produced incompatibilities.

Evolutionary time and energy would be wasted if such unproductive episodes frequently took place in the wild. It is obvious from the integrity of living species that they rarely do. Visible differences in form are often striking enough to prevent hybridization between closely related species living in the same area. But it is clear that other mechanisms may be operating as well. For example such species may be separated ecologically: different feeding habits, the occupation of different levels in woodland, or of different types of ground, often effectively isolate them from one another. Their visual displays, while showing a family resemblance, may have come to differ sufficiently, in combination with plumage changes, to prevent recognition of their significance by the related species.

It is now widely accepted that vocalizations can act as yet another isolating mechanism, as it is called, between species. As we have seen not all vocalizations operate in this way. Alarm calls, for instance, or flight calls, may be very similar in members of the same genus or family. (There may even be a resemblance in such calls between species that are only very distantly related. No one can be certain why, but the reasons may be environmental and acoustic.) These calls, however, are not used in situations where the identity of the species is the only important factor. The vocalizations that act as isolating mechanisms are song (particularly among territorial species) and calls associated with mate selection and courtship. The differentiation of these sound signals is an evolutionary time and energy saver if, with other isolating mechanisms, it helps to prevent unsuccessful hybridization.

Much attention has been paid to the so-called 'sibling species'. The Willow Warbler and the Chiffchaff are a good example of this. Sibling species pass the species test in that they do not normally interbreed in the wild. But they are obviously closely related and are very similar in appearance. They are present in the same habitats over at least part of their ranges. In the cases that have been investigated, the songs have been found to be sufficiently different to prevent cases of mistaken identity in areas where the sibling species occur together. In most cases this has not only been observed but checked by playback experiments to test the reaction of each to the song of the sibling species.

All this applies to the Willow Warbler and the Chiffchaff. These two warblers are so much alike in appearance that few ornithologists, catching only a glimpse of a silent bird, could be sure which it was. Gilbert White, in the late eighteenth century, was the first to establish the fact that these were two species and not one. He noted particularly the difference in song, and in the length of their song-seasons. His observations and the increasing certainty of his identification are recorded in various letters in 'The Natural history and antiquities of Selborne'. It was a splendid piece of detective work at that time. (He also distinguished both from a third very similar species, the Wood Warbler.)

There are many differences in the song of the two species. For example, although some of the elements are similar, others differ greatly; the Willow Warbler strophes are divided into sections with a changing rhythmic pattern while the Chiffchaff's strophe lacks these divisions, has a continuous, simple rhythm and is more variable in length. The Willow Warbler has a greater frequency range and the pitch descends in each strophe while the Chiffchaff maintains a fairly steady pitch within a narrower frequency range.

The possible course of events is that at some period in their evolutionary history, populations of the common ancestor of these two species were separated (perhaps by Ice Age barriers) for long enough to develop the minor visible differences in leg colour and feathering which also distinguish them. In addition, they may have evolved, at least partly, their distinctive types of song. When the two forms began to occupy the same areas once again, they no longer recognized each other so that there was little, if any hybridization.

So far, so good: similar hypotheses are made for other sibling species since two species could hardly evolve from one as long as the birds are in contact in the same area. However the particular interest of the 'Willow-Chiff' story is provided by the Chiffchaff's part in it.

Samples of Chiffchaff song from a very extensive region of northern and central Europe (over 4000 kilometres from north to south) were analysed by Dr Gerhard Thielcke and Dr K. L. Linsenmair, and the lack of geographical variation found was striking. Less rigorous observations confirm that the song is fairly consistent over an even greater part of the species' range. But in Spain and Portugal the Chiffchaff's song is very different. It shares some of the characteristics of the Willow Warbler's song and some of the normal Chiffchaff's.

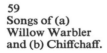

59
Songs of (a)
Willow Warbler
and (b) Chiffchaff.

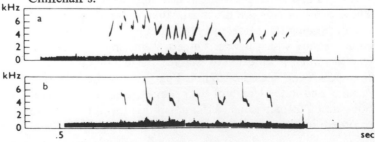

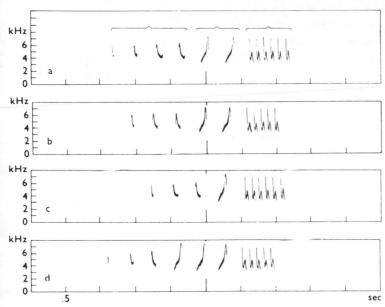

60
Four song-stro-
phes from a
Spanish Chiffchaff
showing the divi-
sion into sections
(horizontal
brackets), as in a
Willow Warbler
song (Thielcke
and Linsenmair,
1963).

Figures 59 and 60 give examples of song from each of the three types for comparison: Willow Warbler, Chiffchaff and Spanish Chiffchaff. Figure 60 illustrates four strophes from a Spanish Chiffchaff in which the division of the strophe into sections (a Willow Warbler characteristic) can be seen. But in its smaller frequency range the song is more like the Chiffchaff's. In yet other ways the Spanish type of song differs from both.

The Spanish song is heard only in the Spanish peninsula, a small area of south-western France and in north-west Africa. As a further complication there is an area of overlap in south-western France where there are some 'mixed singers' among the Chiffchaffs. These birds sing both the song of the Spanish Chiffchaff and the normal song or a mixture of the two which is nearer to the Spanish type. A mixed form of song is heard on the Canary Islands: Figure 61 shows a song recorded on the island of Tenerife.

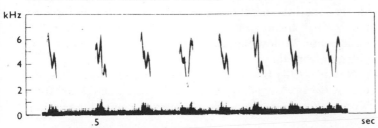

61
Song of a Chiff-
chaff from Tene-
rife, Canary
Islands.

So, possibly, another stage of evolutionary history can be reconstructed. It is known that during the last Ice Age, there were two refuge areas in southern Europe where birds survived – one in the east, the other in the west. It may be that what we now know as the 'normal' Chiffchaff, along with the Willow Warbler, was confined to the eastern refuge where, as sibling species, they may have continued to differentiate vocally even more strongly. But the Chiffchaffs isolated in the western refuge and surviving in north-west Africa and the islands retained more of the characteristics of the ancestral form of song. For it is thought from these, and other studies of the songs and calls by Dr Michael Schubert in Germany, that vocally the Chiffchaff is closer to the common ancestor than is the Willow Warbler. But the Chiffchaff's song, too, probably continued to evolve in the western refuge. By the time the two Chiffchaff groups came together again after the last retreat of the European ice-cap they had not diverged sufficiently to behave as 'good' species. But they were different enough, particularly in song, to restrict interbreeding.

In a series of experimental playbacks in south-west Germany, the three main song types were played to Willow Warbler and normally singing Chiffchaff males. Both species reacted well to the song of their own species and very little to that of the sibling species. Both reacted more strongly to the Spanish song than to the sibling type; confirmation that each recognized characteristics in it which corresponded more closely with their own song.

A slightly different story emerges from a study of the Willow Tits by Herr Willi Thönen in Switzerland. More accurately, perhaps, we may be reading a different chapter in the evolutionary history of this small, black and fawn coloured member of the tit family.

Until fairly recently the Willow Tit of North America (the Black-capped Chickadee) and the Willow Tit of Europe and Asia were regarded as members of the same species with the Latin name of *Parus atricapillus*. The genus *Parus* includes all the true tits and the species are widely distributed over the whole of the northern hemisphere though apart from the problematic Willow Tit the North American tit species are different from those of Europe and Asia.

Nowadays the Black-capped Chickadee retains the specific title of *Parus atricapillus* while the European and Asian form is called *Parus montanus*. Next, however, comes the question of the subdivision of the species into subspecies: forms which differ slightly but which are still capable of interbreeding in the wild. And this is where the song types of the Willow Tit become interesting for there is one European subspecies, the Alpine Tit, which sings quite differently from the rest.

When species are subdivided by the systematists they are given another Latin adjective to describe the subspecies to which they belong. The Alpine Tit is called *Parus montanus montanus* and it is found only in the Swiss Alps and their foothills. Another subspecies (or race) *Parus montanus salicarius* more or less encircles it and, in turn, is replaced by yet other races in the rest of the species range in Europe and Asia.[1] All of these, at least in Europe, sing the 'normal' Willow Tit song. The boundary between the two song types is so sharp that in some Swiss valleys the Alpine song can be heard on one side of the valley and the normal song on the opposite side. But in three places along the boundary there are small mixed zones where the birds sing both types of song and respond to playbacks of both. These three localities are also transitional zones for the other characteristics which distinguish *montanus* from *salicarius*. Elsewhere along the boundary the two races fail to recognize each other's song.

It is thought that the Alpine Tit may have been the older form in Europe, driven by the Ice Age from its mountain home to which it returned as the ice-cap retreated. The Alpine Tit then came into contact with other members of the species but interbred only rarely. It seems therefore as if a development in these two forms of the Willow Tit which might have led to separation into distinct species (as with the Willow Warbler and the Chiffchaff) was halted half way. They are still capable of interbreeding but rarely do so because they have a well defined geographical and altitudinal boundary in the Alps. Their very different songs no doubt help to maintain their separation but do not seem to hinder hybridization in the mixed zones, where both song-types are recognized.

Now comes the problem of their North American Willow Tit relatives. The song of the Black-capped Chickadee is very similar to that of the Alpine Tit. These North American and European/Asian species could never meet in the wild so we cannot know whether they would hybridize in natural conditions. But the similarity of the Black-capped Chickadee and

---

[1] See 'Definitions of Terms' (page 221).

62
Songs of the
Marsh and Willow
Tits of Europe and
Asia and two
related North
American species.
(a) One song-form
of the Marsh Tit;
(b, c) two versions
(same individual)
of the normal
song of the
European Willow
Tit; (d, e) two
versions
(same individual)
of the alpine race
of the European
Willow Tit; (f)
song of Black-
capped Chickadee;
(g) song of
Carolina Chick-
adee (Thönen,
1962).

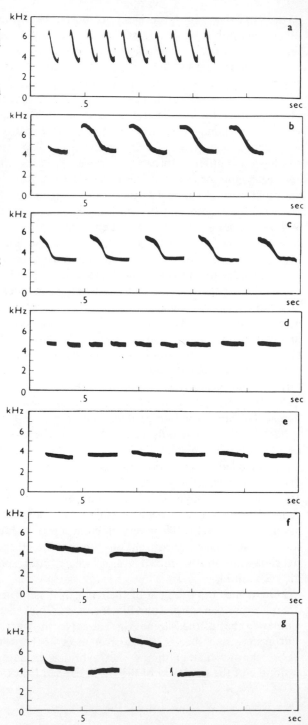

Alpine Tit songs emphasizes their close relationship and perhaps renews the question mark over the separation into two
species. Figure 62 illustrates the songs of the Alpine and the
lowland races of the European Willow Tit and the song of
the Black-capped Chickadee. This figure also shows the
songs of two other close relatives: one in Europe and one in
North America.

Parus palustris, the Marsh Tit, is the sibling species of the
Willow Tit in Europe and Asia. Though very much alike in
appearance the two species can be distinguished visually in
the field, with experience, but the safest clues are their songs
and calls. Even these, however, have some resemblances and
bird listeners often discuss how best to describe the difference
in the sounds of a very similar call that both use, for this call
is often the sole indication of the presence of one or other
species in a wood. It is the *tchay* call, more or less the equivalent of the Great Tit *churr*. (These alarm or scolding calls in
the genus *Parus* are discussed later in this chapter.)

The sonogram of one of the Marsh Tit's song-variants in
Figure 62 shows that though the song is very different, the
elements in this variant are much more like those in the normal
European Willow Tit song than in the Alpine type.

Parus carolinensis, the Carolina Chickadee, replaces the
Black-capped Chickadee in the southern part of the United
States with an area of overlap) and its song contains elements
resembling those of the Black-capped Chickadee and the
Alpine Tit.

The vocalizations of this group of species and races, on
two continents, are just one indication of the complicated
relationships within the *Parus* genus. There are many others.
I should like to draw further examples from this genus to
illustrate some of the main points in evolutionary research
on vocalizations; partly because these studies of *Parus*
species are interlinked and partly because familiar British
species can then be seen in this wider perspective.

Other European and Asian *Parus* species have been studied
for many years, from an evolutionary point of view, by Dr
Hans Löhrl and Dr Gerhard Thielcke at one of the Max-
Planck Institutes for behavioural research (at Radolfzell-
Möggingen in southern Germany). When Terry Gompertz
had the opportunity to breed in captivity two races of the
Great Tit, Dr Thielcke was able to re-test some of her sig-
nificant findings.

63
Some song-motifs from three groups of the Great Tit *Parus major* whose ranges are illustrated in the map (based on information from H. E. Wolters). 'India' is used as a geographical term for the Indian sub-continent. Songs from the same individual are linked by an arrowed line.

It is not certain whether *bokharensis* should be regarded as a separate species (Gompertz, 1968).

These two races, like the Willow Tits of North America and Europe, could not possibly meet in the wild for the male belonged to the British race, *Parus major newtoni*, and the female, *Parus major nipalensis*, came from the northern part of the Indian sub-continent. The many races of *Parus major* spread right across Europe and Asia, and in most cases are linked by populations with intergrading characteristics. In spite of differences from north to south and from east to west in plumage colour, in voice quality, and in the frequency and form of the song-elements, the Great Tits of this vast continent are classified as one species. They are, however, divided into three main groups of races: *Parus major major* in the west and north, *Parus major cinereus* in parts of southern Asia and *Parus major minor* in the Far East. The relationship to them of *Parus bokharensis*, is uncertain. Figure 63 includes a map of this distribution and typical song-variants from each group.

The breeding in captivity of these two representatives of the *Parus major major* and *Parus major cinereus* groups could be described as a reluctant success; reluctant that is on the part of the British male. Even when the *cinereus* female was in full breeding condition and courting him (there were no longer any members of her own race in the house and connecting outside aviary) he paid no attention until the female Great Tits he could see in the garden had virtually disappeared from the scene as they busied themselves with nesting and incubation. Then he formed a pair with her.

The four fledged offspring when adult took after their mother in voice quality and plumage colour: the *cinereus* tits are blueish grey on the back and white to pinkish-fawn underneath, instead of the green and yellow colouring of the *major* group. The black head-cap, neck band and stripe down the front are the same in both. The visual displays and postures of both groups also seemed to be the same.

One of the young *cinereus*-like males paired with the only female in the brood and when they were released from captivity, in January of their first winter, the pair treated a large area as their territory, returning to roost in the house each night. Although the male had heard his father's songs and those of all the other British Great Tit males within earshot, his own six song-variants bore no resemblance to any of them. The elements in four of the variants could be related to call notes of his mother's. The other two, while looking more like *major* songs on sonagrams, sounded completely

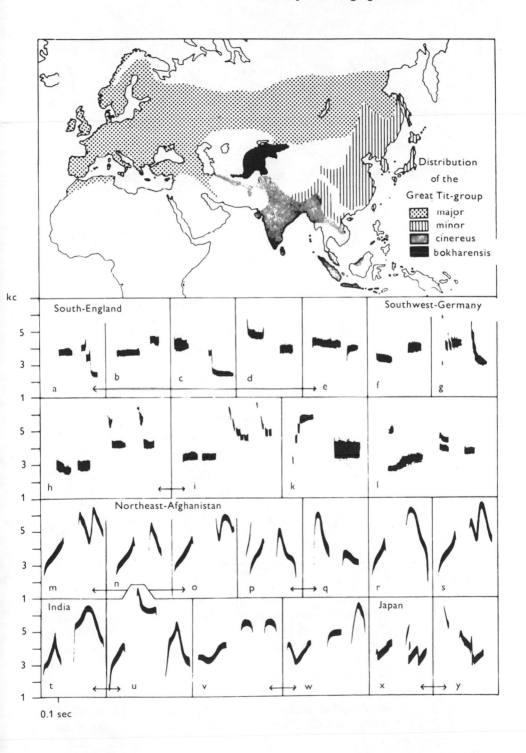

Distribution
of the
Great Tit-group
major
minor
cinereus
bokharensis

kc

South-England

Southwest-Germany

5

3

1

a   b   c   d   e   f   g

5

3

1

h   i   k   l

Northeast-Afghanistan

5

3

1

m   n   o   p   q   r   s

India

Japan

5

3

1

t   u   v   w   x   y

0.1 sec

64
Six songs of the
hybrid male Great
Tit (a, c, d, f, h, i);
(b, e, g) calls
used by his
cinereus female
parent; (k) song of
a captive *cinereus*
male kept by Dr
H. Löhrl in
Germany
(Gompertz, 1968).

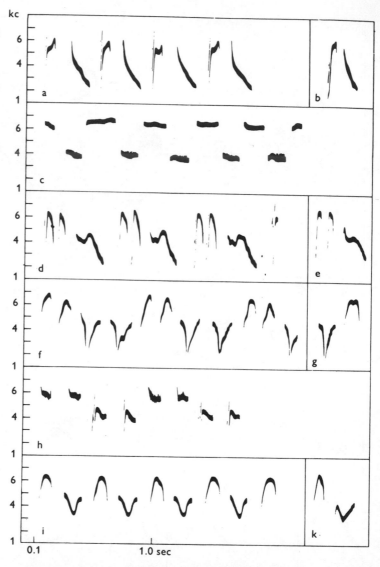

different. All six are illustrated in Figure 64.

None of these songs provoked a response from the local Great Tits and the pair were ignored by all the Great Tit territory holders into whose domains they so freely trespassed. The male could sing, with impunity, from the tree that Johnny most favoured as his own song-post. Nor was there any evidence that either the male or the female attracted attention as potential mates from the unmated British Great Tits of both sexes who were around. These included young Yellow-

Right who was seeking a mate at the time and remained unmated that year.

Some playbacks of the *cinereus*-type songs in other districts suggested that the songs were still not recognized even when there was no possible source of confusion from the strangely coloured plumage of the singer. This was confirmed by a series of playback experiments which Dr Thielcke undertook a year later. He and Dr Löhrl had just spent some months in north-east Afghanistan and brought back song-recordings of the local Great Tit race, *Parus major decolorans*, which is also in the *cinereus* group. The sonagrams in Figure 63 (m to s) show that these songs are not markedly different from those of *nipalensis* (Figure 63 t to w). When they were played to Great Tit males in south-west Germany the lack of response indicated that here, too, they were not recognized as songs of the same species.

It may be, then, that the British race and the two *cinereus* races, located so far apart in the connecting chain of Great Tit populations, have diverged sufficiently – most obviously in plumage colour and voice – to be almost separate species. The evidence suggests that they would behave as 'good' species if they came into contact in the wild.

Parus ater ater

The continuing research of Dr Löhrl, Dr Thielcke, and of an ornithologist from the University of Mainz in Germany (with field work in north Africa and in Nepal) has revealed further interesting *Parus* relationships in the sub-genus which embraces a group of tits with a preference for feeding on conifers. In Europe we have only one of these species: the Coal Tit, *Parus ater*. It is the most widespread, with many races: some connected by mixed populations, others isolated by geographical barriers. In Nepal the local race *Parus ater aemodius*, an isolated one, is found with the four other forms of the tits in this sub-genus. All of them, including this race of our Coal Tit, have crests – tiny, forward-curving feather tufts.

P. ater aemodius

Dr Jochen Martens of the University of Mainz has now suggested, on the evidence of vocalizations and other shared characteristics, that one of these closely related tits may have differentiated fairly recently, in evolutionary terms, from the rest of the sub-genus and should properly be described as a semi-species not a full species as was thought hitherto. Although it has some marked differences in plumage colour from all the other forms, it interbreeds with the Coal Tit

P. melanolophus

65
Song-motifs of the Coal Tit group. (a) European Coal Tit, *Parus ater ater*; (b) *P. ater aemodius*–the race in Nepal: two song-forms from one locality and (c) from another locality; (d) *Parus melanolophus* from a hybrid population; and (e) for comparison *–Parus major decolorans*, the Great Tit race in Afghanistan (Martens, 1975).

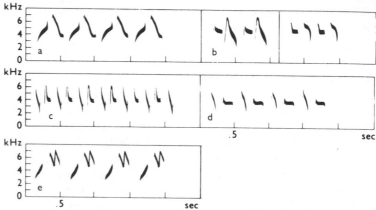

Parus ater aemodius in a narrow zone in the mountains of western Nepal.

This tit is *Parus melanolophus*, known as Vigor's Black-crested Tit. Its song is very similar to that of the Coal Tits; so similar that European Coal Tits react strongly to it. Figure 65 shows a *melanolophus* song, with songs of the European coal tit (*Parus ater ater*) and the Nepalese race (*P. ater aemodius*) for comparison. A song of *Parus major decolorans* is also included because the songs of the *cinereus* Great Tits resemble songs of the Coal Tit group much more than they do those of Great Tits of the *major* group. In fact some British Coal Tits tended to respond mildly to *cinereus* songs. Figure 66 is a map of the distribution of the Coal Tits and the contact zone between *melanolophus* and *ater aemodius*.

Melanolophus helps to provide additional evidence on

66
Map of the distribution of the Coal Tit group of species and the contact zone (arrowed) between *Parus melanolophus* (black) and *P. ater aemodius* (Martens 1975).

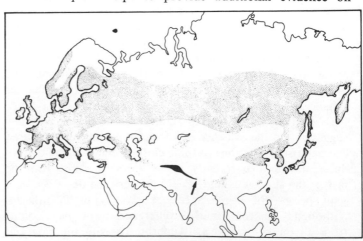

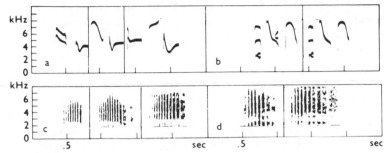

67
Alarm calls
against nest-
predators from
(a) three European
Coal Tits (calls
separated by
vertical line); (b)
*Parus melano-
lophus* – two calls;
(c) Moroccan
Coal Tit, *Parus
ater atlas*; (d)
European Coal
Tit kept in an
aviary with
Moroccan Coal
Tits (Löhrl and
Thielcke, 1973).

relationships in the *Parus* genus. Its alarm or scolding call used against nest-predators and in owl-mobbing (like the calls of other members of its group) is quite different from the equivalent Great Tit *churr*. These calls from *melanolophus* and the European Coal Tit are shown in Figure 67 a and b. But Figure 67 c shows the call given by a North African race of the Coal Tit in the same circumstances. This is a harsh rhythmic drum roll of the same type as the Great Tit *churr*.

Now, the *churr* type of call is shared, with variations, by all the other members of the *Parus* genus whose alarm calls are known. It would seem therefore that this is the older type – one of the ancient links between the numerous tit species. Since they diverged from their common ancestor, their songs have differentiated much more sharply than this call.

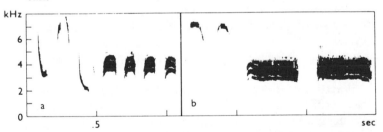

68
Alarm calls of (a)
Marsh Tit and (b)
Willow Tit.

Figure 68 shows the *tchay* calls of the Willow and Marsh Tits mentioned earlier in the chapter. These, like the Great Tit *churr*, seem to indicate a state of agitation. It will be seen that the type of sound resembles the Great Tit *churr* much more closely than do the Coal Tit calls. The alarm calls of other members of the genus also conform broadly to this pattern.

The Coal Tit subgenus alone, it appears, has evolved a different type of alarm call. In this group only the isolated North African Coal Tit races of the Atlas Mountains, as far as we know at present, use the more widespread and presumably older form. However one observation in the wild in Germany by Dr Löhrl, when a newly fledged youngster was seized by a Jay, showed that the European Coal Tit might use the older form of call when in a state of great agitation. Figure 67 d is the call of a captive European Coal Tit, kept in the same aviary as some birds of the North African race, from whom it may have learnt to make their call.

These few examples (and the discussion of the calls of ducks and geese in Chapter 6) illustrate the ways in which vocalizations can be useful indicators of past and present avian relationships.

It seems clear that new species can evolve only when populations are isolated from the main breeding stock for long periods of time during which they diverge sufficiently to prevent mutual recognition if contact is renewed. Dialect variation of songs and calls within a species, as well as slight differences of body form, size and plumage colour – adaptations to varying conditions of climate and habitat – indicate how this process could begin. The present day semi-species and races, which are sometimes more, sometimes less, sharply differentiated, suggest some of the stages through which the evolving species of the past may have progressed.

One human generation is too short a period for the observation of evolutionary trends in birds. We can only guess what the status of these partly differentiated forms might be in several thousands of years from now. The process of divergence could be held in check or speeded up by all kinds of factors.

Nevertheless it is possible to speculate further on the part that vocalizations play both in ensuring the continuity of existing species and the formation of new ones. The examples I have quoted have been drawn from only two passerine families. There are other evolutionary studies: of the estrildid finches for instance and, nearer home, the treecreepers. A broad picture begins to emerge.

In general, calls tend to be fairly stable and to suggest ancient relationships. But the evidence of geographical variability, and of a degree of learning in some calls, shows that their comparative stability is not necessarily due solely to genetic influences. Even if the innate basis of most calls is stronger than that of song, it is likely that tradition also plays a part.

Where calls are not connected with courtship and mating there is probably little evolutionary pressure for each species to have its own highly characteristic version. There is no threat to the species if the messages are more widely understood. Indeed as we saw earlier, it may be an advantage in communication between species. So both the tradition and the genetic basis for such calls are likely to remain unchanged.

Courtship and mating calls, like song, need to be more specific signals. The integrity of the species could be at risk if these produced a response from a related species of similar appearance. In two North American species of meadowlarks whose range overlaps in the centre of the continent it seems that a call used just before copulation is more important than song as an isolating mechanism between them. Song, however, is generally the most significant of all bird vocalizations for the continuity of the species. But because in many species a considerable amount of learning is involved, it is also the most flexible of the sound-signals. The potentiality for change is there.

Song-learning has been described by Dr Thielcke as 'a possible pace-maker of evolution'. It might start off the process of differentiation because, unlike almost any other basic features of bird behaviour, anatomy or physiology, song can be modified fairly rapidly. Once again it is a question of the balance between change and stability.

Whatever the exact process and timing of song-learning in different passerine species, it is evident that, as a rule, young birds perfect their songs by copying the fully-formed song patterns of the older males. Tradition therefore has a stabilizing effect. It may continue unaltered, within the limits of variability recognized by the species, for a long time. It is interesting that a recent sampling of songs in New Zealand, where several European songbird species were transported a hundred years ago, suggests that no significant change has taken place there in that time in spite of occupation of a new habitat and the small initial population of each species.

Tradition may ensure that the signal remains almost as stable as if it were entirely innate. But tradition can be broken. If there is an unusually wide dispersal of young birds before they have completed their song-learning into areas where there are no adults, they have no specific models to copy from. The peculiar songs developed by young birds reared in groups in captivity but isolated from adults of their species, point to the likely outcome in the wild – very swift

69
Songs of Short-
toed Treecreepers
from (a) north
Germany; (b)
southern Spain;
(c, d) Morocco
(Thielcke, 1973).

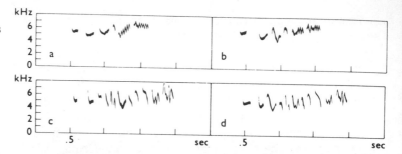

changes in the song could take place and a completely new tradition be established.

It is possible that this happened with the Short-toed Tree-creeper and accounts for the consistent difference in song between European populations of this species and the populations in North Africa (Figure 69). The North African populations may have been built up from juvenile colonizers who arrived there from Europe before they had been imprinted on the songs of adult males in their home area. Their tradition is now so different (though some single elements remain similar to those in Europe) that males in Europe did not respond to playbacks of the North African form of song.

Probably other isolating mechanisms in addition to song would have to evolve before reproductive separation of populations in any species is complete. But as Dr Thielcke suggests 'the potentiality for rapid change in song should increase the speed of the multiplication of species'.

This could, indeed, have been the most important single factor in the extraordinary proliferation of species among the songbirds preceding, and thereby assisting, their finer adaptation in other ways to the equally extraordinary range of habitats they now occupy. In the classification of birds, the passerine Order comprises more species than all the other twenty-six Orders put together and the vast majority of the passerines are true songbirds.

10 Copies and Counterfeits

Some redstarts are accomplished mimics . . . It might be thought that mimicry of others birds' songs would be of advantage to the mimic if the birds mimicked were deluded into supposing that a bird of their own species were holding territory where the song was delivered. But the willow-warbler, which was so often mimicked, is no rival of the redstart either for nesting-site or for food . . . and willow-warblers frequently came near the redstart without being attacked.

Or it might be thought that the redstart would mimic birds it often heard: yet at Eichstätt there were no robins, thrushes or nightingales within earshot. Probably the birds had heard these songs elsewhere – we had a starling that would mimic a golden oriole tirelessly, but there was none near – and continued sometimes to deliver these songs for no worse reasons than because it enjoyed doing so. *John Buxton*

John Buxton's observations of the Redstart were made during the Second World War when he was a prisoner-of-war in Bavaria. In the camps he had as few aids to field study as Gilbert White more than 150 years earlier: no binoculars, no camera, no tape-recorder. But he had the willing help of his fellow prisoners in a continuous watch on the birds whose life he had chosen to study, and his monograph is based on hundreds of hours spent in watching and listening to these summer residents in Britain and Continental Europe. His careful description of the songs of several well-studied individuals is rich evidence of the Redstart's capacity for mimicry.

Although it is more than 25 years since John Buxton's book was published, the questions that he put then are still discussed. No straightforward explanation has yet been found for the curious habit of mimicry, an ability which again links birds and men; for the power of vocal imitation among land mammals, even the Primates, is very limited. (Marine mammals, with their extensive use of sound are a different matter.) Most people have been startled at some time or another by the remarkable speaking ability of captive parrots, budgerigars and mynahs; and there are many reports of pet songbirds and other musically imitative species learning human melodies.

Though mimicry remains a puzzle, both by its presence in some species and by its apparent absence in others, the advances in our understanding of bird vocalizations now offer better evidence of the value of imitation in natural conditions. It begins to look as if the issue may have been confused in the past by the tendency to consider mimicry of other species as a separate phenomenon. This calls for explanation. But the basic skills required are obviously present in a far greater number of species than appears on the lists of habitual mimics.

Learning of songs and calls demands imitative ability even if, in most cases, it is limited in the wild to the sounds of the bird's own species. When it comes to finer detail, as in the signals between Twite pairs who, as seems likely, modify their flight calls to match each other, the imitation must be exact. Parrots are known to be very vocal but were not previously suspected of mimicry in the wild. It is now thought that they make use of this ability in the modification of signals between partners, and other members of the social groups within these mainly gregarious species. Their speech-learning could be part of a substitute relationship with their human companions.

Moreover as we have seen, the Chaffinch in some parts of Europe has added to its repertoire a sound that is probably an imitation of the woodpeckers' *kit*. Perhaps similar borrowings are still passing unnoticed for lack of sufficiently close observation of individual birds and because of the belief that such-and-such a species does not mimic. Unobtrusive or occasional mimicry may be more widespread than we think.

At present we can only ponder on the significance of imitation, examining the well-attested cases to see whether there are any connecting threads between them. In this chapter there are some varied examples of mimicry of other species; of the matching of sound signals between paired birds (antiphonal singing or duetting); and co-ordinated vocal displays by groups of birds of the same species. The skills required for all these vocalizations seem to involve learning, and imitation of some kind.

The Imitators

An amusing example of the imitation of another species is provided by a local population of Blackbirds at Garmisch-Partenkirchen in West Germany. It was detected by an ornithologist with a keen musical ear and a special interest in vocalizations, Professor Erwin Tretzel. At the time he had just published a paper on a population of Crested Larks in Germany which had learnt to imitate a shepherd's whistles so successfully that his dogs sometimes responded to whistled commands from the Larks.

On Easter Sunday evening in 1966 Professor Tretzel was driving slowly through the streets of the town, listening to Blackbirds (whose song-structure and dialect formation he had studied for many years). As he says, when you are very familiar with the song of any species, you develop a sensitivity to what is or is not normal – even in songs as varied as the Blackbird's. It is often hard to explain the basis for such judgements; they must come from expectations of sequences of notes, pitch-changes, rhythms and tone-qualities accumulated half-consciously over a long period.

On this occasion Professor Tretzel heard a Blackbird giving a particularly emphatic, sonorous and lengthy whistle which, he was immediately convinced, was an imitation of a human whistle. He stopped the car, got out and made a tape-recording. The next morning he returned to record it again. He then discovered that two Blackbirds nearby had also incorporated the whistle into their song-phrases in a similar or only a slightly altered form.

He continued his auditory exploration and found that yet other Blackbirds used the whistle; but the further away their territories lay from the district where the first three Blackbirds lived, the greater the transformation of the sound. This suggested to him that on the first evening he had picked up the sound somewhere near the centre of its area of radiation. The more distant Blackbirds had probably learnt it at second, third and fourth hand from each other.

If it was an imitation therefore the human originator was most likely to live somewhere in the vicinity of Blackbirds A, B and C, as Professor Tretzel had by this time labelled them. So with the help of his wife and the evidence on the tape-recorder, he embarked on a house to house enquiry. Finally he was directed to a small house lying just off the right street but only reached by crossing a yard with a notice saying 'No entry'. It was so well hidden in trees and bushes that he had missed it. The neighbours knew that Herr Herbert Schreiber had a cat.

Herr Schreiber, it seemed, had always whistled to his eight-year-old cat 'Mohrle' when he wanted it to come indoors. He was most co-operative and recorded his whistle many times over, sometimes directly into the microphone and sometimes when actually calling the cat. It was a four-note whistled call but Herr Schreiber, as recordings and sonagrams proved, varied the pitch and rhythm somewhat. The nearest Blackbird (A) provided the most faithful copy. But it was

70
Imitation of
human whistle by
a Blackbird. (a)
The man's whist-
led call to his cat;
(b) Blackbird A's
imitation of it.
The elements are
numbered. (Tret-
zel, 1967).

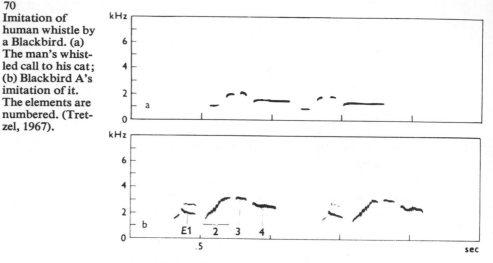

transposed upwards by an interval of about a fifth and
ornamented. A little introductory element was added and the
second element of the human whistle was transmuted into a
long, rising, slurring sound which emphasized the higher
pitch of the Blackbird motif.

Professor Tretzel then wondered if Herr Schreiber had ever
pitched his own whistle higher. But test recordings revealed
that he was unable to whistle the high second and third
elements of the call at the pitch of the Blackbirds' versions.
So that deviation from the model was also entirely their own.
Figure 70 gives sonagrams of the human whistle and Blackbird A's copy, and Figure 71 examples of the motif woven into
Blackbird phrases.

71
Different ways of
incorporating the
imitation (ele-
ments 5–7) in two
phrases (a and b)
from the same
Blackbird
(Tretzel, 1967).

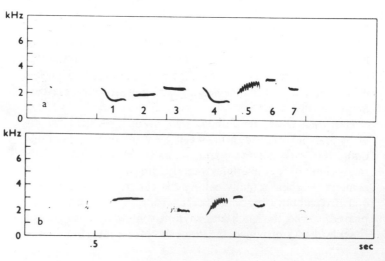

Blackbirds, as we shall see in the next chapter, alter and adjust their song in the course of a season and seem to string their motifs together in such a way that they fall into a balanced pattern of phrases within each strophe. It is likely therefore that even good and clear imitations may be modified slightly to make them 'fit'.

Other observations of Blackbird imitation were made by Dr Thielcke and his wife. In the aviary in their workroom they had a Pekin Robin. They noticed one day that a male Blackbird in the garden, then at least six years old, mimicked calls of this bird, which it could have heard only during the preceding two years – evidence of learning at a mature age. They also noticed, in the course of experiments on song-learning by hand-reared Blackbirds, that two males who adopted fragments of melodies played to them on a flute, transposed them differently: each placed them in the pitch range of his individual song.

Jay

There are mimics more exact in their copying methods than the Blackbird. One of the entries in my field notebook, describing a particularly good songster among the Sedge Warblers on the East Anglian Broads, reads 'lots of trills and musical elements and a section labelled "on living with Chiffchaffs" '. The most accurate of our local counterfeiters was a Starling that imitated the call of a vixen, a frequent night-time visitor to the gardens. This sound became a regular component of the Starling's song. When we played a recording of it to a neighbour one afternoon, her Alsatian started to pound up and down the room with excitement.

Lanceolated Jay

Derek Goodwin has heard both the European Jay and (in captivity) its relative from the western Himalayas, the Lanceolated Jay, bark at the sight of a dog. Wild Jays are notable and ear-deceiving mimics. During his observations he has often been 'mobbed' by parent Jays imitating predators such as the Tawny Owl, or the alarm notes of other species. They are very good at copying the chattering of their relatives, the Magpies. The Jay's habit of mimicry seems to be deployed in situations of alarm and excitement. In contrast, they also mimic when they are foraging or resting, interspersing their imitations with quiet versions of their own appeal notes. However this is a different mode of imitation from that of species where the mimicked notes, accurately copied or not, are woven into the song.

The Starling might be expected to be less particular than the Blackbird in its choice of models. Its own range of sounds runs from wheezes and clicks to whistles and any or all of these may be incorporated in the variable, loosely-structured song. Charles Hartshorne, an American Professor of Philosophy who has studied bird song as an intensive hobby for more than 50 years, suggested that imitation is most likely to be found in species with songs of this kind:

A highly imitative species must be one with no very strong fondness for any one musical pattern; and hence it must have a rather loose sense of overall musical form. It cannot care too much whether a sound be harsh, a sprawling handful of notes, a mediocre or brief tune, or an elaborate musical structure; except – and this is a notable exception – that it will somewhat disfavor the last. For even an imitative species has to have some style, some unity of pattern, of its own; hence, like all medleyists, it must utilize other compositions (of any length) only in snatches.

There are further questions about the origin and possible biological value to the species of these lengthy songs which incorporate imitations. Many species with such songs live in habitats with a good deal of vegetation. They include the Australian lyrebirds which, it has been estimated, borrow up to 70 % of the material of their very beautiful songs.

One explanation of a link between complicated, imitative songs and a fairly dense habitat has been that the males need to keep up a continuous stream of sound to advertise their whereabouts. The extension of their own sound-repertoire by borrowing helps this along and adds variety to the song. (A tendency to vary song in one way or another during long bouts of singing has been noted already and is discussed further in the next chapter.) This explanation applies, for example, to the imitative warblers of the marshes and reed-beds of Europe. It does not account for mimicry in the Starling, a gregarious species of more open country.

A possible problem is how the females recognize songs with such an indiscriminate content. But as Professor Hartshorne suggests, borrowings are always incorporated in a characteristic way into a song structure which, however loose, characterizes the species and even the individual. The specific tone-quality of some, at least, of the elements in such songs is evident to human ears. Probably even the most accurately mimicked borrowings can be recognized as such by females of the mimics' own species; for it comes more and more evident that tone-quality is a very important parameter in both species and individual recognition.

Foster Parents and Fosterlings

The role of imitation in song learning, already well established, is emphasized by the discovery that young birds of some songbird species, when reared in captivity by foster parents of another species, acquire the song of their foster father. Learning, in these cases, seems to depend on the personal bond between the young bird and the parent. When fostered the young birds choose the strange song rather than the songs of males of their own species, even when these can also be heard.

This preference has been shown to occur for instance in Bullfinches and in Zebra Finches. Moreover some Zebra Finches reared only by females, but in the same bird-rooms as males of their own and other grass-finch species, developed their songs in yet another way. Their versions consisted of elements of the right type for their species but these were selected from the songs of a number of their neighbours. No complete song patterns were taken as models.

In the wild the satisfaction of these two, apparently innate, preferences of the young Zebra Finches – for the song of the bird that rears them and for the right type of element (or perhaps merely the right tone-quality) – is provided by their natural father. They learn the song of their own species just as surely as the young of species like the Chaffinch whose learning process and innate preferences are different. Nevertheless the vocal adaptability of these fostered young is evidence of a rather special kind of the imitative propensities of birds.

A similar adaptability is well demonstrated in the wild by some of the species that habitually lay their eggs in the nests of others. The Estrildidae, the family to which the grass-finches belong, are again involved because they provide the nests and the foster parents. The fosterlings come from the Ploceidae – the weaverbird and sparrow family – of which the House and Tree Sparrows are the only British representatives.

In Africa, estrildid species share some of the same habitats with a special group of species in the Ploceidae – the indigo-birds and whydahs – which have all evolved this parasitizing habit. The fosterlings grow up as members of a mixed brood and their adoption is helped by a close resemblance in plumage and in mouth patterns (a stimulus to the parents to feed them) between the young of both species concerned. For in general it seems that each species of the indigobirds and whydahs concentrates its attention on one estrildid host species for fostering its young, who therefore learn this song, including any dialect variation there may be. Specialization, however, is not complete.

Study of the vocalizations offers revealing evidence of the habits and evolutionary history of these birds. Adult females seem to show a preference for the song of the species that reared them and this works in two ways. For instance if a female Paradise Whydah is attracted by the song to approach a male of her host species she may find the nest and lay an egg. But if she is attracted by the song of a male of her own species mimicking the same song, she often mates with him because in this case the other signals are right: plumage markings and colour, and the calls he gives as he displays over the trees.

The mimicked songs, together with plumage differences, appear to ensure reproductive isolation between the indigo-bird and whydah species as effectively as the songs of a normally singing species. But, not surprisingly, ornithologists specializing in this very closely related group of parasitizing birds have found it difficult to decide where the lines between some of these species are to be drawn. Recent studies by Dr Robert Payne of the University of Michigan in the United States have highlighted the problems.

For example, in parts of southern Africa three different forms of indigobirds each mimic a different host species (almost always) and the females mating with each of them also differ in appearance. In fact these forms look and behave like 'good' species. But in parts of West Africa, where some of the same forms of indigobirds are present, the situation is more complicated. Some indigobirds that look different mimic the same host species, while others that look alike but live in different places mimic different hosts.

Why should one apparent species of indigobird mimic four host species of fire finches? A suggested explanation is that because of northward and southward shifts in the narrow vegetation belts in West Africa during the last few thousand years, some estrildid species were replaced by others, better adapted to the drier or wetter conditions. Local populations of indigobirds may have switched successfully from one host to another more than once. Their behavioural and vocal adaptability has been swifter in its effects than the genetic changes needed to complete their separation into full species.

There is obviously a great deal more to be found out and it

looks as if arguments over the correct classification of particular population groups and species have a long time to run. Analyses of the songs these indigobirds and whydahs have learned from their foster parents and of their own characteristic sound repertoires are a fundamental part of the investigation.

Mynahs in the Wild

The ability of the Indian Hill Mynah, or Grackle, to imitate a great variety of sounds in captivity – human speech, noises and musical fragments – has often aroused wonder and curiosity. It might be thought that they would be superb mimics in the wild. In fact they are not. Wild Mynahs have now been studied in Assam and in other parts of their range in India, Bhutan and Sri Lanka by Dr Brian Bertram of Cambridge. The results of the study have shown yet another pattern of learning and suggest a different explanation of the Mynah's imitative ability in captivity.

Mynahs have no basic song or call pattern. Their *loud calls* in the wild are short and sudden and are all acquired by imitating other individuals of their species. Since these birds are easily hand-reared and become very tame, they are often taken straight from the nest for sale as pets. At this early age, they probably become imprinted to humans, so they might naturally imitate sounds associated with or made by these new social companions: in particular, short, sharp noises such as swear words, wolf-whistles and coughs which come nearest in form to their own vocalizations. In any case it seems that Mynahs have to learn by imitation if they are to call at all; in captivity the models can only be the sounds around them. In the wild, however, this imitative capacity is used in a highly selective way. Young Mynahs not only limit their learning to the sound repertoire of their species; they tend to learn the call-types of birds of the same sex.

As adults they have four categories of vocalizations, including long-distance and close-range signals, covering a wide range of situations. But the most interesting and fully studied category is the *loud calls*. These are most commonly made when the bird sees other Mynahs, whether its mate or neighbours.

To some extent these calls could be considered as the equivalent of song but they are used in an even wider variety of situations than the songs of most species: even, for example, in winter flocks. Mynahs are semi-gregarious and not strongly territorial even in the breeding season. Though paired birds have other vocalizations when they are close together, the loud calls seem to be their method of keeping contact at a distance. They call more frequently if they are more than about 35 metres apart.

The calls are extremely varied in pattern – most birds have a repertoire of between 5 and 12 different types. None of these is the same as the call-types of its mate but some types are shared with one of the birds in a few of the pairs in the immediate neighbourhood. Since both sexes of the Mynah have the same plumage they could not always be distinguished in the field during the study, but all the evidence suggests that this sharing of call-types was between members of the same sex. Figure 72 gives some examples of shared call-types in the repertoires of two neighbouring pairs.

These calls were individually recognized within the neighbourhood group. A bird tended to respond immediately to a call from its mate with a standard reply – it chose a particular type from its own repertoire to answer each of its partner's call-types. In responding to neighbours, a bird used the same call-type if it was a shared one. If not, the reply tended to be one of the more similar types in its own repertoire. Playbacks established that the Mynahs could distinguish between a single call made by a neighbour and a single call of the same type made by their mates.

It was found that the call-types were very localized. Even at a distance of only 14 kilometres or so, they were completely different. But there was no problem of species identification, despite the great variability in the pattern of the sounds. Call types from widely separated areas produced a response though it was less strong than to the known calls of neighbours.

It seems therefore that species recognition is ensured by the tone-quality of the sound. The only other common factors are the shortness of the calls and the lack of rapid or regular repetition. This is one of the most interesting points to come out of the study. The other is the Mynah's apparently total

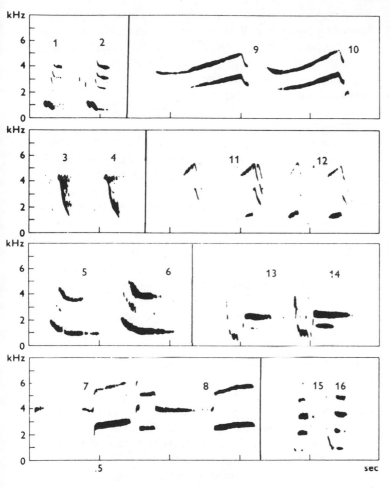

72
Loud calls of the Indian Hill Mynah: call types shared between pairs 2 and 5. Sonagrams show two examples of each of eight call types in the repertoire of these pairs. The first call of a type was recorded from pair 2 and the second from pair 5. The calls were produced by one member of each pair. Bird 2A or 5A made calls 1–8 and bird 2B or 5B calls 9–16 (Bertram, 1970).

dependence on imitative learning during the development of its vocalizations, combined with the limitation of its choice of models (in the wild) to members of its own species and sex.

Duets and Trios

Vocal adaptability, imitation and learning among birds who are old enough to form pairs are displayed by the species that engage in antiphonal singing or duetting. This form of vocalization has so far been found most commonly in tropical species living in habitats with plenty of cover. Here the need for mutual identification and for maintaining contact between mates is paramount in species that remain paired for all or most of the year. It is thought that these highly synchronized duets may also serve to form and strengthen the bond between them. It is possible, as Konrad Lorenz and others have suggested, that pair-bonding is one of the principal functions of the imitative ability of birds. However, some species at least sing their duets to proclaim territorial ownership and in actual disputes with neighbours so the message carried in these co-operative signals is not necessarily directed solely to the partner.

Antiphonal singing has been studied by Professor W. H. Thorpe, at first with the help of the late Myles North whose recordings of African birds have added so much to our knowledge. The species that Professor Thorpe worked with most was the Tropical Boubou Shrike of Africa of which there are several races.

Once a pair is established in a territory, the partners spend weeks, possibly months, working out and practising their duets. Each pair has several duets, some simple, others more elaborate. One pair near Lake Nakuru in Kenya sang 17 duet patterns in a single day. Some of the simple patterns can be heard from a number of pairs in a population but with so large a repertoire some are probably characteristic of each pair.

In these duets, contributions from the two birds are combined in a formalized, repeated pattern or motif. One bird starts the phrase and the mate completes it, or the second bird alternates with its partner in a rapid interchange which sounds as if it came from one singer. Figure 73 illustrates six duets of the Tropical Boubou Shrike. Because of the purity of tone and exact pitch of the elements in these songs it is possible to transcribe them in musical notation and this makes it easier to see the rhythmic precision of the interchange and the separate contribution of each bird. As it is difficult to distinguish between the sexes the birds are labelled X and Y. A duet may be started by a bird of either sex but each is aware of the whole pattern. If alone either bird can sing the complete duet, apparently to recall the missing partner.

A puzzling feature of antiphonal singing in the Boubou Shrike is the occasional occurrence of trios. Sometimes the third bird is quite a distance away but on one occasion all three birds were perched on the same tree. Figure 74 illustrates two such trios.

Professor Wolfgang Wickler and his colleagues at the Max-Planck Institute for behavioural research at Seewiesen in

73
Duets of the
Tropical Boubou
Shrike transcribed
in musical nota-
tion (all from the
race *Laniarius
aethiopicus major*).
The contributions
of each bird are
marked X and Y
(W. H. Thorpe).

74
Trios of the
Tropical Boubou
Shrike. Contribu-
tions of each bird
are marked X, Y
and Z (W. H.
Thorpe).

West Germany have also studied duetting in shrikes and in species in Africa belonging to other families. These include the drongos (another song-bird family), the Robin Chat (thrush family) and barbets – small gaily-coloured species often kept in aviaries in Europe, and not even passerines. Their family, which inhabits the southern parts of the world, with many species in Africa, is related to the woodpeckers.

Like the Shrikes, these duetting partners perform stereo-typed, precisely synchronized phrases, though the female Robin Chat has only one reply to her partner's several motifs. But she can affect the speed of his singing by changing her own, and he hers by changing his motif. Barbet pairs may use the duet as part of a greeting ceremony with special body and feather postures and mutual bill-wiping. Observations of several species show that, for them at least, contact and mutual identification at a distance are not the main function of the signal for they start to sing only when they come to-gether. Then there was one extraordinary vocal encounter when a drongo and a Slate-coloured Boubou Shrike performed a perfect duet, the drongo adjusting its interventions to the shrike's pattern (the sexes of the two birds were not known). The noisy sounds of the drongo are too dissimilar from the musical shrike notes for a mistake in species identity to be an explanation.

None of these observations is inconsistent with the idea that duets and trios are a form of communication between paired birds or, on occasion, social companions. In Professor

Thorpe's aviaries in Cambridge, two young hand-reared birds – both females – who had been placed in the same aviary developed a strange little duet which one sang, in full, for several days after the early death of the other.

Nevertheless this is not the whole story, for the duets are also sung in territorial encounters between neighbouring pairs. Professor Wickler and his colleagues (among them Dr Uta Seibt who studied the Flappet Lark) have conducted playback experiments, in addition to the normal field observations, which have demonstrated that the signal carries a territorial message. Male and female – for both take part in the defence of the territory – fly straight to the loudspeaker and start duetting.

More subtle evidence of the territorial message is also being found, for several species, in the sound-structure of the signal itself. Measurements of the intensity of the sounds the birds utter and of the distances over which they respond to the duets of other singers provide material for an interesting speculation. In simple terms the argument runs as follows: why sing so loudly if you are only addressing a partner who is perched beside you or in the next tree, when you respond to sounds that are no louder (and much less so by the time they reach you) from another pair 50 metres away? Possibly therefore these duets evolved in the first place as joint proclamations of territorial ownership.

Detailed investigation of the separate elements in some of these duets supports this argument, because a variation in the intensity of different elements has been found. One element uttered by the Slate-coloured Boubou Shrike would carry no further than ten metres and seems to be used when there is some slight disturbance in the territory: it must have communicative value for the partner alone. Perhaps in some of these species, with variable duets, part of the repertoire is for communication between mates and represents a more sophisticated development of duetting behaviour, evolved after the basic need for a joint territorial proclamation had been met. It appears, then, that the more that is found out about this fascinating form of co-operative signalling, the more flexible its social functions are seen to be, differing, maybe, in different species.

True duetting has been found less often among species living in temperate zones. The Little Grebe, which is quite common in Britain and Continental Europe, is a notable exception with a long Trill Duet. However, other races of this

Little Grebe

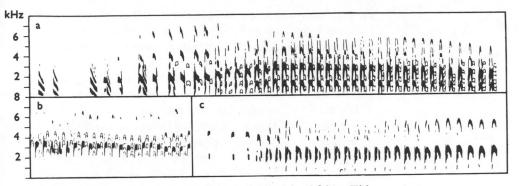

species are to be found in tropical Asia and in Africa. This small relative of the Great Crested Grebe is roundish and squat, lacking eartufts, neck-frill and even a tail. It differs in several ways from the majority of grebe species. It holds a very large territory (on average 1900 square metres) with sharply defined boundaries and most of the breeding period is spent among thick vegetation in or near the water. Perhaps this is why, in spite of its small size, the Little Grebe can safely be so strenuously vocal.

75
Trill duets of the Little Grebe: (*a*) a complete duet; (*b*) part of another one; (*c*) trill of a Little Grebe delivered without its partner (Bandorf, 1968).

The trill, which is usually delivered as a duet by both partners (though one part may be performed as a solo) is an important courtship ceremony between pairs. Up to 80 duets an hour have been heard from a pair. Trill duetting may also accompany or follow visual displays on the water: the partners swim or dive towards one another, duetting when they meet, or swim side by side, trilling as they go.

Figure 75 shows the length and complexity of this vocal display. The contribution of each bird is indicated on the traced sonagram, one by black traces, the other by white outlines. The birds keep perfect time as they speed up and then slow down in the course of the trill. Such a performance demonstrates vocal adaptability of a high order.

Communal Singing

Finally, a curious form of communal vocalization needs to be considered here – the so-called 'singing-assemblies'. These gatherings, sometimes of considerable numbers of birds, are known to occur in only a few bird families.

Singing assemblies have been observed in some of the forest humming-bird species. Dr David Snow studied one of these, the Little Hermit, in the forested mountain ridges of northern Trinidad. Many of the assemblies took place high up on these ridges, always on traditional sites. The assemblies are most common between November and July, when the birds moult after the breeding season. A report from another part of the species' range – in western Colombia – suggests that the displays there continue vigorously all the year round but in this area there is a more consistent climate.

The generally accepted explanation of these highly vocal gatherings is that they are a form of 'lek'. Each male bird has its own perch on the assembly ground and they counter-sing for quite long periods. The females come to the assembly-ground for mating. As the sexes are virtually indistinguishable in the field it is difficult for observers to be certain of exactly what is happening, especially since these tiny birds move extremely rapidly. But it seems that the females approach a perch, hover above it and finally alight beside the male. Copulation probably takes place on the perch after some moments of rapid display flights above it.

In each song-bout there is a period of uninterrupted singing, followed by more intermittent song. As the singing tails off, there is an increase in the number of aerial displays between two birds who then usually leave the assembly ground together. It looks as if the males, at first aggressive in song, engage in courtship displays with the females towards the end of each session.

The song is 'a brief, high-pitched, chittering phrase', individually varied. Interestingly, birds occupying neighbouring perches tend to have similar songs: when a bird manages to get a perch on the assembly ground, it develops and retains a song resembling those of its nearest neighbours. The effect of this is that the assembly consists of groups, each of which has its own dialect and these group song-traditions may persist for several years. A very similar distribution of song-types, with different variants in groups as little as 150 feet apart, has been found in another forest species of Central and South America, Guy's Hermit Hummingbird.

In terms of vocalizations alone, this pattern resembles that of the local song-groups of the New Zealand Saddlebacks but the social organization of the two species – one engaged in a vocal lek, the other an unaggressive territory-owner with an enduring bond between mates – is entirely different.

David Snow and Derek Goodwin also observed the song-behaviour of the Black-and-Gold Cotinga. The Cotingas are another forest-dwelling family of the southern United States, Central and South America and the West Indies. The Cock-of-the-Rock, sometimes seen in captivity in Britain, is another member of this family.

The Black-and-Gold Cotinga itself lives only in the forested mountain ranges of south-eastern Brazil and little was known about it except that it had a long, plaintive, whistled call which left a deep impression on earlier observers. The evidence that David Snow and Derek Goodwin were able to obtain in a short visit to its home terrain indicates that these birds have a remarkable form of lek display, probably unique in the Cotinga family.

There is concerted singing but it is initiated and sustained (as far as they could tell) by one, presumably dominant, male. One or two other males would appear and join in with the leading singer. From time to time they fell silent while he was still calling. In the early morning, or in dull weather, the birds called from exposed perches, but in the heat of the sun they called invisibly from within the leaf canopy.

When a female arrived, sometimes from a distance of a few hundred metres, one or more of the males would fly to her perch and call. In this type of forest country visual observation is perpetually obstructed, and it was impossible to be certain whether calling in chorus was stimulated only by the presence of a female or occurred spontaneously in support of a calling male. There seems to be little doubt, however, that the dominant male's vocal display is enhanced with the help of attendant males.

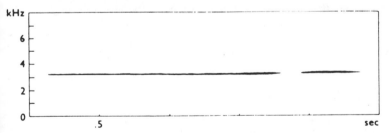

76
Call of the Black-and-Gold Cotinga (Snow and Goodwin, 1974).

The song, or call, is a long-drawn-out, very pure whistle lasting about two seconds. This is followed by a brief pause and then a second, shorter whistle, which is sometimes omitted. The full call is shown in Figure 76. The pitch rises slightly and the volume increases, but over distances, or if the bird turns its head, the signal inevitably fluctuates. Normally there is only a two-second pause between each two-note call, so if at least two birds call, more or less alternately, there is a continuous stream of sound and this was the effect achieved in some of the sustained choruses that the two observers heard.

More observation is needed before this performance can be fully interpreted. To my mind it raises a tantalizing question: have these birds evolved an acoustic triumph over their environment by co-operative signalling? The augmented, continuous sound could certainly be an extra stimulus to the female in courtship and this might be explanation enough. But it might also more easily attract her from a greater distance to the source of the sound. Here, the dominant male in his black plumage, with a pure yellow patch on his wings and a bright orange bill, can effectively present his visual displays.

The varied forms of vocal behaviour described in this chapter are linked, so far, by tenuous threads. Evidence of imitative learning and co-operative social skills recurs in most of these examples and others that could be chosen.

It would be an illusion to suppose that a single explanation could account for the multitude of vocal behaviour patterns that have been, or are still to be, examined. What we can detect in all of them, surely – when we know enough – is a relationship between the vocalizations of a species, its social organization and the environment in which it lives. So the species, the 'unit of evolution', remains the unit of study.

11   Airs and Variations

There are just two possibilities for evolutionary theory concerning the musical sensibility and capability characterizing man: Either it is entirely unique to human life, or there are precedents and analogies in the older forms of animal life. *Charles Hartshorne*

When we listen to bird songs we are conscious that many of the individual sounds are pleasantly musical to our ears. But beyond that many people find that the longer and more complicated song patterns, brief though they may be by our standards, take a form which we also find satisfying. This chapter is a tentative exploration of the musical qualities of birdsong and of the birds' use of this highly developed vocal skill.

Some of the acoustic reasons for our response to bird sounds have been given in earlier chapters. For example the frequency range of most bird songs, though higher than the fundamental frequencies of the human singing voice and of most musical instruments, is well within the compass of our hearing and many of the sounds are in the frequency range to which we ourselves are most sensitive. People reared in the broad cultural traditions of either western or eastern music hear notes and pitch-intervals, or gliding transitions of pitch, that are familiar to them; for birdsong has features in common with both traditions.

We are also sensitive to other characteristics of birdsong. As we can now see, the elaboration of these long-distance signals has been both stimulated and constrained by a combination of influences: the kind of information that songs convey; the need for each species to have a distinctive type of song; the role of song in the life of the species; and the acoustic properties of different environments. The effect of these, and possibly of additional influences that we are not yet aware of, has been the evolution of a multiplicity of sound patterns in which rhythm, tempo, pitch and tone-quality are varied within different types of sound composition. These basic characteristics of structured sound are the stuff of which all forms of human music are made.

The significance of speech is extended by similar modifications in the flow of sound: in some languages the same word, even, has a different meaning when it is spoken with a different tone. During the earliest stages of human evolution, before verbal language and music began to develop in divergent and ever more sophisticated ways, rhythmical and pitch changes must have shaped the sound signals of the emerging genus *Homo* for, at the simplest level, the physical properties of sound affect the use that all animals can make of it in their communication systems. The instrumental signals of insects, the vocalizations of frogs, and of land- or sea-living mammals are subject to variations in the same fundamental sound parameters. However, it is the development of the musically elaborate sound-patterns of the songbirds that arrests our attention.

There is nothing mysterious about this evolutionary parallel: a refined capacity to shape sounds, and sensitivity to them, must evolve together in a group of animals adapting to a way of life in which communication by sound becomes especially important. Early man, like the evolving songbirds so much earlier in time, lived with the sounds and sensations of rhythmic processes – heartbeat and breathing; the movements of walking and running (or hopping and flying). The sounds of the natural environment, crucial for his safety, must have stimulated his awareness – leaves and grasses vibrating in the wind, falling rain or flowing water: all changing in rhythm, pitch and quality as the driving forces and acoustic conditions altered. And for early man the songs and calls of the birds were already there. Nowadays many people in the advanced countries spend much of their lives in conditions which obliterate these natural sounds and much contemporary music, from pop to the most experimental forms, reflects a man-made sound environment. This music could be a response to the insistent beat of machines and to the otherwise arhythmic din of industrial and urban life.

Despite the small scale of the musical patterns of birdsong, it is possible to discover in them many of the same rhythmic and melodic devices that human composers in all musical traditions have used to achieve tension, contrast and balance in their phrases. Sometimes this comparison has to be made on a micro-scale: the new tools of study were needed to reveal the wealth of musical detail compressed into so short a timespan. Nevertheless man's appreciation of birdsong probably springs from a recognition of these congruencies between avian and human music; the songs of the Nightingale, the Willow Warbler and the Blackbird, for example, are musically interesting to us before their full detail is revealed.

The analysis of the songs of many species in terms of

sound alone is a necessary first step towards a better understanding of the formal resemblances between bird music and
human music. Professor Hartshorne, in his book 'Born to
sing' has made a magnificent beginning, with a worldwide
survey of all the birdsongs known from the ever-lengthening
catalogue of recordings, or from adequate field descriptions.

By applying standard criteria to the evaluation of songs
and assessing characteristics such as complexity, organization
and tone-quality, some of which are measurable, he has tried
to rid the process of comparison of vague, subjective judgements such as 'beautiful' or 'musical'. He has made a list,
compiled on this basis, of the 200 or so best singers of the
world among approximately 5000 species which can be said
to sing.

This list, incidentally, includes nine species that breed in the
British Isles: the Nightingale, Robin, Blackbird and Song
Thrush; the Garden Warbler, Marsh Warbler and Blackcap;
the Skylark and Woodlark. Our runners-up – good but not
superlative singers – are the Sedge Warbler, Wren, Willow
Warbler, Tree Pipit, Pied Flycatcher and, more doubtfully,
the Dipper and the Linnet. This selection accords well with
the song-ratings of earlier authorities who had perforce to
confine themselves to a smaller number of species, and often
to regional groups, within their travelling experience. Most
bird-listeners in Britain would agree with the choice.

Yet though his criteria are as objective as possible, they are
still derived from human responses to the sounds. This makes
another of Professor Hartshorne's findings even more significant. When the habits and habitat of the excellent, the
reasonably good and the merely passable singers are considered, there is a relationship with the quality of the song:
songs that are musically most interesting to us are found in
species in which biological pressures seem to account for a
greater elaboration of the signal. This means that where
greater elaboration has been evolved, bird music has anticipated, in a very simple way, the development of human
music.

These, then, are separate questions that need further
clarification – how far the elaborate songs of some species are
adequately explained by particular biological pressures and
how musical, in our sense, this elaboration is. Before I give
a few examples from the songs of species that have already
been well studied there are two other points which I have not
discussed so far and which are relevant here because they

probably apply to all acoustic signals.

One is 'redundancy'. This term is used by communications engineers to cover any extensions of a message necessary to ensure that the required information gets through to the recipient, in spite of interruptions or interference with the signal. It has turned out to be a useful concept in the analysis of bird vocalizations. Repetition, a marked feature of all birdsong, is an obvious form of redundancy. Again, the wide frequency range of many songs, or of the elements in them, is probably a form of redundancy – an adaptation to the environment: enough of the signal gets through for identification even if some frequencies are lost – for instance in temporarily poor acoustic conditions such as a high wind. Some, at least of the elaboration in song could be explained as redundancy. It could also be a means of achieving variety in the signal.

This is the second point that needs to be considered. On the evidence, nearly all birds that sing a good deal vary their songs in some way or another. This is another feature of long-distance signalling: a change in the signal reawakens attention. But it is also a musical principle: tension followed by relaxation, changing rhythms and dynamics, dissonance and resolution. And it applies to speech. We all know the effect of a speaker who is literally monotonous; only one who has a good range of vocal inflexions is likely to hold our interest. But it is fair to ask whether these two principles, of redundancy and variety, are enough to account for the degree of elaboration and variation that has been found. It seems unlikely.

The first example of an elaborate song – and one that raises a very interesting question – is the Blackbird. An analysis of the song by a professional musician, Joan Hall-Craggs, has done much to explain in precise terms our musical satisfaction in listening to it. Her method was to record song from the same individual adult male Blackbird practically every day from the beginning to the end of its song season. Then she analysed the recordings in chronological order so that she was able to discover not only how the song was structured but how it changed in the course of the season. This procedure was repeated over several years and with a number of birds. Many details of Blackbird song are lost to us in the field and in recordings played back at normal speed. Figure 77 illustrates this with the same phrase presented first in musical notation, as it was heard at normal and at slower speeds, and on a sonagram.

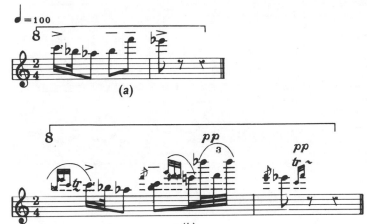

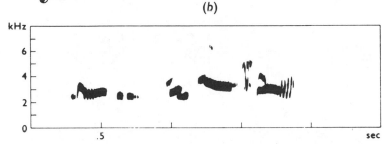

77
Blackbird song:
(a) an approximate
rendering in
musical notation
of a phrase as
heard at normal
song speed; (b)
notational repre-
sentation of the
same phrase after
listening to it at
one-eighth and
one-sixteenth
normal speed; (c)
sonagram of the
same phrase (Hall-
Craggs, 1962).

Earlier work by other students of Blackbird song had shown
that young Blackbirds learn their motifs, or phrases, from
their father and from neighbouring Blackbirds; and we have
seen already that occasionally, at least, new motifs can be
acquired at a later stage. Mrs Hall-Craggs found that one of
her Blackbirds, fully adult when she started to record him in
early spring, had a repertoire of 26 basic phrases and that
these, with 24 variants on them, were all recorded in the first
week that he sang in that year. Some of the phrases had a
little flourish – a terminal decoration – tacked on at the end,
composed of chuckles, squawks or other non-musical sounds.

At first the Blackbird tended to sing a variant immediately
after the related basic phrase, or to repeat a basic phrase
several times in succession, suggesting a form of practice or
'working-up'. But this habit disappeared after he had been
singing for a fortnight. Even in the practice period, he combined two or more phrases into a longer sequence and some
phrases appeared to have a special position: he almost always
sang three of them only at the beginning of combined phrases;
three others occurred only at the end.

However, there was a great deal of development to come.

78
Blackbird song:
development of
phrases by one
male in the same
year. (a) Basic
phrase 7; (b) basic
phrase 9; (c)
developed phrase
7a with two new
notes; (d) 7/9–a
new form com-
bining the first
part of phrase 7
and the second
part of phrase 9;
(e) developed
form 7/12 with a
long terminal
decoration; (f)
approximate
musical notation
of compound
phrase 7/12;
(g) phrase 7a
(adapted from
Hall-Craggs,
1962).

This formation of combined, or compound phrases went on throughout the season. Moreover extracts from basic phrases were combined to form further phrases. With two particular phrases and their variants, the process of merging and re-combining went on for 12 weeks, as if the bird were experimenting all the time. The most extended form was not recorded until the beginning of June. Some of the interme-diate forms remained in the bird's repertoire but were not sung very often. The non-musical terminal decorations were tried out at the end of different phrases until one combination became a permanent item in the repertoire. Chains of phrases were established which the bird sang frequently but even these were not inflexible. As the season progressed, new series were created, with many phrases occurring in more than one series. So the song, though never stereotyped, be-came progressively more highly organized.

The development of phrases is illustrated by the sonagrams in Figure 78. First comes basic phrase number 7, as it was sung at the beginning of March (the start of the season), and a compound phrase in which it was linked with phrase 12.

Then there is a variant of 7 in which two notes were added to the end of the basic phrase, one in early April and the second nearly three weeks later. Phrase 7 was sometimes linked with phrase 9. Phrases 7 and 12 are also shown in musical notation in the Figure, for this demonstrates more clearly the rhythmical symmetry and well-balanced melody of this combination.

The extended variant of Phrase 7 (with the two extra notes which, to our musical sense, would have disturbed the symmetry) was never used in this compound phrase though it remained in the repertoire in other contexts. Nor, apparently, did the Blackbird ever reverse the order of these two musical phrases. Again, this would be far less satisfying musically to us.

This example is not an isolated one. Over and over again, combinations of phrases, and longer series, occurred with a rhythmic and melodic balance which could be related to the larger scale structures found in widely different forms of human music. In Figure 79, phrase 7 is compared with two human melodies. One is the opening phrase from J. S. Bach's Suite no 3 in G and the other is the sea-shanty 'Blow the man down'. All three have been transposed to the same octave and key to simplify the comparison. Next comes a question that Joan Hall-Craggs' study has raised. She noted, as have other observers, that when a Blackbird is intimidating an intruder, the song is 'loose and disjointed' and phrases are cut short. The song is musically at its best and most complex in the morning when the bird sings more continuously, and usually with fewer outside interruptions, than at other times of day. However, her recordings of the same indi-

79
A Blackbird's phrase (phrase 7/12) compared with two widely divergent types of European music. Each has been transposed to the same octave and key (Hall-Craggs, 1969).

viduals showed that the song improves in form and musical quality (in our sense) throughout the season. In the earlier weeks when the bird is occupied with territorial and mating affairs, it is less elaborate. So, as Joan Hall-Craggs puts it:

It is later in the season, when these immediate and pressing needs have been fulfilled, that the song becomes organized in a manner so closely resembling our own ideas about musical form. It would appear, then, to be moving towards the realm which we call art music – where our experience of musical form enables us to predict what is likely to happen next.

We must suppose that the primary biological functions of song in the Blackbird, as in many species, are to obtain and hold a territory and a mate for though visual displays are important in the Blackbird's way of life, song is certainly used in these contexts. It seems unnecessary for the form of the signal to be further elaborated after all these requirements have been met. A similar development in song – the expansion of the earlier forms of song-strophe, late in the season and after the conclusion of breeding – has been reported in the Willow Warbler (this was referred to in Chapter 4).

A contrast with the Blackbird in both the form and function of the song is provided by another of our good songsters, the Sedge Warbler. According to Dr Clive Catchpole of Bedford College, London, who has analysed it in detail, the song could well be thought of as 'an acoustic Peacock's tail'. In the semi-open habitat on the edge of water or marshland where the Sedge Warbler lives, it usually sings from prominent song-posts on a bush or at the top of a reed, and during short song-flights – simply to attract a female. This restricted function is evident because song practically ceases after pairing and visual threat displays are commonly used in territorial confrontations between males.

A single song-strophe may last for over a minute and contain about 300 syllables: as with the Cardinals, these are often complex structures made up of several distinct elements. The strophe has three sections: at the beginning, one or two syllables are alternated and repeated in an unpredictable sequence; in the middle, five to ten additional syllables are introduced and combined in very varied patterns, and one or two of these new syllables are used in the closing sequence and at the start of the next strophe. But this is not the limit of invention. One bird was still introducing previously unused syllables in the 26th consecutive strophe out of 32 that were analysed and there were plenty in reserve; for, like several other Sedge Warblers whose songs were fully studied, he had between 60 and 70 types of syllable in his repertoire. On song-flights, the structure of the song is even more complicated than that of the normal song and twice as many syllable types are introduced in each strophe.

Though the Sedge Warbler's song contains harsh sounds as well as notes of musical quality, and we cannot appreciate all its refinements in the field, it is an exciting aural experience. Its build-up of speed and loudness to a peak in the middle section, and then the gradual fading of the closing sequence, are musically right as a framework for the stimulating variety of sounds.

Dr Catchpole suggests that the extraordinary elaboration of this song, with its limited function of mate attraction, has evolved because female Sedge Warblers have opted for the best singers when choosing their partners. This explanation, advanced since Darwin's time to account for a number of phenomena in the appearance and behaviour of avian males, could well apply in this case though species whose songs function primarily as territorial proclamations must be subject to other evolutionary pressures as well.

To turn to another type of elaboration – why should Song Sparrows and Cardinals have so many variants in their individual repertoires and why, in a species such as the Great Tit, does one male have more variants than others? Why, for that matter, does one Sedge Warbler structure his sound patterns rather more freely than another?

The comparatively simple and not very highly rated song of the Great Tit helps to demonstrate these puzzles even more clearly than some of the better singers. The maximum number of song-variants that each Great Tit has in its repertoire seems to be eight or nine but many birds have only four or five. One bird in our local population had just a single variant though this was the only case we knew of in 17 years. Yet this bird obtained a territory, found a mate and bred successfully for at least three years. Johnny, one of our most 'musical' singers, had eight variants but his breeding record over the years was no better than that of males with only four or five. This kind of evidence, which has been confirmed by other observers, suggests that a large song repertoire is not essential for individual survival and reproduction. It may have incidental advantages that we do not yet understand.

Dr John Krebs of the Edward Grey Institute at Oxford, in a bold speculation, has recently suggested one possible advantage. We know already that a young, unestablished male takes swift advantage of the death of a resident to occupy his territory and Dr Krebs has also found that if several resident Great Tit pairs are removed by capture, pairs living in a marginal habitat nearby may decide to improve their position by transferring to the more favourable vacant territories. The absence of song is the cue for moving in. But such birds – on the local waiting list for good territories, as it were – are in a position to know the individual repertoires of residents within earshot. Before breeding starts, however, birds already in the locality are not the only candidates for vacancies and in Dr Krebs' field experiments some of the new occupants were thought to have come from further afield.

He suggests therefore that birds prospecting in one area after another for somewhere to settle may use the songs they hear as an indicator of residential density and thus of the chances of success in their search. If only a few song variants are to be heard they might assume that there are not many residents and the opportunities good. If this were so a greater number of variants could be an advantage for the singing bird – the passing intruders are tricked into believing that the residential density is higher than it is and do not attempt to settle; so the owner is spared extra trouble in territorial defence.

There are difficulties in this hypothesis: for example certain forms of behaviour are required, such as singing in different parts of the territory – as the Great Tit does – for the system to work. It could not apply to all species nor account for all forms of song elaboration. No single explanation, however, is likely to do this and since we still understand so little about the precise mode of operation of these long-distance signals, hypotheses which suggest new lines of enquiry are worth having.

There is still the puzzle of individual mastery of the art of sound composition. As a species, Great Tits manage to do everything that a human composer could achieve with the same limited material by varying the rhythm, and the pitch and intervals of the notes, in their simple two or three-note motifs. But some do rather more than this. In one of our distant study areas we found a Great Tit with a motif containing 25 elements in rapid succession (Figure 80). Johnny himself had in his repertoire a beautiful four-note motif (already mentioned in Chapter 7). In musical terms it was

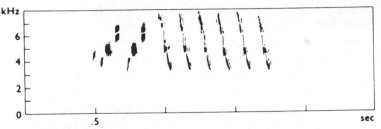

80
An unusually
complicated Great
Tit song-motif,
recorded in
Hertfordshire in
1968.

the common chord in the key of F♯ sung in arpeggio form.
In our experience comparatively few Great Tits in any one
population have motifs as elaborate as these.

For seven years Johnny's 'Common chord song' was not
acquired by any of his neighbours. Then young Yellow-
Right learned it during his first spring as a mateless holder of
a small territory next door to Johnny. He practised away at it
hard for a long time. Finally he produced a version that was
slightly different from his model – to us it sounded rather
more jaunty. His version and Johnny's are shown again in
Figure 81.

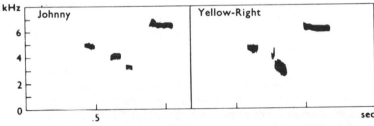

81
Great Tit 'Com-
mon chord' song-
motif, learned and
modified by
Yellow-Right
from Johnny.

Yellow-Right, too, developed a repertoire of eight variants,
possibly because he had few demands on his time and energy
while he was still learning some of his variants. Young Great
Tits who mate and breed in their first year as adults are a
good deal busier than he was and this may be one of the
factors that contributes to variations in repertoire size.

As Great Tits go Johnny and Yellow-Right were good
singers, with large repertoires and an unusual motif which
one learned from the other. Since Johnny brought his 'Common chord' motif into our area when he arrived to mate with
a widowed female in the late spring of 1959, it has been
copied only by Yellow-Right and two other males: one who
held a territory adjoining Yellow-Right's after Johnny's
death, and Redblack (Yellow-Right's son) who developed
his repertoire, and then held a territory, within earshot of
his father. Redblack is still singing this song in 1977. Each
bird modified it slightly and each had learnt it from the sur-

viving bearer of this tiny musical tradition, confined to some three acres of well-wooded gardens in Middlesex.

Perhaps there is some evolutionary advantage for the species as a whole in a capacity for sound variation which, in many individuals, is not fully extended. But it may be that this apparent surplus is not directly necessary at all. We do not have to find an immediate function to explain every phenomenon we observe. If bird sounds evolved primarily for communication there could still be a surplus of vocal skills which the individual will exercise because it is there; and some may be better endowed with it than others. The same argument applies to the senses of touch, smell and taste or to muscular strength and flexibility: all these attributes have been highly developed in various animal orders as an adaptation to their particular way of life. Why should such skills be employed only when there is a pressing need for them?

We cannot ever know, for certain, whether birds share, to however limited an extent, our enjoyment of patterned sound; whether in Charles Hartshorne's words they have musical sensibility as well as capability. But some of the examples quoted in this chapter suggest that this might be so.

We know that the substructure of a species' song is, in some cases, genetically determined and that the need for species recognition sets limits to the range of variation. But within these constraints the selection of models for imitation, and the combination of elements or motifs – especially in the more freely structured types of song – appears to be a matter for the individual bird. There is also the evidence of the apparently functionless forms of subsong in which the bird, in a relaxed state, appears to be playing with sound.

We are presented with some tantalizing possibilities: that in some species at least, these sound signals have evolved beyond the point which is necessary (so far as we can tell) for survival and reproduction; and that the birds may be exercising a rudimentary sense of musical form, very like our own, in the shaping of their songs.

Here the challenge of anthropomorphism must be met. All students of animal behaviour and many laymen have been made aware that it is misleading to interpret the actions of animals in human terms; to attribute thought and purposefulness where none may exist or feelings too complex for the level of mental awareness that we suppose the animal to have. But it is just as erroneous – for it inhibits deeper understanding – to assume that an organism as highly evolved as a bird is devoid of the simple emotional reactions and physical sensations of fear, anger, frustration and pleasure. It is the human content of these experiences that we must try to discard when we attempt to enter a bird's world. As Edward Armstrong has expressed it:

Let us not be scared by the bogey of anthropomorphism into the arms of the spectre of Cartesian mechanism. It is not anthropomorphism to believe that man and the higher animals have much in common so far as instinct and emotion are concerned but an acknowledgment of truth scientifically demonstrated.

Nevertheless the possibility that birds enjoy not just the act of singing but the shaping of the song is likely to remain controversial. In future, perhaps, further evidence of song development similar to that of the Blackbird's may make it seem more likely. Meanwhile I should like to cite some opinions from experts whose work has already been quoted in this book.

Charles Hartshorne:

If specifically human aesthetic responses are beyond the capacity of the other animals, this is not because the responses are aesthetic, but because of the intellectual element which pervades them. I have every sympathy with the caution contemporary ornithologists show regarding any attribution of human-like thought to birds (in spite of the navigational feats of migratory species), but I distinguish between aesthetic feeling and aesthetic thought. When a baby babbles rhythmically he is not doing much thinking, aesthetic or otherwise; but I believe he is enjoying certain sensations which I term aesthetic.

W. H. Thorpe:

The idea that bird song is often an expression of irrepressible joy can be supported with some plausible arguments and is certainly not without some scientific justification. In so far as this is true, the songs of birds can be regarded as a first step towards true artistic creation and expression.

And John Buxton concluded the passage on the Redstart's song which appears as the epigraph of Chapter 10, with these words:

For we should not be so inhuman or unscientific as to suppose birds do not enjoy their abilities as do we and other creatures. And they have much leisure (a fact that is often overlooked), since they have so few occupations or necessities. The hen, when brooding, can get all the food she needs, can stretch and preen and attend to any other wants she may have, in at most a quarter of every hour of daylight. If we allow the cock a little longer (because he has to defend his territory) we may be sure that for at least half of every waking hour he has nothing that he must do. Why not spend it in singing, and if so, why not elaborate the rather meagre song with which he is naturally endowed? What else should he do to amuse himself and employ his best abilities?

The use of sound is an aspect of a bird's behaviour that human beings can perhaps understand more readily than any other. As Terry Gompertz wrote in a passage which expresses the view that she and I had formed of the link between bird music and human music:

Sounds are for survival, both for birds and men. One of the greatest human achievements has been to shape sounds into forms and uses far beyond the demands of mere survival. But within the strict limitations of their way of life, the song birds also fashion sound in ways we recognize as musical. In the case of the Great Tit the material may be simple: but an experience such as listening to young Yellow-Right shaping his songs to his own satisfaction makes a distant kinship seem very much less remote.

12 How and Why?

It is an irony of history that the great powers should have discovered the unity of nations at Cairo in 1943. The geese of the world have had that notion for a longer time, and each March they stake their lives on its essential truth.

In the beginning there was only the unity of the Ice Sheet. Then followed the unity of the March thaw, and the northward hegira of the international geese. Every March since the Pleistocene, the geese have honked unity from China Sea to Siberian Steppe, from Euphrates to Volga, from Nile to Murmansk, from Lincolnshire to Spitsbergen. Every March since the Pleistocene, the geese have honked unity from Currituck to Labrador, Matamuskeet to Ungava, Horseshoe Lake to Hudson's Bay, Avery Island to Baffin Land, Panhandle to Mackenzie, Sacramento to Yukon.

By this international commerce of geese, the waste corn of Illinois is carried through the clouds to the Arctic tundras, there to combine with the waste sunlight of a nightless June to grow goslings for all the lands between. And in this annual barter of food for light, and winter warmth for summer solitude, the whole continent receives as net profit a wild poem dropped from the murky skies upon the muds of March. *Aldo Leopold*

Aldo Leopold, one of America's great naturalists and conservationists, died in 1948 fighting a marsh fire on a neighbour's land. His writings, and the tributes of those who knew him, speak of a man who was practical, humble and wise in his approach to the understanding of living communities: plants, animals and men. He accepted the discipline of science without agreeing with all its dogmas. He remained free in mind to enjoy the birds and mammals he studied: unafraid of emotional involvement so long as the observations were objective; his delight intensified by scientific insight.

The mystery of bird migration which puzzled scientists from Aristotle onwards has been gradually clarified by the scientific method of observation and experiment, and by worldwide cooperation among observers. I believe that the 'wild poem' is to be fully apprehended only by those who find the clarification more moving than the mystery. So Aldo Leopold's image of the geese in flight over time and space epitomizes for me the ideas that I have tried to convey.

There remain a number of questions which need to be considered further in this final chapter: how much is still to be found out about bird vocalizations and what the amateur can do; the methods of work; and how these studies contribute to our understanding of human behaviour. Running through all these is the question of our attitude to animals whose wellbeing, as we are at last beginning to realize, is the responsibility of our own dominant species.

Collecting Bird Sounds

It has been obvious at many points in this book that so far as bird vocalizations are concerned we have not yet completed the descriptive stage in this new science of bio-acoustics which includes the collection, categorization and study of the sounds that animals make. Adequate theories can only be founded on the widest possible evidence.

The first bird song recordings, so far as we know, was made as long ago as 1889 by Ludwig Koch, when he was eight years old. It was of the Indian Shama, a beautiful singer and a member of the thrush family. Dr Koch published 'sound-books', with text and recordings, for many years before he came to Britain from Germany. In 1936 he collaborated with E. M. Nicholson, who later became the Director-General of the Nature Conservancy, on the first and classic sound-book in English, 'Songs of wild birds'.

Older listeners will remember Ludwig Koch's birdsong programmes on radio, introduced with verve and enthusiasm in his highly individual accent. In spite of his musicality and aural experience with the birds he retained an engaging non-mastery of the sounds of the English language. His collection of wildlife recordings formed the core of the BBC's natural history library. With the help of indefatigable engineers, the cumbersome equipment of those days was transported, and kept working, up and down mountains, in and out of boats and onto remote islands, to record species found only in these inaccessible habitats.

Even so, a more extensive collection of animal sounds and their proper study had to await the postwar technical developments: tape-recording, miniaturization of equipment, parabolic reflectors and the rest. In 1951 Eric Simms took over the natural history section of the BBC's Sound Archives. With his wide experience as a naturalist and the continuing support of the engineers, he skilfully exploited these new techniques in the service of the birds and other animals and greatly increased the number of species whose songs and common calls are represented. In 1954 he reported on these activities to the eleventh meeting of the International Ornithological Congress in Basle which he attended with Bob Wade, the engineer who worked with him in the field. This was the first time that the BBC had been officially represented at the Congress.

Since those pioneering days – for that is what they were in the short history of the scientific recording of natural sounds – other excellent ornithologists on the staff of the BBC's Natural History Unit have still further expanded this fine collection which also includes recordings made by professional and amateur recordists from all over the British Isles and many parts of the world. Now there is the British Library of Wildlife Sounds, a London-based research library, to complement the older Library of Natural Sounds in the Cornell Laboratory of Ornithology at Ithaca in the United States, and the more recently established centres in Australia, South Africa and a few other countries. Copies of the BBC's natural history recordings are deposited in the Library, together with many commercially produced records, and fully annotated material on tape from recordists who have specialized in wildlife sounds.

All these recordings are accessible for scientific purposes but many more are needed to provide the evidence on which future research may be based. Some species have not yet been even adequately studied. Those that have are not always well represented in recordings because the studies were made before good field equipment was available to amateurs or to young professional research workers on a slender grant.

There is no doubt that the amateur who is prepared to work with scientific care, however limited his time, has still a great deal to contribute; not least, as Professor Niko Tinbergen has pointed out in his book *Social Behaviour in Animals*, in a freshness of approach. A number of remarkable behavioural studies have started from the curiosity and enjoyment of an amateur presented with an opportunity. What particular line of investigation you follow and how far you pursue it is a matter of time and means.

Some people are better at single-minded concentration on one species. This will always take a very long time: no one can know much about even one species without several years of close acquaintanceship. Other people might prefer to spread their interests more widely over some aspect of behaviour in a group of related species, or to study an ecological community. Yet others would be happier to join in the cooperative efforts of the various local or national ornithological societies. There is plenty of scope for all these forms of research at many levels of complexity.

There are certain themes on which there can never be too much information because even local differences may help to demonstrate some point of general biological interest. These themes include song variation in individuals and in populations; seasonal and daily rhythms of vocal behaviour; calls related to the circumstances of their use; and the correlation of all these with other forms of behaviour and with changing factors in the environment. Some of these topics can be investigated with only the simplest technical equipment and regular observations.

Research Methods

For the proper study of animal behaviour there are three complementary approaches: fieldwork; the study of animals in captivity, within an environment that is as spacious and as natural as possible; and laboratory experiments.

The methods for bird vocalization studies are no different from those in any other scientific study of animals. Everything begins with long and patient observation and recording of wild-living birds. 'Controls' must always be used: the study of a sufficient number of individuals, or of populations in different areas, to make sure that the observations are not biassed by aberrant individuals or unusual circumstances.

The observer must be quick to take advantage of evidence from natural experiments: the unexpected events which switch a bird's behaviour from one pattern to another and thereby suggest an explanation for some aspect of it (like Redblack's loss of his mate, or the Yorkshire Great Tit's sudden change from full song to *tinking* when it was startled by a gunshot). A very great deal can be learned in this way. Contrived experiments, such as playbacks, are needed to confirm critical conclusions or to solve puzzles that cannot be elucidated naturally, such as the testing of response to songs from a different area or from a geographically-remote species.

Most people who study one species closely have found the need for additional work at close quarters with birds that are unafraid of them. This gives the opportunity for hearing quiet sounds, seeing small movements, and for controlling changes in the birds' environment. Some form of captivity is essential. In this, as in the wild, the greatest care must be taken to avoid distorting the birds' behaviour by interference which distresses or exhausts them. Scientifically, deductions made from distorted behaviour are useless and more importantly, in my view, we have no right to interfere in this way.

In the United Kingdom legislation on bird protection is good and was improved by 'The Conservation of Wild Creatures and Wild Plants Act, 1975'. Under the various Acts, no one can take protected wild birds into captivity, or eggs or nestlings for hand-rearing, without a licence from the Nature Conservancy Council. A licence and training are also required before birds can be ringed, or colour-ringed for identification in field work.

When Terry Gompertz and I first started the hand-rearing and natural breeding in captivity of some of the tit species, we were lucky in the possession of a house and garden that could readily be adapted for the birds. Their main living quarters were in a big outside aviary with growing shrubs and other plants to attract insects, and a structure of natural branches for perching. The aviary was linked through open windows with a large room where the birds usually roosted. This was also liberally decorated with branches and had the minimum of normal furniture required for our comfort when we were in the room. Interesting objects were added as bird furniture. The tape-recorders were elsewhere, with long cables leading to the on-site microphones. One practical reason for this was that the birds found the recorders highly attractive: tape-pulling came naturally, and squeaky spools were a stimulus to vocalization, particularly warbling subsong. A few books were the only casualties, during paper-tearing periods. But they could not be removed because the box-like cavities between books of appropriate height and the shelf above were much sought-after roosting holes.

The birds were completely fearless. To some extent we were their social companions though for this they relied mainly on each other's company. Mostly, we were interesting 'props' for their explorations. The satisfaction of this relationship, and the scientific interest, were out of all proportion to the trouble we took to provide for the birds' wellbeing. This 'free captivity' permitted them to breed and rear young, and to carry on their other activities in a fairly normal way. The changes they were forced to make in comparatively confined and artificial surroundings were in themselves revealing to us. But, as we already knew or were able to confirm, these were adaptations, not distortions, of natural behaviour.

Work with captive animals is necessarily an important part of behaviour studies by professional scientists. Many research projects require more precise experimentation than amateurs could or should carry out. This means, however, that the professionals have ethical problems to solve. Certain types of extreme experiments possibly involve more subtle forms of cruelty than those against which existing legislation protects laboratory-kept animals.

Behavioural scientists themselves hold differing views on how far it is right to go in experiments with animals and I think the issues should be more widely understood and debated. I do not want to enter, here, into the enduring and more difficult controversy about the use of animals in medical experiments which immediately benefit man. Nor do I underrate the argument that research which appears to have no relevance to human medical or psychological problems, later turns out to have a useful application. But I believe that it is very important to ask whether in behavioural studies which, in the main, answer questions only of long-term biological interest any procedures which unduly distress or permanently damage animals should be used.

A German scientist friend once said to us in the course of an argument on the deafening of birds in learning experiments 'The results are very interesting, but I could not do it.' This, I think, is the crux. The temptation to satisfy our human curiosity is great and our moral susceptibilities, as the events of the last half-century have shown, are too easily blunted. Ethical restraints need to be worked out and exercised in good time. For our own good, as well as for the sake of the animals, I feel we ought to think very seriously before embarking on such experiments. If they only produce, quickly, results which could be achieved by more laborious means, surely we could wait? And if the results are unobtainable in any other way, must we know everything, at the expense of other species over which our temporary evolutionary success has given us such power?

We have still so much to learn about animals and from them, in a more natural setting and by simpler means, that we could afford to hold our zeal for experimentation more firmly in check.

Animal Studies and Human Behaviour

Animal behaviour has been studied for its intrinsic interest and for the understanding of general biological and evolutionary principles which it offers. Much research has also been undertaken in the hope of increasing our comprehension of our own behaviour.

There are probably four main areas in which zoologists, psychologists, anthropologists, sociologists and linguists hope to find evidence from animal studies which is relevant to the human behavioural sciences. The first is behaviour itself, in the strict sense of how we act as individuals and interact with each other. There is the question of animal communication and the origin of human language. Next, our understanding of the basic processes of learning is illuminated by observing them at an elementary stage in animals. Finally there is the hope that a clear picture of the population-regulating mechanisms evolved by animals might indicate where we should look for unexplored causes of our failure to control the increase in human population.

For the first of these, psychologists and others primarily concerned with human behaviour must draw freely from the whole range of ethological work. For many of their purposes studies of our close relatives the mammals, and especially the Primates, are the most relevant. There they can see in simpler, more overt form the conflict between aggressive and cooperative tendencies. They can observe ritualization of behaviour and examine possible parallels with our own. They can note parent-child and other family relationships and differing forms of social structure. But when it comes to the role of communication in human affairs birds, which make such a highly developed use of sound, must be specially considered.

As we have seen birds use sound when alone and, as far as we can tell, for pleasure. Socially, sound signals stimulate and maintain the relationships between individuals on which reproduction and the rearing of offspring depend. Sound signals function, both in antagonism and in cooperation, as part of the systems which regulate the social structure of communities. The vocal codes of a species and even of a local population are, in many cases, at least partly learned. Sound signals also act as a form of crowd control and, presumably, stimulation; for instance in the mass aerial manoeuvres of flocking species. They help to maintain organization at communal roosts and breeding grounds.

These are suggestive comparisons with human vocalizations. Moreover in intimate situations, in individual or group antagonism and in crowds, we often use non-verbal sound signals to replace, or in addition to, the spoken word. We have been less successful than many bird species in the substitution of sound signals for direct conflict. We appear to be an excitable species and communal war-whoops have too often stimulated physical aggression instead of preventing it.

There has been considerable interest in the last few years in the role of non-verbal communication, both visual and vocal, in human relationships. By observation, filming and recording of conversations between individuals and in groups, psychologists have followed Darwin's lead in 'The Expression of the Emotions in Man and Animals'. They have shown how the meaning of the spoken word is amplified – and sometimes contradicted – by tones of voice, emphases, pauses, eye movements, facial expression, body posture and gestures.

This emotive communication was very fully exploited by birds and mammals for tens of millions of years before our time. It was unlikely that we should shed so useful an inheritance in our brief evolutionary span. But with our capacity for conscious control of our behaviour it is better that we should understand the emotional strength of the forces we can employ for social good or evil.

Closely related to this is the question of the origin of human language for which no satisfying explanation has yet been proposed. Did it emerge as an extension of the non-verbal communication systems of animals with which it shares some fundamental features? Or did it appear, in however simple a form, as an evolutionary innovation by some saltation: a sudden leap from one level to another which no previous development seemed to foreshadow?

Most modern evolutionary theorists are wary of saltation as an explanation of a difficulty. It can too easily mask the more complex situation which further knowledge reveals. The 'missing link' between ape and man was an intellectual illusion. Long chains of links connecting particular characteristics are emerging as more and more of the evidence from the pre-human and early human past is assembled. But vocal communication systems leave no trace in the fossil record.

In one of his contributions to a recently published symposium on 'Non-verbal Communication', Professor W. H. Thorpe comments on this problem:

We may never come to know how this great gap between the highest animal 'language' and the language of man was bridged by the human ancestral stock. No anthropologist nowadays ever hopes to find a language which is primitive in the sense of forming a link between the language of man and the communication systems of animals. The search for a primitive language was abandoned by sociologists and anthropologists fifty years or more ago. And this recognition of the uniqueness of the human language and still more, the understanding of those respects in which it is unique, constitute a great step forward in comprehension of the relationship or lack of relationship between man and the animals. But if we are ever to find out how such a gap might possibly have been bridged it seems, to some of us at least, that the fullest possible study of bird language is an essential preliminary.

The level of communication at which the language of birds and man most nearly converge is to be found in the utterances of that expressive non-verbal communicator, the human baby. As we have seen the ritualized, communicatory signals of birds are capable of carrying a greater number of messages than the baby can convey vocally in its first few months of life. But the simple cries of pain, hunger, distress and contentment are exactly paralleled.

It seems that we have to learn to distinguish accurately the significance of these sometimes intergrading cries of the human infant. Some medical workers in Scandinavia, using techniques similar to those of bird vocalization studies, have analysed the sounds and shown that groups of midwives, of nurses with less specialized experience of babies, and of mothers, varied in the success of their identification of different cries. Midwives were in general the best at recognizing all types of cry. Mothers quickly learn to identify the cries of their own babies and pick them out from recorded sequences which include cries from other babies. The great value of this work for the future is in the recognition of special cries which may help in the early diagnosis of abnormalities.

Various theories about the origin of language have invoked babies' cries. One, sometimes referred to as the 'Pooh-pooh' theory, suggests that language grew out of such simple interjections, expressing an emotional state. Another (the 'Contact' theory) sees language arising from gregarious man's need for social contact. The call, as when the baby cries out for its mother, led on to the word symbolizing a specific need. (A nestling bird's begging call, incidentally, is symbolic in the same way: the sound bears no relation to the need expressed.) In the Contact theory the earliest verbal utterances were simple imperatives. But none of these – not even the attractively named and plausible 'Yo-heave-ho' theory (the parallel development of cooperative manual effort and the sound signals required to coordinate it) are able to explain the more difficult transition from single-word signal to structured sentence.

Many linguists have also been interested in the pre-speech

babbling of infants. This, too, might have something to tell us about the origin of language. More certainly, it is important for the development of language in the individual child. Here, there is a link with the third area in which human behavioural scientists are making useful comparisons with animals: the study of the process of learning.

Infant babbling presents interesting parallels with bird vocalizations. Oddly enough, the ways in which it helps the child to develop verbal language are not precisely understood, though there are many theories. Babbling occurs in a number of different situations. One is when the baby is alone and at ease with the world, its needs temporarily satisfied. This is very similar to the bird, juvenile or adult, warbling in a relaxed and solitary state when living conditions are easy enough to permit leisure. Another situation is when the baby or very young child is playing – the equivalent, perhaps, of the young bird's exploratory activity when it is not sufficiently hungry for real food-searching. This seems to have the quality and function of useful play and is likewise often accompanied by a vocal commentary.

The learning parallel that has aroused particular interest is the development of song, in certain bird species, out of the juvenile warbling or subsong. Some of the same mechanisms appear to operate in the child as it shapes sounds into signals during its own apprentice stage of vocal practice. These parallels, as Professor Peter Marler has suggested 'perhaps point to a set of conditions to which any system of vocal learning should conform, if it is to function effectively'. However, as he also comments 'That there should be even a suspicion of basic similarities in physiological machinery and learning strategy is remarkable when the specific problems confronting a child and a young bird are so vastly different'.

The widely discussed linguistic theories of Professor Noam Chomsky pose the learning problem in a different way. In his view there are fundamental features of language – basic logical and grammatical 'rules' – to which all languages, however different, conform; children have an innate capacity to respond to and use these fundamental features of language when they are learning to talk.

There is a resemblance here, too, to the model that has been proposed to explain song development in some bird species: a genetically controlled programming for a particular form of song, with the details to be mastered by listening, imitation and practice. The child, like the young bird, needs social stimulation if its very generalized predisposition is to develop into an effective act of communication.

Exploration of the origin and individual acquisition of language has an especial fascination. But if we never deduce how language began, the result is merely a tantalizing gap in our evolutionary history. The processes by which children acquire linguistic skills are of practical importance. The more that is found out about language learning the better and here, it seems, the study of bird sounds is a fruitful source of ideas.

It may be significant for future research that just as some psychologists have worked with animals or even permanently changed disciplines to elucidate processes that are easier to study in animals so, more recently, several ethologists have transferred their attention to the study of babies and young children. Direct experience on both sides of a borderline is likely to be more productive than even the most effective exchange of information between researchers in different disciplines.

Lastly there is the study of animal populations: of the mechanisms that keep numbers within the limits that the environment can support. Among these mechanisms vocalizations clearly play only a minor, though possibly a significant, role in the regulation of bird numbers. In territorial species they are part of the behavioural system which controls the spacing out of individuals; and they help to maintain the social structure of a community, whatever form this may take in different avian species.

A theory which incidentally attaches even greater importance to sound signals as population regulators has been put forward by Professor V. C. Wynne-Edwards in a remarkable book, *Animal Dispersion in Relation to Social Behaviour*. In this theory, occasions for mass vocalization – such as the regular morning and evening song periods, communal roosting, and certain types of aerial and ground flock displays – function partly as an aural census of numbers. The birds would respond to this assessment and make adjustments in their population density on the ground.

The theory as a whole has been disputed, particularly by the late Dr David Lack, and has not aroused the interest among biologists which it may yet turn out to deserve. However, these are matters too complex and important to be skimmed over and they lie beyond the scope of this book: the evidence and the arguments over its interpretation should be read by anyone who is seriously interested. We need to know a great deal more about animal populations and the ways in which their numbers are regulated before the arguments can be resolved and conclusions reached which might help us in our own dilemma.

But the impetus to resolve these and the other questions so briefly referred to in this chapter is there: in the emerging, synthesizing science of sociobiology. As threads are gathered together from studies of social organization among animals, and linked by modern evolutionary theory, sociobiologists are reaching forward to make a contribution to our understanding of human societies which, if it comes in time, could be crucial for our survival.

In the light of this greater question, the study of bird sounds might seem a trivial, if enjoyable, occupation. But broad theories are constructed from fine detail. Knowledge of how its members communicate is essential for the understanding of any society; and only when the structures of animal communities are thoroughly comprehended, can the sociobiological contribution to our thinking about the future of the human community be fully and convincingly made.

I return to Aldo Leopold, for he realized our need for a far-seeing and truly scientific approach to animals:

For centuries this rich library of knowledge has been inaccessible to us because we did not know where or how to look for it. Ecology is now teaching us to search in animal populations for analogies to our own problems. By learning how some small part of the biota ticks, we can guess how the whole mechanism ticks. The ability to perceive these deeper meanings, and to appraise them critically, is the woodcraft of the future.

To sum up, wildlife once fed us and shaped our culture. It still yields us pleasure for leisure hours, but we try to reap that pleasure by modern machinery and thus destroy part of its value. Reaping it by modern mentality would yield not only pleasure, but wisdom as well.

Postscript

This is really a book by two people and it only bears my name because Terry Gompertz did not live to write it herself. The research on the Great Tits, in its imaginative direction and execution, was all hers but in my spare time I, too, enjoyed the excitements of fieldwork in all weathers, a house and garden festooned with cables, international conferences, record-keeping, carpentry, bird-catering and – above all – listening. We shared our ideas and experiences in daily talk and often only a note has reminded me that I was not present during some episode with the birds that is vivid in my memory. Yet there was much that I had to miss and twenty-five years of companionship were not long enough for all that we wanted to do and to talk about. This book is the best that I could make, without her, to honour the birds we knew.

Readers will appreciate the variety of skills that such studies demand and will realize that without unstinted help and teaching from people who possessed them, we could neither have done our own work nor had the opportunity to understand that of others. Some of our ornithological colleagues and friends are referred to in the text and I hope that they, and many more from whom we also learned, will accept my gratitude. If I single out a few – Frank Fraser Darling, Derek Goodwin, Joan Hall-Craggs, Patrick Sellar, Gerhard Thielcke and Margaret Vince – it is because they have given their expert help in the preparation of this publication as well as the advice and encouragement over the years that meant so much to us.

Robert Windsor and Gerald Ramshaw supervised our technical plans, responding inventively to impossible demands, and kept our equipment in good order. In the course of my own work at the BBC and from specialist colleagues there, I acquired many ideas and techniques that could be applied to the study of bird sounds. We both appreciated the understanding, as well as the opportunities, that the BBC offered us.

I am grateful, too, to Margery Llewellyn and Charles Rolfe who helped with the house-living birds; to many past and present residents on Pinner Hill, Middlesex, who allowed us to use their gardens for observation; to the Fisheries Angling Club, West Hyde, for access to their fishing lake and for their care of the habitat, and to staff of the Forestry

Commission – in particular Arthur Cadman, George Ryle, Gordon Simpson and Norman Terry – who welcomed us to the forests.

Edward Armstrong, J.-C. Brémond, Evelyn and Alan Charnley, Daphne and Anthony Dorrell, Janet Kear, Eric Knowles, John Krebs, David Pye, Eric Simms, David Snow, W. H. Thorpe and B. Tschanz gave time to reading all or parts of the book and I thank them warmly for their thoughtful comments. Simeon Potter, my mentor in linguistics for many years, also gave the text his characteristically meticulous scrutiny only a few weeks before he died, unexpectedly, in August 1976.

I am indebted to Raymond A. Stefanski and John Brackenbury for much information and drafting help in the section on voice production. I also acknowledge, with particular pleasure, permission from all those – named here or elsewhere – who have allowed me to draw on their work and to use their illustrations and recordings because in every case it was given with such sympathetic enthusiasm. If errors of fact or interpretation remain they are my responsibility.

Jeffery Boswall of the BBC Natural History Unit kindly provided the note on bird recordings that are available commercially.

Peter Campbell of BBC Publications, and the staff of the Cambridge University Press, have expertly made light of the problems of this complicated project.

Definitions of Terms

1   The structure of songs and calls

There are as yet no standard terms for bird sound analysis though a number of useful systems have been proposed. Most of the terms I have chosen are in fairly widespread use, particularly in France and Germany.

Element: a single sound in the sequence of sounds of which a song or call is composed, represented by an unbroken trace on a sonagram made from a recording reproduced at normal speed. Some calls consist of only one element.

Syllable: a combination of two or more elements which always occur together, usually with a very small time-separation, in the songs or calls of some species.

Note is sometimes used as a comprehensive term for any element or syllable which is musical in tone-quality, to emphasize the contrast with a harsh or noisy sound.

Motif: a sequence of elements which may be repeated immediately or recur periodically in some types of song.

Phrase: for its definition in the analysis of Blackbird song, see Chapter 11. In other contexts phrase is used colloquially for any short, well-defined sequence of sounds.

Strophe: either a complete song pattern which is usually repeated with or without variation after a short pause (as in the Chaffinch or the Wren); or an uninterrupted song utterance which is resumed in the same or a varied form after a pause (as in Great Tit or Sedge Warbler song).

Song-variant denotes one of the song forms used by an individual of a species.

Song type refers to the basic structure or pattern of the song of a species. Song types can be classified in various ways.

2   Acoustic analysis

The technical terminology of acoustics has been avoided as far as possible and is unnecessary for an aural classification and comparison of bird sounds. However, refined analysis depends on physical measurements and it is useful to have some idea of the relationship between these and our aural perceptions. There are two matters in which this is particularly important – the frequency of a sound and its power.

Frequency is a physical measurement – the number of vibrations per second of a sound: 1 vibration per second = 1 Hertz (1000 Hertz = 1 kiloHertz). Sounds of lower frequency have longer wavelengths and those of higher frequencies have shorter wavelengths. These physical characteristics of sound affect the way in which it is absorbed or deflected by obstacles in its path and therefore the distance it can travel in different acoustic environments.

Pitch is a subjective assessment. We hear a sound as low or high in pitch and this corresponds in a particular way with low and high frequencies. The bottom C on a piano has a frequency of 32·7 Hertz (Hz) and the top C – seven octaves higher – is 4186 Hz. The frequency of a sound is doubled every time to produce a sound one octave higher, so the difference in frequency between sounds that we hear as semitones in the highest octave of the piano is much greater than in the lowest octave. The difference, however, is proportional: each upward step of a semitone in pitch increases by a factor of 1·06 in frequency (in the 'equal temperament' system for tuning keyboard instruments which has been in use since the time of Johann Sebastian Bach).

Intensity is the power of a sound and is expressed in *decibels* (dB), familiar from reports of acceptable noise levels in factories or from aircraft. A sound that is 10 times more powerful than another has a sound intensity 10 dB higher; if it is 100 times more powerful it has an intensity 20 dB higher, and so on. An *intensity curve*, which can be useful in comparison of bird sounds, shows fluctuations in the intensity of the sound measured in dB.

Amplitude is the measure of changes in sound pressure and is related to changes in intensity: intensity is proportional to the square of the pressure amplitude. For example, a sound that is 100 times more powerful than another (= +20 dB) has a sound pressure level 10 times higher. Fluctuations in the amplitude of a signal are displayed on oscillograms and these, too, have proved useful in bird sound analysis.

Loudness is a subjective matter and what we hear as degrees of loudness relate to, but do not correspond exactly with fluctuations in intensity. Our assessment varies with the frequency of sound. For example, we hear as sounds of equal loudness:

a tone of 100 Hz at 75 dB
a tone of 1000 Hz at 50 dB
a tone of 6000 Hz at 70 dB.

Tone-quality, or timbre, depends on the physical structure of the sound and this is affected by the materials and construction of the sound source, whether it is a human or avian voice or a musical instrument. A *pure tone* is a sound of a single frequency and though it can be produced by an oscillator or a tuning-fork is seldom, if ever, heard otherwise though piping or fluting notes can often be remarkably 'pure'. Most sounds, however, are *complex tones* consisting of the lowest or *fundamental frequency* which sets the pitch we assign to the sound, and a mixture of mathematically related higher frequencies (overtones or *harmonics* – see below). The relative intensity of these higher frequencies has a profound effect on tone-quality.

Some bird notes maintain a fairly steady pitch and have clear harmonics – it is these that we are most likely to compare with the sounds of musical instruments. But in general bird sounds have a much greater vibrato round the fundamental frequency, and are therefore less constant in pitch, than any humanly produced musical note. The extent of this, too, affects the tone-quality.

Harmonic. The first harmonic is an alternative term for the fundamental frequency. The second harmonic is an octave higher, the third at an interval of a fifth higher still and the fourth at the second octave above the fundamental – and so on through the whole *harmonic series* as it is called; for each harmonic occurs in arithmetical progression from the fundamental frequency. For example, the A above middle C on the piano, with a fundamental frequency of 440 Hz has its second harmonic at octave A = 880 Hz and its third harmonic at E above = 1320 Hz (3 × 440 Hz). The higher harmonics follow at equal frequency intervals and therefore at ever-decreasing pitch intervals.

While some bird sounds are too high for even the second harmonic to show on a standard sonagram, harmonics have been detected, when present, by other means. The most interesting point, however, is that when there are two separate and simultaneous traces on a sonagram, one above the other, whose frequencies do not form a simple ratio, we know that the sounds must have been independently generated in the bird's vocal organs since one cannot be a harmonic of the other. This is the equivalent of double stopping on a violin but a human singer is incapable of such a feat.

Parameter – a term borrowed from mathematics – is used in bio-acoustic work to cover any one of the independently variable characteristics of a sound-sequence such as frequency, intensity, duration, rhythm and tone-quality.

3   Taxonomic terms

Order, Sub-order, Family and Genus. These higher taxa, in descending order, represent increasingly close relationships between species. They are classifications based on the probability of such relationships because of similarities in, for example, the structure of the skeleton and the musculature. They also indicate probable lines of evolution since specialized adaptations in shared characteristics must have evolved later than the basic form.

Passerines is the term commonly used, collectively, for members of the large order of 'perching birds' – the Passeriformes. The remaining bird orders are often referred to collectively as non-passerines.

Oscines are the true songbirds and are a sub-order of the Passeriformes. In terms of families, genera and species, they far outnumber the rest of the passerines.

Species can be defined as a group of animals whose members are capable, in the wild, of mating and of producing viable and fertile offspring (see Chapter 9).

Sub-species are geographical populations within a species that show recognizable but usually rather slight differences from populations found elsewhere within the species' range. In some cases they may be a stage in the continuing evolution of new species. Sometimes, as on islands, a sub-species has been completely isolated from the main stock in which case the differences may have become fairly sharply defined. More commonly, sub-species are connected by populations with inter-grading characteristics so that there is no clear division between them.

Geographic race. In ornithology *race* is commonly used as a synonym for a formally recognized sub-species and in most contexts is so used in this book. Since, however, recent evidence from many sources, including ecological, behavioural and vocalization studies, is altering some of the earlier classifications of sub-species (and even of species) the term race has also been preferred because it is less rigidly defined.

Wader, in the plural, is commonly used in the British Isles for species belonging to a group of families (the sub-order Charadrii) in the order Charadriiformes. Snipes; plovers, sandpipers, phalaropes, avocets and oyster-catchers, for example, are all 'waders' on this definition.

Classification of the Great Tit to illustrate some of these terms.

Order	Passeriformes
Sub-order	Oscines
Family	Paridae
Genus	*Parus*
Species	*major*
Sub-species, e.g.	*newtoni*
	(in British Isles)

Notating Bird Sounds

The inadequacy of phonetic transcriptions of bird songs and calls is generally agreed. Nevertheless, supplemented by verbal descriptions, they have been until recently the only method in widespread use for representing bird sounds. Now that there are gramophone records and cassettes of the songs and common calls of an ever increasing number of species, we do not have to depend on these verbal symbols for identification. But listening is a fleeting experience and aural memories are only too easily obliterated; a permanent, visual record of sound is invaluable. There is no clear cut answer to the question of the form this should take. Before recording and analytic equipment were available it was much debated – and still is. However, the emphasis has changed and it is now possible to choose a method of visual presentation suited to the job in hand.

The sonagram, oscillogram and intensity curve quickly superseded all the earlier methods of transcription for the scientific analysis of vocalizations. Most of the work described in this book could not have been done without them and they are likely to be used more and more in ornithological handbooks and field guides. Further sources of information about these methods of analysis and presentation are given in the references (p. 252). Professional equipment, however, is not available everywhere or to everyone and some form of written notation is needed as well.

Orthodox musical (staff) notation was widely used in the past by those who were mainly interested in bird song for its musical qualities and a few advocates still retain the belief in its efficacy to which their skill in this form of transcription entitles them. Certainly the songs of some species can be beautifully represented in this way but the method has disadvantages – mainly that it cannot cover the whole range of avian sounds and that comparatively few people are able to read or apply it adequately.

Various diagrammatic systems – some including verbal descriptions and relying to a certain extent on musical notation – have been proposed, from the turn of the century onwards. An article by Dr Trevor Hold (see p. 252) lists and reviews them as well as providing a recommendation for a sophisticated compromise system. This retains useful features of musical notation within a more flexible format. All these

systems take time to write and assume the need for considerable accuracy. This is important for some purposes and
in the absence of a tape recorder: for example individual
birds can be identified and relocated on subsequent visits to
an area if the detailed characteristics of their vocalizations
are transcribed. Anyone who needs a comprehensive written
notation should consult these sources: there are interesting and
helpful ideas in all of them, especially those of A. A. Saunders
and M. E. W. North.

In my experience, however, a system of sound-notation is
most frequently required nowadays for the learning of new
songs and calls and as a running annotation of recordings or
of sound sequences in the field. For such purposes it should
be simple, adaptable and quickly written. It is likely to be
used only by the individual concerned or a small group of
colleagues and as long as the code is clearly set down and
easy to decipher, the details are unimportant. My aim here is
to suggest a few guidelines for the construction of such a code
to help beginners and any amateur fieldworkers who would
find it useful.

Easily written symbols for different types of element, and
markings to indicate other features of a sound sequence, are
the basis of any system. Symbols for musical elements are
simple to devise. Several diagrammatic systems, including
the one that Terry Gompertz and I worked out for our own
use, anticipated or followed the equivalent sonagram trace
for an element. Notes gliding upwards or downwards in
pitch can be represented by curves of varying length and
steepness; single notes of short duration by something like
a large full stop and single notes of longer duration by a
horizontal line. Trills, or very vibrant notes and glides, become a wavy line whose length and degree of curvature give
some idea of duration and of speed of fluctuation. Relative
pitch is suggested by setting each symbol above, below or
level with the preceding one. For greater accuracy the nearest
major or minor interval in the western musical scale can be
indicated but inability to do this, or lack of time in the field,
need not be a cause of despair. Any visual representation is
better than none.

Non-musical elements can take various forms. A vertical
line, as on a sonagram, stands for a click and an x for a single
noisy or harsh element. For species with several distinctive
types of non-musical element different symbols should be
allocated as each sound is separately identified. Any special
sound frequently made by a species needs its own symbol.

As soon as we had differentiated the Great Tit aggressive *tink* from the somewhat similar social calls, we gave it a special symbol. As a result we could glance through the annotated card-index to the tape recordings and quickly pick out an example of this call.

Rhythmic patterns are most satisfactorily indicated by adopting signs from musical notation and adding crotchet, quaver or semi-quaver tails, the point for the dotted note and so on, to the basic symbols. This was essential for noting Great Tit song-variants among which several motifs may be similar in speed, the pitch of the elements and tone quality (to the unaided ear) and differ only in their rhythm. However, few species have songs that are as persistently and conventionally rhythmical as those of the Great Tit and in many cases an accent mark to indicate a strongly emphasized note may be enough.

Examples of other markings which may usefully be adopted from musical notation are the staccato sign for a short, abrupt note, rests to indicate a definite break in the flow of sound and crescendo and diminuendo marks. They are quick to write and easy to learn for those who are not practised in musical notation. These and other signs are illustrated below, together with some of the suggested symbols.

It must be re-emphasized that these are not proposals for a precise system of representing bird sounds. They are intended simply to offer a basis for a practical, easily written code for use when a shorthand reminder of the sound is all that is necessary. I have among my notes a lengthy field annotation of a Great Tit territorial border dispute which clearly charts the progress of the vocal battle. The dispute was recorded but the annotation is particularly valuable because

82
Sonagram of the Golden Oriole call described in Chapter 1 (E. D. H. Johnson).

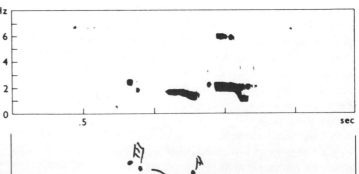

Rough field notation of the same call. The first two short notes are not heard at a distance and might be omitted.

Some symbols for different types of sound element

|	a click
——	long, pure, whistled note
•	short note of definite pitch
⌒⌒⌒	long, slow trill
⋏⋏⋏⋏	short, fast trill
ᴡ	vibrant note
\ \ ⟍	downward glide
⟋ ⟋ ⟋	upward glide
⟋ᴍ	vibrant, downward glide
✕ ⊐ ⊐	examples of symbols that can be allocated to
‖ ○ ✓	short, non-musical elements in the repertoire of a species
♭	symbol used for Great Tit *tink*
♭	symbol used for Chaffinch *pink*
	a rough, *churring* sound: approximate duration
⋀⋀⋀⋀	indicated by length of symbol

Some signs from staff notation which are useful in the field

>	accent for a stressed element
⟍	short rest indicating break in flow of sound
⁚	staccato dot below a short, abrupt musical element
♩. ♪	two-note Great Tit motif in uneven, skipping rhythm; the second note higher in pitch
♪	two-note motif in even rhythm: the notes flow smoothly and the first one is strongly emphasized; the second is lower in pitch
↑ ——	sustained whistled note preceded by a very short musical note
↑ ⟋	as above but whistle gliding upwards in pitch. This example can often be heard from a Song Thrush
<	crescendo
>	diminuendo
ƒ p	loud and soft signs placed under elements or phrases in a song

it bridges the gap when the tape ran out and a minute or two was missed while it was changed. To judge from some field notebooks that I have seen and the scribbled patterns which colleagues often enclose as a guide to their recordings, other ornithologists have thought along the same lines when devising their own codes and with very similar results.

Beginners need not be so concerned about speed but they may find, as we did, that the essential experience of listening, both to recordings and in the field, is reinforced by the attempt to transcribe the sounds. There are suggestions in Chapter 4 (page 60) about the different aspects of a song pattern that should be noted as a key to recognition. These are more easily recalled if they have been indicated, however roughly, in a diagrammatic form which can be checked in a field notebook.

Voice Production

At first sight a bird's skeleton looks quite unlike that of any mammal. Nevertheless it is easy to understand that foreleg (or arm) bones have merely evolved somewhat differently to form the wings and that leg and foot bones have been modified for perching or swimming, and for bi-pedal walking – a method of progression not generally favoured by mammals other than ourselves. The structures associated with breathing and voice production show much greater differences.

In the first place the lungs are partly surrounded by, and connected to, structures that are unique to birds – large, thin-walled air sacs. There are also air spaces instead of bone marrow in some of the bones of the skull and limbs and these help to lighten the weight of the bird – an advantage in flight. The air sacs are in two groups: a posterior group behind the lungs and extending into the abdominal cavity; and an anterior group of somewhat smaller sacs in the breast cavity and at the level of the collar-bones (the clavicles). The result is that although the lung capacity of birds is smaller, size for size, than that of mammals, the total volume of air in the avian respiratory system is about three times that of a mammal.

As the bird breathes in, some of the air flows from the main bronchial tube straight into the posterior air sacs. But part of the same intake of fresh air goes into the lung and ventilates it, and then flows on into the anterior sacs. When the bird breathes out, the fresh air stored in the posterior sacs is driven through the lungs and out into the main bronchial tubes. There it is joined by the stale air from the anterior sacs and all the air is then exhaled through the mouth. Air, in fact, flows through the lungs in one direction only – outwards – and the sacs act as bellows to keep it moving through the complicated network. As a result of this system, incidentally, there is a higher intake of oxygen to the blood, and a greater loss of carbon dioxide, than mammals can achieve and this accounts for the ability of birds to remain active in the rarefied atmosphere at very high altitudes.

The relevance here is the effect on vocalization. The air sac surrounding the bird's vocal apparatus (the interclavicular air sac) is essential for sound production: if it is punctured the bird loses its voice. It is possible that the sac also acts as a resonator. Another point is that a bird, unlike a mammal,

83
Simplified diagram
of a bird showing
the main features
of the breathing
and sound-
production
system (the air
sacs are grouped
and not given in
detail).

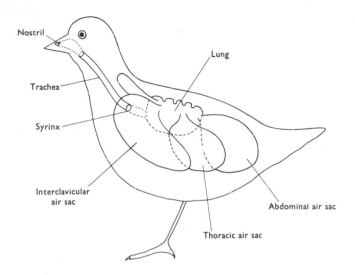

breathes actively during both inspiration and expiration. In general, sound is produced on the outbreath.

The vocal organs themselves are also quite different from ours. The larynx is not directly involved in bird vocalization: at most it affects resonance and its main function is to act as a valve, regulating the flow of air into and out of the trachea, or windpipe. A bird's voicebox is another unique anatomical feature – the syrinx. This is basically a bony enlargement of the bottom end of the trachea just where it divides into the two main bronchial tubes. Some of the component parts are set in the walls of the trachea and bronchi. The syrinx, there-fore, lies deep in the breast cavity in front of the heart, separated from the bird's mouth and the outside air by the length of the trachea; in species with long necks, like swans, geese and cranes, the trachea is very long indeed (Figure 83).

The exact placing of the syrinx in this junction between trachea and bronchi, the form of its component parts, and the number of muscles associated with it, differ considerably in the various bird orders – from the primitive to the more recently evolved. The greatest complexity is found in the most recently evolved of all – the songbirds.

The actual source of sound within the syrinx is some thin tympaniform membranes, so called because they resemble the membrane of a drum, the tension of which can be changed to produce notes of higher or lower pitch. The striking force that sets these pairs of membranes in vibration is air expelled from the lungs by the action of the air sacs. Their tension is

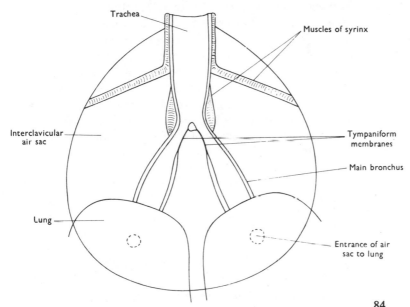

Trachea

Muscles of syrinx

Interclavicular
air sac

Tympaniform
membranes

Main bronchus

Lung

Entrance of air
sac to lung

controlled by muscles. These membranes are located, in
different species, in the outer walls of the trachea or the
bronchi (external membranes) or the inner walls (internal
membranes). Their sound-producing function was first de-
duced from the fact that they seem to be the only structures
in the syrinx able to vibrate at the frequencies found in bird
vocalizations (Figure 84).

Variation between bird orders in the number of muscles
associated with the syrinx was known long before work on
their function in voice production began. Indeed it was one
of the features on which the higher classifications were based.
Non-passerine birds have at most three pairs of muscles
while most passerines have as many as seven pairs. Some of
the muscles connect the syrinx with other parts of the bird's
anatomy (extrinsic muscles) and hold it in position. Intrinsic
muscles adjust the various parts of the syrinx itself.

The vocal apparatus of the Domestic Goose is a good

84
Enlarged view of
a bird's syrinx
inside the inter-
clavicular air sac,
seen from the
front.

85
Sonagram of a
Greylag Goose
call.

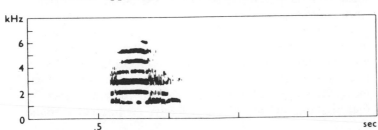

kHz

6

4

2

0

.5

sec

example of the simpler forms of syrinx (Figure 86). There are large internal and external tympaniform membranes, similar in size. When the bird is breathing normally, the membranes are taut and well separated, but when it makes a sound, muscles bring the internal and external membranes close together. Air expelled from the lungs draws them even closer and sets them vibrating in a kind of hand-clapping motion. The fundamental frequency produced in the column of air as it moves past them varies within a narrow range and depends on the tension of the membranes. The sound, however, is a complex one with strong harmonics (Figure 85). This is because the various structures surrounding the sound source, and the subsequent movements of the sound waves through an enclosed space – the trachea – all contribute to the sound and have a decisive influence on its tone-quality. A wind instrument with a vibrating reed performs in the same way as the syrinx and the trachea, for the quality and volume of the sound is affected both by the size and materials of the tube and by the player's precise control of the airflow.

The songbird, or oscine, syrinx is much more complicated than that of the goose. Besides the increase in the number of controlling muscles there are additional anatomical features – for instance external 'lips' which are not generally found in non-passerines. Figure 87 illustrates the Great Tit syrinx. The large external lips (labia) are very obvious but there are only internal tympaniform membranes, one in each bronchus. The structures marked A1 and A2 on the diagram are formed from cartilage and are attached to intrinsic muscles. Contraction of the muscles can rotate these structures, which then push the external labia further out into the empty space in the bronchial tube. They are thus brought nearer to the internal tympaniform membranes: the importance of this is explained below. But first compare the Great Tit syrinx with that of the Blackbird in Figure 88. They are very similar except that in the Blackbird there is a cavity behind each of the external labia, and external as well as internal tympaniform membranes. Notice the large area of muscle shown in both diagrams.

Now come the more difficult and not fully resolved questions about the use of these structures in sound production. During normal breathing the bronchial passages are open and no sounds are made because the tympaniform membranes are well separated from the external labia, so that air flows in and out quite freely. To produce a sound

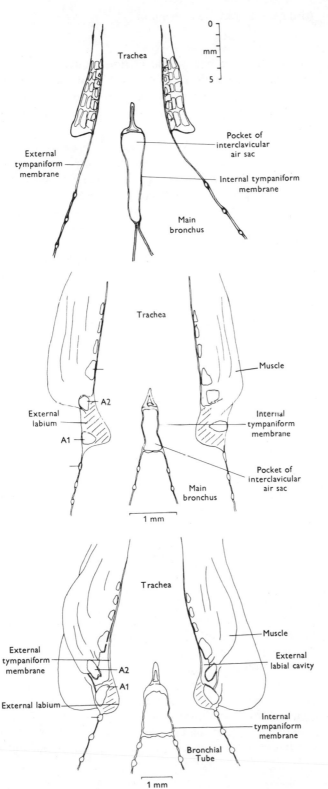

86
Greylag Goose
syrinx seen from
the front. The
scale in millimetres
is shown beside
the diagram.

87
Great Tit syrinx.
The scale is shown
below the diagram.

88
Blackbird syrinx.
The scale is shown
below the diagram.

the tube must be partly, and at times fully, closed, in order to regulate the airflow. This is just what the external labia might do if they were pushed outward into the tube. Adjustments could be made, at the same time, to the tension of the internal tympaniform membranes.

With the bronchial tubes closed, air pressure builds up in the lungs. If the external labia are then partly drawn back, the released air rushes through the narrow openings and sets the membranes in vibration. They oscillate in a simple, regular pattern and this produces corresponding sound waves in the column of moving air. These are sine waves of a single frequency and would be heard as a pure tone of steady pitch. But the frequency can be altered by changing the tension of the membrane. This basic process accounts, for example, for the musical glissandi which show up on sonagrams as fine upward- or downward-sloping traces. These are present in some of the elements in the Great Tit and Blackbird song extracts in Figures 89 and 90.

89
Sonagram of a Great Tit song: a three-note motif sung twice with the first note of a third motif (G. Thielcke).

90
Sonagram of a Blackbird song-phrase (J. Hall-Craggs).

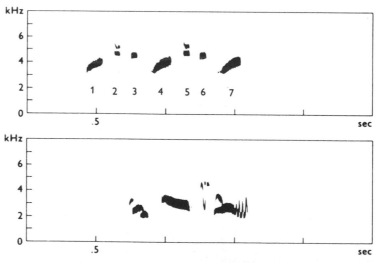

As we know, however, both these species produce a large number of differently structured elements. The three long elements in this Great Tit song motif (nos. 1, 4 and 7) are more complicated sounds. Detailed analysis demonstrates that they are made up of complex waves superimposed on the sine wave 'carrier frequency' produced by the internal tympaniform membrane and described above. The wave pattern shows that there are modulations in both amplitude and frequency: that is, further changes in volume and pitch are added to the carrier frequency, thus changing the tone-quality of the sound.

In these three song elements the carrier frequency is around 3000 Hertz and the amplitude- and frequency- modulating waves vary together 220 times a second. Amplitude- and frequency-modulated sounds are quite a common feature and the coupling of these two distinct forms of modulation has been demonstrated in many oscine species. It is not certain, however, exactly how the modulations are produced or how they are synchronized. Changes in the size of the air space in the bronchi as the external labia move to and fro, and vibrations in the muscles associated with the tympaniform membranes, are probably involved. Experimental investigations of the way in which the syrinx works in the living animal may well produce explanations in the next few years.

The presence of another phenomenon in bird vocalizations can be more easily related to the structure of the syrinx. The second and fifth elements in the Great Tit song in Figure 89 are composed of two separate though virtually simultaneous sounds. Their frequencies lie close together, so the higher sound cannot be a harmonic of the lower and must have been produced by a different sound source. This, in fact, is possible because of the pairing of structures in the syrinx. The two internal tympaniform membranes, it seems, can be adjusted independently to produce a different fundamental tone in each bronchial tube. Moreover these two sounds can be independently varied: one might be a pure tone, the other a modulated one. These are true 'double elements'.

In the Blackbird song, too, the first and fourth elements in Figure 90 consist of overlapping tones which are not harmonically related. As the sonagrams in Chapter 11 also show, Blackbird song elements are notable for their variations in frequency and the presence of overlapping tones. The functions of the Blackbird's external tympaniform membrane, so far unknown, may be connected with the great variety of sounds that this species makes.

On the other hand – and this is a further unresolved question – to what extent can the diversification of bird songs and calls, involving such clear-cut distinctions between species, be attributed to differences in the vocal apparatus? The Domestic Goose with its comparatively simple syrinx, and the Great Tit and Blackbird – strongly contrasted in the form of their songs – all produce acoustically complex sounds. And, despite small variations in the syrinx, songbird species of comparable size could make the sounds of virtually any of the others: mimicking species often do so.

Some workers believe that the richly varied vocal achievements of songbirds owe less to minor structural differences in the syrinx than to an increasingly sophisticated use of the basic apparatus under the control of the central nervous system. Given that these species are all physically capable of producing a gamut of sounds, social and environmental selective pressures, as we have seen, are continually at work: usually increasing diversity; sometimes narrowing, sometimes extending, the range of frequency and complexity in the elements, to form signals that are better adapted for a particular habitat and function.

Further Reading

This selection is not a comprehensive guide to the wealth of excellent books on birds and their way of life. It is intended for readers who would like to know more about some of the general questions in biology, ethology, ecology and physics which the study of bird sounds raise and which could only be touched on here. Other useful books of more than specialized interest are included in the Chapter References, pp. 246–53.

* indicates books requiring some knowledge of the subject for their full appreciation. They are best tackled after a more simply written book in the same category has been read.

** indicates textbooks or works written mainly for specialists. These are invaluable for reference.

General Ornithology

DORST, JEAN. *The life of birds.* 2 vols. London: Weidenfeld and Nicolson, 1974.

FISHER, J. and FLEGG, J. *Watching birds.* Berkhamsted: T. and A. D. Poyser, revised edn. 1974.

RAND, A. L. *Ornithology: an introduction.* London: Penguin Books, revised edn. 1974.

ROBERTS, M. B. V. *Biology: a functional approach.* London: Nelson, revised edn. 1976.**

THOMSON, A. LANDSBOROUGH ed. *A new dictionary of birds.* London: Nelson for the British Ornithologists' Union, 1964.

VAN TYNE, J. and BERGER, A. J. *Fundamentals of ornithology.* New York and London: John Wiley, 2nd edn. 1976.**

WELTY, J. C. *The life of birds.* Philadelphia and London: W. B. Saunders, 2nd edn. 1975.

YAPP, W. B. *The life and organization of birds.* London: Edward Arnold, cased and paperback, 1970.

Animal Behaviour

ARMSTRONG, E. A. *Bird display and behaviour – an introduction to the study of bird psychology.* London: Dover Publications, revised edn. 1965.

BAERENDS, G., BEER, C. and MANNING, A. eds. *Function and evolution in behaviour – essays in honour of Professor Niko Tinbergen, F.R.S.* Oxford: The Clarendon Press, 1975.*

GOODWIN, DEREK. *Instructions to young ornithologists,* vol. 2, *Bird behaviour.* London: Museum Press, 1961.

Instructions to young ornithologists, vol. 6, *Domestic birds.* London: Museum Press, 1965.

HINDE, R. A. *Animal behaviour – a synthesis of ethology and comparative psychology* (International Students edn.). Tokyo and London: McGraw-Hill Kogakusha. 2nd edn., paper back, 1970.**

LORENZ, KONRAD. *King Solomon's ring.* London: Methuen, 1952; University paperbacks, 1961.

MANNING, AUBREY. *An introduction to animal behaviour.* London: Edward Arnold, 2nd edn. 1972.

MORRIS, DESMOND. *Patterns of reproductive behaviour – collected papers.* London: Jonathan Cape, 1970; Panther, 1972.*

THORPE, W. H. and ZANGWILL, O. L. eds. *Current problems in animal behaviour.* Cambridge University Press, 1961.*

TINBERGEN, NIKO. *Social behaviour in animals.* London: Chapman and Hall, 2nd edn., cased and paperback 1965.

WILSON, EDWARD, O. *Sociobiology: the new synthesis.* Cambridge, Mass. and London: The Belknap Press of Harvard University Press, 1975.

Bird Vocalization and Communication

ARMSTRONG, E. A. *A study of bird song.* New York and London: Dover Publications, 2nd edn. 1973.

Discovering bird song. Aylesbury: Shire Publications, 1975.

BROWN, A. M. and PYE, D. S. *Acoustic communication* (Studies in biology). London: Edward Arnold (in preparation).

BUSNEL, R.-G. ed. *Acoustic behaviour of animals.* Amsterdam and London: Elsevier for the International Committee of Bio-Acoustics, 1963.**

GREENEWALT, C. H. *Bird song: acoustics and physiology.* Washington, D.C.: Smithsonian Institution Press, 1968.

HARTSHORNE, CHARLES. *Born to sing: an interpretation and world survey of bird song.* Bloomington and London: Indiana University Press, 1973.

HINDE, R. A. ed. *Bird vocalizations: their relations to current problems in biology and psychology. Essays presented to W. H. Thorpe.* Cambridge University Press, 1969.

Non-verbal communication. Cambridge University Press, 1972.

SEBEOK, T. A. ed. *Animal communication: techniques of study and results of research.* Bloomington and London: Indiana University Press, 1968.**

THIELCKE, GERHARD. *Bird sounds* (Ann Arbor Science Library). University of Michigan Press, 1975. (translated from the German).

THORPE, W. H. *Bird-song: the biology of vocal communication and expression in birds.* Cambridge University Press, 1961.

Evolution and Systematics

GRUSON, E. S. *Checklist of the birds of the world – a complete list of the species, with names, authorities and areas of distribution.* London: Collins, 1976.

LACK, DAVID. *Evolution illustrated by waterfowl.* Oxford: Blackwell Scientific Publications, paperback, 1974.

MAYR, ERNST. *Animal species and evolution.* Cambridge, Mass.: Belknap Press of Harvard University Press, 1963.*

VAURIE, CHARLES. *The birds of the palearctic fauna: – a systematic reference:* Vol. 1. *Order Passeriformes.* London: H. F. & G. Witherby, 1959.**

Ecology

CLOUDSLEY-THOMPSON, J. L. *Terrestrial environments.* London: Croom Helm, 1975.

DAVIS, D. E. ed. *Behavior as an ecological factor* (Benchmark papers in ecology, 2). Stroudsburg, Pa.: Dowden, Hutchinson & Ross, 1974.*

(This book is a compilation of extracts from key papers of the last 50 years or so on a wide range of behavioural and ecological topics.)

LACK, DAVID. *Ecological adaptations for breeding in birds*. London: Methuen, 1968.*

LISTER, MICHAEL. *A bird and its bush*. London: Phoenix House, 1962.

OWEN, D. F. *What is ecology?* London: Oxford University Press, cased and paperback, 1974.

MURTON, R. K. *Man and birds*. London: Collins, 1971.

SIMMS, ERIC. *Woodland birds*. London: Collins, 1971.

Birds of town and suburb. London: Collins, 1975.

SNOW, DAVID. *The web of adaptation – bird studies in the American tropics*. London: Collins, 1976.

STONEHOUSE, B. S. and PERRINS, C. M. eds. *Evolutionary ecology*. London: Macmillan (in press).*

YAPP, W. B. *Birds and woods*. London: Oxford University Press, 1962.

Acoustics and Music

JEANS, JAMES. *Science and music*. Cambridge University Press, 1937: London: Dover Publications, 1969.

JONES, G. R. and others, eds. *Teach yourself acoustics*. London: English Universities Press, 1967.

TAYLOR, C. A. *The physics of musical sounds*. London: English Universities Press, 1965.*

Sounds of music. London: British Broadcasting Corporation, 1976.

VAN BERGEIJK, W. A., PIERCE, J. R. and DAVID, E. A. *Waves and the Ear* (*Science Study*). London: Heinemann, 1961.

Guides to Bird Watching

Identification

There are numerous field guides and, at least for the birds of the British Isles and Continental Europe, choice is a matter of preference for a particular format. There are also excellent popular books with more detailed descriptions of each species on the British Isles, its behaviour and habitat; among them:

CAMPBELL, BRUCE. *The Oxford book of birds*. London: Oxford University Press, 1964; pocket edn. 1972.

COWARD, T. A. *Birds of the British Isles and their eggs*, edited and revised by J. A. G. Barnes from the original three-volume work. London: Frederick Warne, 1969.

For more extensive reference, there is *The handbook of British birds* (in five volumes) by H. F. Witherby, the Rev. F. C. R. Jourdain, Norman F. Ticehurst and Bernard W. Tucker, first published by H. F. and G. Witherby in 1938–41. A successor to the Handbook is in preparation (it is referred to in Chapter 3):

CRAMP, STANLEY and SIMMONS, K. E. L. S. eds. *The birds of the western Palearctic*. London: Oxford University Press, volume 1 is due for publication May 1977.

and BANNERMAN, D. A. *Birds of the British Isles*. 12 vols. Edinburgh: Oliver and Boyd, 1953–63.

Distribution

The first book on this list bridges this categorization, for it describes identifying features of each species as well as where to look for them:

FITTER, R. S. R. *Collins guide to bird watching.* London: Collins, 2nd edn. 1970.

Useful books concerned with the numbers and distribution of the birds of Europe are:

FERGUSON-LEES, JAMES, HOCKLIFFE, QUENTIN and SWEERES, KO, eds. *A guide to bird-watching in Europe.* London: The Bodley Head, 1975.

GOODERS, JOHN. *Where to watch birds.* London: André Deutsch, rev. edn. 1974.

PARSLOW, JOHN. *Breeding birds of Britain and Ireland: a historical survey.* Berkhamsted: T. & A. D. Poyser, 1973

SHARROCK, J. T. R., ed. *The atlas of breeding birds of Britain and Ireland.* Tring: British Trust for Ornithology/Irish Wildbird Conservancy, 1976.

VOOUS, K. H. *Atlas of European birds.* London: Nelson, 1960.*

Bird Sound Recordings Available

Since the turn of the century about a thousand gramophone records, reel-to-reel tapes, cassettes and cartridges presenting the voices of birds have been published. All that can be done in this summary is to suggest a selection. It includes a number from Britain, a few from Europe, and one (or at most two) from each of the other major bird continents of the world.

For British users the best less expensive set of records is undoubtedly *Witherby's Sound-Guide to British Birds* comprising two 12-inch LPs and a 104-page book. It was compiled by M. E. W. North and Eric Simms who present 300 recordings of 194 species. The publisher is H. F. and G. Witherby of London.

Eric Simms, with the BBC Records as publisher, has also produced a number of 12-inch long-players including *Highland Birds, Sea and Island Birds* and two discs of *Woodland and Garden Birds.* The Stone Curlew 'conversation' (Chapter 6) is included in *Wildlife of East Anglia.* The BBC has also issued, in both LP and cassette form, *British Wild Birds in Stereo,* with recordings by John F. Burton and David Tombs.

John Kirby has personally published (from 10 Wycherley Avenue, Middlesbrough) eight cassettes under the title *Wild Life Sound Tracks,* most of the recordings being of birds. Another British LP, *Bird Song Adventure,* with recordings by Patrick Sellar and Victor C. Lewis, is put out by Pye as one of their Golden Guinea series.

A more encyclopaedic work is the *Peterson Sound Guide to the Bird Songs of Britain and Europe* which includes on fourteen 12-inch LPs recordings of over 500 species. It was published in Sweden but is available in the United Kingdom from the Royal Society for the Protection of Birds. The records are designed to accompany the famous Peterson pocket field guide (Peterson, R., Mountfort, G. and Hollom, P. A. D. *A field guide to the birds of Britain and Europe.* London: Collins, 3rd edn 1974).

The International Centre for Ornithological Sound Publications will send (on application to its address: 04 Aubenas-les-Alpes, Haute-Provence, France) a catalogue of its prodigious output. Sound guides are available for northern Europe, southern Europe and north Africa, as well as discs from many other countries.

A set of five 10-inch LPs can be got from the Soviet Union, complete with a booklet in English. The recordings were made in European Russia, Siberia and the Soviet Far East. Address to write to: All-Union Studio of Disc Recording, Mezdunarodnaja Kniga, 32/34 Smolensk Square, Moscow 200, USSR. The title is *The Voices of Wild Nature*.

In bird-conscious Japan many discs and tapes have been commercially issued. One of the many good publications as *100 Singing Birds*. It comprises four 3¼ inch diameter tapes (reel-to-reel) and a 136-page book. It is compiled by Reiji Nakatsubo of the Japan Broadcasting Corporation and can be obtained from Akio Abe, 2–33–19 Umegaoka Setagaya-ku, Tokyo.

One of the more comprehensive Australasian compilations is John Hutchinson's *Australian Bird Calls Index* available from him, as either LP or cassette, at Brockman Street, Balingup, WA6253, Western Australia.

Among the many gramophone records of African bird voice are M. E. W. North's LPs *Voices of African Birds* and *More Voices of African Birds*, both available from the Laboratory of Ornithology, Sapsucker Woods Road, Ithaca, New York, USA. This laboratory also sells a very wide range of records of sound production by North American birds. There are *Peterson Field Guides* to the birds of eastern and western North America and many other discs. Write for a catalogue which will also show a number of excellent specialist records compiled by W. W. H. Gunn and Donald H. Borror.

In South America the most active recordist has been J. D. Frisch of Brazil who has issued a number of LPs including *Songs of the Birds of Brazil* (with sleeve text in Portuguese). The publishing company is SOM in Sao Paulo.

Anyone interested in pursuing further the availability of bird sound on commercial disc could start by consulting a bibliography of avian discographies published in *Recorded Sound*, the journal of the British Institute for Recorded Sound, number 54 (see p. 245).

JEFFERY BOSWALL

Societies and Journals

British Ornithologists' Union, c/o The Zoological Society of London, Regent's Park, London, NW1 4RY.
Journal: *The Ibis*. The Union has two scientific meetings a year and members may join the British Ornithologists' Club which meets regularly for talks and discussion and publishes a *Bulletin*.

The British Trust for Ornithology, Beech Grove, Tring, Hertfordshire, HP23 5BR.

Journal: *Bird Study*. The BTO also publishes a bulletin for birdwatchers: *BTO News*, and guides on subjects such as nest-boxes; binoculars, telescopes and cameras; the care of injured birds, and the arrival and departure dates of summer migrants. It organizes meetings and many co-operative research projects.

The Royal Society for the Protection of Birds, The Lodge, Sandy, Bedfordshire, SG19 2DL.
Journal: *Birds*. The RSPB has a Young Ornithologists' Club for members of 15 and under. It manages a large number of nature reserves, engages in research and educational activities, helps to enforce the protection laws and organizes local activities, including film shows.

The Wildfowl Trust, Slimbridge, Gloucestershire, GL2 7BT.
Annual publication: *Wildfowl*. In addition to the main collection at Slimbridge, the Trust has smaller collections and wildfowl refuges in several parts of the country and is a centre for international research schemes.

British Birds: a monthly journal published by Macmillan Journals Limited, 4 Little Essex Street, London WC2R 3LF; obtainable from the publishers by annual subscription.
The Council for Nature, Zoological Gardens, Regent's Park, London, NW1 4RY.

Newsletter: *Habitat*. The Council acts as a forum for natural history and conservation. Many societies are affiliated to it and the newsletter is also sent to individuals who are Subscribers or Associates.

The Society for the Promotion of Nature Conservation, The Green, Nettleham, Lincoln, LN2 2NR, was granted a new Royal Charter in 1976, enabling it to widen its objectives, after 60 years of activity as the Society for the Promotion of Nature Reserves. It works with the County Naturalists' Trusts and these, with the local natural history societies, are the focus for local activities. Most trusts and local societies organize field excursions for members on which experienced naturalists help beginners to identify bird species and their vocalizations.

The Wildlife Sound Recording Society, c/o The British Library of Wildlife Sounds (address below).
Journal: *Wildlife Sound*. This society for active field recordists provides information and discussion on techniques, equipment, and recording projects through its journal, meetings, contests, and tapes circulated among members.

The International Bio-acoustics Council, c/o The Natural History Museum, Universitetsparken, Aarhus 8000 C, Denmark.
Journal: *Biophon*. The function of the Council is to keep in touch with research workers throughout the world, for exchange of information, and to encourage and co-ordinate new sound recordings in the field. It holds a meeting every other year, in a different country.

The British Library of Wildlife Sounds, c/o The British Institute of Recorded Sound, 29 Exhibition Road, London SW7 2AS. The Library was set up in 1969 as a department of the Institute which is recognized as the national collection of sound recordings. 'BLOWS' is international in scope but assumes special responsibility for British recordings and those made in the Antarctic. It maintains links with libraries of wildlife recordings in other parts of the world. It welcomes properly documented tape-recordings from individual recordists. Copies of these and many of the BBC recordings which are deposited in the Library are available for scientific study and the whole collection, including all the commercially published records, can be listened to on the premises.

Two numbers of the Institute's journal *Recorded Sound* – nos. 34 (April 1969) and 54 (April 1974) were devoted entirely to wildlife sound to mark, respectively, the opening and the fifth anniversary of BLOWS.

All enquiries should be directed to the BLOWS Librarian.

Further information about all these bio-acoustic activities, and advice on equipment, can be found in an article by Patrick Sellar who, with Jeffery Boswall, was co-founder of BLOWS. (Sellar, P. J. (1976). 'Sound recording and the birdwatcher.' *British Birds* 69, 202–14.)

Chapter References

These are limited to studies described or mentioned in the text since such papers contain references to earlier work on the same, and related, topics. In some cases, and for the same reason, only the most recent paper by an author on a particular topic is listed.

The source of the epigraph for each chapter is given first. *Op. cit.* indicates that the book is included in the 'Further Reading' section above.

1 Listening to Birds

ARMSTRONG, E. A. 'The evolution of man's appreciation of bird song' in HINDE, R. A. ed. *Bird vocalizations*, op. cit.

2 The Communication System

HOWARD, H. ELIOT. *An introduction to the study of bird behaviour.* Cambridge University Press, 1929.

CHAPPUIS, C. (1971). 'Un exemple de l'influence du milieu sur les émissions vocales des oiseaux: l'évolution des chants en forêt équatoriale.' *La Terre et la Vie*, 2–71, 183–202.
GOMPERTZ, TERRY (1957). 'Some observations on the Feral Pigeon in London.' *Bird Study* 4, 1–13.
GOODWIN, DEREK (1956). 'Observations on the voice and some displays of certain pigeons.' *Avic. Mag.* 62, 17–33, 62–70.
Pigeons and doves of the world. London: British Museum. (Natural History), 1967.
HOGAN-WARBURG, A. J. (1966). 'Social behaviour of the Ruff *Philomachus pugnax* (L.)' *Ardea* 54, 8–229.
HJORTH, INGMAR (1970). 'Reproductive behaviour in the Tetraonidae.' *Viltrevy* 7, 183–596.
(1974). 'The lek of the Black Grouse.' *Brit. Birds*, 67, 116–19 and plates 13–20.
HUXLEY, JULIAN. *The courtship habitats of the Great Crested Grebe.* 1914. Reprinted London: Jonathan Cape, cased and paperback, 1969.
LACK, DAVID. *The life of the Robin.* London, H. F. & G. Witherby, 4th edn. 1965; Fontana, New Naturalist series, 1970.
PALMAR, C. E. *Blackgame.* London: Forestry Commission, Forest Record no. 66, H.M.S.O. 1968, amended edn. 1971.
SIMMONS, K. E. L. S. 'The Great Crested Grebe' in BOSWALL, J. ed. *Private lives: studies of birds and other animals.* London: British Broadcasting Corporation, 1970.
(1975). 'Further studies on the Great Crested Grebe, 1. Courtship.' *Bristol Ornithology* 8, 89–107.
SNOW, DAVID. *A study of blackbirds.* London: Allen and Unwin, 1958.

3 The Sounds Birds Make

THIELCKE, GERHARD. *Vogelstimmen.* Berlin and Heidelberg: Springer-Verlag, 1970 (passage translated by Rosemary Jellis).

BERTRAM, B. C. R. (1977). 'Variation in the wing song of the Flappet Lark.' *Anim. Behav.* 25 (in press).

BLUME, D. *Die Buntspechte* and *Schwarzspecht, Grünspecht, Grauspecht*. (Die neue Brehm-Bücherei) Wittenberg Wutherstadt: A. Ziemsen Verlag, 1963 and 3rd edn. 1973 resp.

GOMPERTZ, TERRY (1967). 'The hiss display of the Great Tit *Parus major*.' *Vogelwelt* 88, 165–9.

PAYNE, R. B. (1973). 'Wingflap dialects in the Flappet Lark *Mirafra cinnamomea*.' *Ibis* 115, 270–4.

SEIBT, U. (1975). 'Instrumentaldialekte der Klapperlerche *Mirafra cinnamomea*.' *J. Orn.* 116, 103–7.

THONEN, W. (1969). 'Auffallender Unterschied zwischen den instrument alen Balzlauten der europäischen und nordamerikanischen Bekassine *Gallinago gallinago*.' *Orn. Beob.* 66, 6–13.

4   Songs

CHAUCER, GEOFFREY. Prologue to *The Canterbury Tales* in the *Complete Works*, edited by Walter W. Skeat, London: Oxford University Press, 1929.

ARMSTRONG, E. A. *The Wren.* London, Collins, 1955.

BONDESEN, POUL. *Fuglesangen: en verden af musik.* Copenhagen: Rhodos, 1967.

BREMOND, J.-C. (1967). 'Reconnaissance de schémas réactogènes liés a l'information contenue dans le chant territorial du rouge gorge *Erithacus rubecula*.' *Proc. XIV Int. Ornithol. Cong.*, 217–29.

(1968). 'Recherches sur la sémantique et les éléments vecteurs d'information dans les signaux acoustiques du rouge-gorge *Erithacus rubecula*.' *La Terre et la Vie* 2–268, 109–220.

(1976). 'Specific recognition in the song of Bonelli's Warbler *Phylloscopus bonelli*.' *Behaviour* 58, 99–116.

GOMPERTZ, TERRY (1961). 'The vocabulary of the Great Tit.' *Brit. Birds* 54, 369–94, 409–18.

(1971). 'Sounds for survival.' *Birds* 3, 178–82.

SCHUBERT, M. (1967). 'Probleme der Motivwahl und der Gesangsaktivität bei *Phylloscopus trochilus*.' *J. Orn.* 108, 265–94.

SIMMS, ERIC. *Birds of town and suburb*, op. cit.

THORPE, W. H. and PILCHER, P. M. (1958). 'The nature and characteristics of subsong.' *Brit. Birds* 51, 509–14.

THORPE, W. H. *Bird-song*, op. cit.

5   Moods and Events

THORPE, W. H. 'Vocal communication in birds' in HINDE, R. A., ed. *Non-verbal communication*, op. cit.

FISCHER, HELGA (1965). 'Das Triumphgeschrei der Graugans *Anser anser*.' *Z. Tierpsych.* 22, 247–304.

FRIEDMANN, H. (1955). 'The Honey-guides.' *U.S. Nat. Mus. Bull.* 208, 1–292.

GOMPERTZ (1961) and (1971). See Chapter 4 references, above.

MARLER, PETER (1956). 'The voice of the Chaffinch and its function as language.' *Ibis* 98, 231–261.

(1965). 'Behaviour of the Chaffinch, *Fringilla coelebs*.' *Behaviour* Suppl. 5, 1–184.

'Developments in the study of animal communication' in BELL, P. R., ed. *Darwin's biological work: some aspects reconsidered*. Cambridge University Press, 1959.

MARLER, PETER and MUNDINGER, P. C. (1975). 'Vocalizations, social organization and breeding biology of the Twite *Acanthus flavirostris.' Ibis* 117, 1–17.

MEDWAY, LORD (1967). 'The function of echonavigation among swiftlets.' *Anim. Behav.* 15, 416–420.

MEDWAY, LORD and PYE, J. D. (in press). 'Echolocation and the systematics of swiftlets' in STONEHOUSE, B. S. and PERRINS, C. M. eds. *Evolutionary ecology*, op. cit.

MUNDINGER, P. C. (1970). 'Vocal imitation and individual recognition of finch calls.' *Science* 168, 480–2.

SPENCER, K. G. *The Lapwing in Britain.* London and Hull: A. Brown, 1953.

STAHLBERG, BRITT-MARIE (1974). 'The development of rank order and aggressiveness in Greylag Geese.' *Wildfowl* 25, 67–73.

TINBERGEN, NIKO and FALKUS, HUGH. *Signals for survival.* Oxford: The Clarendon Press, 1970.

6 The Early Stages

This translation of Akhenaten's 'Hymn to Aten' is quoted from ALDRED, CYRIL, *Akhenaten – Pharaoh of Egypt.* London: Thames and Hudson, 1968; Abacus Books, 1972.

FREEMAN, B. M. and VINCE, M. A. *Development of the avian embryo.* London: Chapman and Hall, 1974.

GOTTLIEB, GILBERT. *Development of species identification in birds – an enquiry into the prenatal determinants of perception.* Chicago and London: University of Chicago Press, 1971.

GUYOMARC'H, J.-C. (1962). 'Contribution à l'étude du comportement vocal du poussin de *Gallus domesticus.' J. Psych. Norm. Path.* 3, 283–306.

KEAR, JANET (1968). 'The calls of very young Anatidae.' *Vogelwelt,* Beiheft 1, 93–113.

LACK, DAVID. *Evolution illustrated by waterfowl*, op. cit.

MARLER, PETER. 'On strategies of behavioural development' in BAERENDS, G., BEER, C. and MANNING, A. eds. *Function and evolution in behaviour*, op. cit.

NOTTEBOHM, F. (1968). 'Auditory experience and song-development in the Chaffinch *Fringilla coelebs.' Ibis* 110, 549–68.

(1969). 'The "critical period" for song learning.' *Ibis* 111, 336–7.

(1970). 'Ontogeny of bird song.' *Science* 167, 950–6.

SCOTT, PETER and The Wildfowl Trust. *The Swans.* London: Michael Joseph, 1972.

SIMMS, ERIC. *Voices of the wild.* London: Putnam, 1957.

THIELCKE, GERHARD (1973). 'Uniformierung des Gesangs der Tannenmeise *Parus ater* durch Lernen.' *J. Orn.* 114, 443–54.

THORPE, W. H. (1958). 'The learning of song patterns by birds, with especial reference to the song of the Chaffinch *Fringilla coelebs.' Ibis* 100 535–70.

VINCE, M. A. 'Embryonic communication, respiration and the synchronization of hatching' in HINDE, R. A., ed. *Bird vocalizations*, op. cit.

7 Dialects

POTTER, SIMEON. *Modern linguistics*. London: André Deutsch, 1957; revised edn. 1967.

CONRADS, KLAUS (1966). 'Der Egge-Dialekt des Buchfinken *Fringilla coelebs* – ein Beitrag zur geographischen Gesangsvariation.' *Vogelwelt* 87, 176–81.

JENKINS, PETER (in press). 'Cultural transmission of song behaviour in a free-living bird population.' *Anim. Behav.*

LEMON, R. E. (1971). 'Differentiation of song-dialects in Cardinals.' *Ibis* 113, 373–7.

(1974). 'Song dialects, song matching and species recognition by Cardinals *Richmondena cardinalis*.' *Ibis* 116, 545–8.

(1975). 'How birds develop song-dialects.' *Condor* 77, 385–405.

MARLER, PETER (1952). 'Variation in the song of the Chaffinch.' *Ibis* 94, 458–72.

'The voice of the Chaffinch' in *New Biology* no. 20. London: Penguin Books, 1956.

METZMACHMER, M. and MAIRY, F. (1972). 'Variations géographiques de la figure finale du chant du pinson des arbres, *Fringilla coelebs*.' *Gerf.* 62, 215–44.

NOTTEBOHM, F. (1970). 'Ontogeny of bird song.' *Science* 167, 950–6.

THIELCKE, GERHARD (1969). 'Geographic variation in bird vocalizations' in HINDE, R. A. ed. *Bird vocalizations*, op. cit.

References for the Black Grouse and Hazel Grouse are listed in Chapter 2 (HJORTH and PALMAR).

8 Individual Recognition

NICE, MARGARET MORSE. *The watcher at the nest*. London: Macmillan, 1939; Dover Publications, 1967.

BROOKS, R. J. and FALLS, J. B. (1975). 'Individual recognition by song in White-throated Sparrows.' *Can. J. Zool.* 53, 879–88, 1412–20, 1749–1861.

FALLS, J. B. (1969). 'Functions of territorial song in the White-throated Sparrow' in HINDE, R. A. ed. *Bird vocalizations*, op. cit.

HARRIS, M. A. and LEMON, R. E. (1976). 'Responses of male Song Sparrows *Melospiza melodia* to neighbouring and non-neighbouring individuals.' *Ibis* 118, 421–4.

HUTCHINSON, R. E., STEVENSON, J. G. and THORPE, W. H. (1968). 'The basis for individual recognition by voice in the Sandwich Tern *Sterna sandvicensis*.' *Behaviour* 32, 150–7.

MULLIGAN, J. A. (1966). 'Singing behavior and its development in the Song Sparrow *Melospiza melodia*.' *University of California Publications in Zoology* 81, 1–76.

NICE, MARGARET MORSE (1937 and 1943). 'Studies in the life history of the Song Sparrow', parts 1 and 2. *Trans. Linn. Soc. New York*, IV and VI.

THORPE, W. H. (1968). 'Perceptual basis for group organization in social vertebrates, especially birds.' *Nature, Lond.* 220, 124–8.

TSCHANZ, B. (1968). 'Trottellummen.' *Z. Tierpsych.* Beiheft 4, 1–103.

SCHOMMER, M. and TSCHANZ, B. (1975). 'Lautäusserungen junger Trottellummen.' *Vogelwarte* 28, 17–44.

WHITE, SHEILA J., WHITE, R. E. C. and THORPE, W. H. (1970). 'Acoustic basis for individual recognition by voice in the Gannet.' *Nature, Lond.* 225, 1156–8.

WHITE, SHEILA J. (1971). 'Selective responsiveness by the Gannet *Sula bassana* to played-back calls.' *Anim. Beh.* 19, 125–31.

9 Far Away and Long Ago

DARLING, FRANK FRASER. *Bird flocks and the breeding cycle.* Cambridge University Press, 1938.

A naturalist on Rona. Oxford: The Clarendon Press, 1939; New York: Kraus Reprint, 1969.

DIXON, K. L. (1963). 'Some aspects of social organization in the Carolina Chickadee.' *Proc. XIII Int. Ornithol. Cong.* 240–58.

DIXON, K. L. and STEFANSKI, R. A. (1970). 'An appraisal of the song of the Black-capped Chickadee.' *Wilson Bull.* 82, 53–62.

GOMPERTZ, TERRY (1968). 'Results of bringing individuals of two geographically isolated forms of *Parus major* into contact.' *Vogelwelt*, Beiheft 1, 63–92.

HALL, M. F. (1962). 'Evolutionary aspects of estrildid song.' *Symp. Zool. Soc. Lond.* 8, 37–55.

LOHRL, HANS and THIELCKE, GERHARD (1973). 'Alarmlaute europäischer und nordafrikanischer Tannenmeise (*Parus ater ater, P. ater atlas, P. ater ledouci*) und der Schwarzkopfmeise *P. melanolophus*.' *J. Orn.* 114, 250–2.

MARTENS, J. (1975). 'Akustische Differenzierung verwandtschaftlicher Beziehung in der *Parus*- (*Periparus-*) Gruppe nach Untersuchungen im Nepal-Himalaya.' *J. Orn.* 116, 369–433.

SCHUBERT, M. and SCHUBERT, G. (1969). 'Lautformen und verwandtschaftliche Beziehungen einiger Laubsänger.' *Z. Tierpsych.* 16, 7–22.

SZIJJ, L. J. (1966). 'Hybridization and the nature of the isolating mechanisms in sympatric populations of meadowlarks (*Sturnella*) in Ontario.' *Z. Tierpsych.* 23, 677–90.

THIELCKE, GERHARD (1968). 'Gemeinsames der Gattung *Parus* – ein bioakustischer Beitrag zur Systematik.' *Vogelwelt*, Beiheft 1, 147–63.

(1969). 'Die Reaktion von Tannen- und Kohlmeise (*Parus ater, P. major*) auf den Gesang nahverwandter Formen.' *J. Orn.* 110, 148–57.

(1970). 'Lernen von Gesang als möglicher Schrittmacher der Evolution.' *Z. f. zool. Systematik u. Evolutionsforschung* 8, 309–20.

(1973). 'On the origin of divergence of learned signals (songs) in isolated populations.' *Ibis* 115, 511–16.

(1974). 'Stabilität erlernter Singvogel-Gesänge trotz vollständiger geographischer Isolation.' *Vogelwarte* 27, 209–15.

THIELCKE, GERHARD and LINSENMAIR, K. E. (1963). 'Zur geographischen Variation des Gesanges des Zilpzalps *Phylloscopus collybita* in Mittel- und Südwesteuropa mit einem Vergleich des Gesanges des Fitis *Phylloscopus trochilus*'. *J. Orn.* 104, 372–402.

THONEN, WILLI (1962). 'Stimmgeographische, ökologische und verbreitunggeschichtliche Studien über die Mönchmeise *Parus montanus* Conrad.' *Orn. Beob.* 19, 101–72.

WHITE, GILBERT. '*The natural history and antiquities of Selborne*', 1789. Various editions.

10 Copies and Counterfeits

BUXTON, JOHN. *The Redstart*. London: Collins, 1950.

BANDORF, H. (1968). 'Beiträge zum Verhalten des Zwergtauchers *Podiceps ruficollis.' Vogelwelt* Beiheft 1, 7–61.
BERTRAM, B. C. R. (1970). 'The vocal behaviour of the Indian Hill Mynah *Gracula religiosa.' Anim. Behav. Monog.* 3, Pt. 2.
GOODWIN, DEREK (1949). 'Notes on voice and display of the Jay.' *Brit. Birds* 42, 278–87.
(1956). 'Further observations on the behaviour of the Jay *Garrulus glandarius.' Ibis* 98, 186–219.
Crows of the world. London: British Museum (Natural History), 1976.
HILTY, STEPHEN (1975). 'Year round attendance of White-whiskered and Little Hermits, *Phaethornis* spp. at singing assemblies in Colombia.' *Ibis* 117, 382–4.
IMMELMANN, KLAUS (1969). 'Song development in the Zebra Finch and other estrildid finches', in HINDE, R. A., ed. *Bird vocalizations*, op. cit.
PAYNE, R. B. (1976). 'Song mimicry and species relationships among the West African pale-winged indigobirds.' *Auk* 93, 25–38.
SNOW, B. K. (1974). 'Lek behaviour and breeding of Guy's Hermit Hummingbird *Phaethornis guy.' Ibis* 116, 278–97.
SNOW, DAVID (1968). 'The singing assemblies of Little Hermits.' *Living Bird* 7, 47–55.
SNOW, DAVID and GOODWIN, DEREK (1974). 'The Black-and-Gold Cotinga.' *Auk* 91, 360–9.
THIELCKE, GERHARD and THIELCKE-POLTZ, HELGA (1960). 'Akustiches Lernen verschieden alter schallisolierter Amseln *Turdus merula* und die Entwicklung erlernter Motive ohne und mit künstlichem Einfluss von Testosteron.' *Z. Tierpsych.* 17, 211–44.
THORPE, W. H. (1967). 'Vocal imitation and antiphonal song and its implications.' *Proc. XIV Int. Ornithol. Cong.* 245–63.
(1972). 'Duetting and antiphonal song in birds – its extent and significance'. *Behaviour Monograph Supplement*, no. 18.
TRETZEL, ERWIN (1965). Imitation und Variation von Schäferpfiffen durch Haubenlerchen *Galerida c. cristata* L. – ein Beispiel für spezielle Spottmotive-Prädisposition.' *Z. Tierpsych.* 22, 784–809.
(1967). 'Imitation und Transposition menschlicher Pfiffe durch Amseln *Turdus m. merula* L. – ein weiterer Nachweis relativen Lernens und akustischer Abstraktion bei Vögeln.' *Z. Tierpsych.* 24, 137–61.
WICKLER, WOLFGANG (1972). 'Aufbau und Paarspezifität des Gesangsduettes von *Laniarius funebris.' Z. Tierpsych.* 30, 465–76.
(1976). 'Duetting songs in birds – biological significance of stationary and non-stationary processes.' *J. Theor. Biol.* 61, 493–7.
WICKLER, WOLFGANG and VON HELVERSEN, DAGMAR (1971). 'Uber den Duettgesang des afrikanischen Drongo *Dicrurus adsimilis* Bechstein.' *Z. Tierpsych.* 29, 301–21.

11 Airs and Variations

HARTSHORNE, CHARLES. *Born to sing*, op. cit.

ARMSTRONG, E. A. (1969). 'Aspects of the evolution of man's appreciation of bird song' in HINDE, R. A. ed. *Bird vocalizations*, op. cit.
CATCHPOLE, CLIVE (1976). 'Temporal and sequential organisation of song in the Sedge Warbler *Acrocephalus schoenobaenus.' Behaviour* 59, 226–46.

HALL-CRAGGS, JOAN (1962). 'The development of song in the Blackbird *Turdus merula.*' *Ibis* 104, 277–300.
(1969). 'The aesthetic content of bird song' in HINDE, R. A. ed. *Bird vocalizations,* op. cit.
KREBS, JOHN (in press). 'Song and territory in the Great Tit' in STONEHOUSE, B. and PERRINS, C. M. eds. *Evolutionary Ecology,* op. cit.
(1976). 'Habituation and song repertoires in the Great Tit.' *Behav. Ecol. Sociobiol.* 1, 215–27.
MATHEWS, F. SCHUYLER, *Field book of wild birds and their music.* New York: Dover Publications, 1967.
THORPE, W. H. (1972). 'Vocal communication in birds' in HINDE, R. A. ed. *Non-verbal communication,* op. cit. (This article includes a short contribution by Joan Hall-Craggs from which the passage on page 200 is quoted.)
TURNBULL, A. L. *Bird music: an introduction to the study of vocal expressions of British birds with appreciations of their songs.* London: Faber, 1943.

The quotations in the text on pp. 205–6 are taken from the following sources:

ARMSTRONG, E. A. *Bird display and behaviour,* op. cit.
BUXTON, JOHN. *The Redstart.* London: Collins, 1950.
GOMPERTZ, TERRY (1971). 'Sounds for Survival.' *Birds* 3, 178–82.
HARTSHORNE, CHARLES. *Born to sing,* op. cit.
THORPE, W. H. (1958). 'The learning of song patterns by birds with especial reference to the song of the Chaffinch *Fringilla coelebs.*' *Ibis* 100, 535–70.

12 How and Why?

LEOPOLD, ALDO. *A Sand County almanac and sketches here and there.* New York: Oxford University Press, 1949; enlarged edition 1966; Galaxy Books, 1968. (The quotation at the end of this chapter is taken from the same source.)

CALDER, NIGEL. *The human conspiracy: new research into forms of social behaviour.* London: British Broadcasting Corporation, 1976.
LACK, DAVID. *The natural regulation of animal numbers.* Oxford: The Clarendon Press, 1954; paperback 1970.
Population studies of birds. Oxford: The Clarendon Press, 1966; paperback 1969.
LYONS, JOHN. *Chomsky* (Modern Masters). London: Fontana, 1970.
KOCH, LUDWIG. *Memoirs of a birdman.* London: Phoenix House, 1955.
MARLER, PETER (1970). 'A comparative approach to vocal learning: song development in White-crowned Sparrows.' *J. comp. Physiol. Psychol. Monogr.* 71, 1–15.
'Animal communication' in KRAMES, L., PLINER, P. and ALLOWAY, T., eds. *Advances in the study of communications and effect,* vol. 1, *Non-verbal communication.* New York, Plenum Press, 1974.
(1975). 'On strategies of behavioural development' in BAERENDS, G., BEER, C. and MANNING, A. eds. *Function and evolution in behaviour,* op. cit.
NICHOLSON, E. M. and KOCH, LUDWIG. *Songs of wild birds.* London: H. F. and G. Witherby, 1936.
SIMMS, ERIC (1955). 'The conversational calls of birds as revealed by new methods of field recording.' *Acta XI Congr. Int. Orn.* 623–6.
Voices of the wild. London: Putnam, 1957.
Birds of the air. London: Hutchinson, 1976.

WASZ-HÖCKERT, O. and others. *The infant cry – a spectrographic and auditory analysis*. London: Heinemann Medical Books, 1968.

WILSON, EDWARD O. *Sociobiology: the new synthesis*, op. cit.

WYNNE-EDWARDS, V. C. *Animal dispersion in relation to social behaviour*. Edinburgh: Oliver and Boyd, 1962; paperback, 1972.

Notating Bird Sounds

GREENEWALT, CRAWFORD H. *Bird song: acoustics and physiology* Washington, D.C.: Smithsonian Institution Press, 1968.

HOLD, TREVOR (1970). 'The notation of bird-song: a review and a recommendation.' *Ibis* 112, 151–72.

HOLST, IMOGEN. *An ABC of Music*. London: Oxford University Press, 1963.

NORTH, M. E. W. (1950). 'Transcribing bird-song.' *Ibis* 92, 99–114.

SAUNDERS, A. A. (1929). *New York State Mus. Handb.* 7, 1–121.

Guide to Bird Songs. New York: Doubleday, 1935; new edn. 1951.

THIELCKE, GERHARD (1966). 'Die Auswertung von Vogelstimmen nach Tonbandaufnahmen.' *Vogelwelt* 87, 1–14.

Voice Production

GREENEWALT, C. H. *Birdsong: acoustics and physiology*. Washington, D.C.: Smithsonian Institution Press, 1961.

MISKIMEN, M. (1951). 'Sound production in passerine birds.' *Auk* 68, 493–504.

SCHMIDT-NIELSEN, K. *How animals work*. Cambridge University Press, 1972.

STEIN, R. C. (1968). 'Modulation in bird sounds.' *Auk* 85, 229–43.

Acknowledgements

Sonagrams are attributed either to the recordist, in the case of figures especially prepared for this book, or to the publication from which the figure is reproduced (these are listed in the chapter references). The BBC gives grateful acknowledgement to the Editors and Publishers of the books and journals from which these figures have been taken.

Unacknowledged figures are from recordings by Terry Gompertz (Great Tits) and Dr Gerhard Thielcke (other species) who also made the sonagrams for them. Mrs Joan Hall-Craggs prepared the musical illustrations in Figures 73 and 74 and made the sonagrams for Figures 5, 32, 34a, 48 and 82; Dr Raymond A. Stefanski those for Figures 55, 85, 89 and 90.

Derek Goodwin wishes to make acknowledgement to Robin Prytherch and A. J. Hogan-Warburg, whose illustrations he consulted for his drawings of the Great Crested Grebe and the Ruff, respectively.

Index of Species

Species are listed under the first letter of the common name unless they share a group name, e.g. tit, thrush, woodpecker, warbler. The scientific name of each species is also given (with alternative in brackets where either may be found). Scientific names of families appear only when inter-family relationships have been referred to in the text or for some species not normally resident in Europe, since these are more difficult to trace in generally available bird books.

Abbreviations: f. = family; sp. = one species; spp. = several species.

[254]